This unique book offers a comparative analysis of three market economies – the United States, Germany and France – providing valuable insights into how economic ideas, embedded in national cultures, shape policy-making. It is mandatory reading for anyone trying to understand why markets and welfare arrangements take different forms.

– **Niclas Berggren**, Research Institute of Industrial Economics (IFN) and Prague University of Business and Economics

This book is a must read for scholars interested in comparative analysis of economic systems in Western countries and their roots in economic ideas and culture. It provides a unique and thorough analysis of the free market traditions in US, Germany and France, and how they work out in economic policies and practices.

– **Johan J. Graafland**, Tilburg University, The Netherlands

This book relates the economic system of Western societies to their cultural background in an innovative, fresh way. It's central thesis—that cultural differences are reflected in the dominant economic theories in France, Germany and the USA—is thought-provoking and sheds new light on the evolution of schools of economics. This book is of interest to both scholars of cultural economics and historians of economic thought.

– **Robbert K.J. Maseland**, University of Groningen, The Netherlands

Economic Ideas, Policy and National Culture

All human beings develop a certain view on the world. Inhabitants of the same country are likely to develop similar worldviews. The common part of these views constitutes the country's national culture. Consequently, academic economists, policymakers, and the population at large are consistently exposed to the same opinions on the preferred way of organizing an economy. This book explores the economic impacts of these shared cultural values, focusing on the economies of the United States of America, Germany, and France.

These three countries broadly represent three different types of economic organization and their corresponding economic ideologies: a free market economy, a coordinated market economy, and a hierarchical market economy. The contributors to this edited volume have examined the extent to which the shared worldviews between academic economists, policymakers, and the wider population impact these economies. In particular, the chapters investigate the consequences for the design of the labor market, the financial system, competition policy, and monetary policy. The work also explores the extent to which the shared views on national culture and economic systems and policies in these countries contribute to the population's well-being overall.

This book makes an invaluable contribution to the literature on comparative economics, economic policy, well-being, and cultural economics.

Eelke de Jong is Professor in International Economics at the Radboud University, Nijmegen, The Netherlands.

Routledge Frontiers of Political Economy

Financialisation in the Automotive Industry
Capital and Labour in Contemporary Society
Marcelo José do Carmo, Mário Sacomano Neto and Julio Cesar Donadone

Political Economy of Financialization in the United States
A Historical-Institutional Balance-Sheet Approach
Kurt Mettenheim

The International Political Economy of the Renminbi
Currency Internationalization and Reactive Currency Statecraft
Hyoung-kyu Chey

Explaining Wealth Inequality
Property, Possession and Policy Reform
Benedict Atkinson

The International Political Economy of the Renminbi
Currency Internationalization and Reactive Currency Statecraft
Hyoung-kyu Chey

Financialization of the Economy, Business, and Household Inequality in the United States
A Historical–Institutional Balance-Sheet Approach
Kurt Mettenheim with Olivier Butzbach

Economic Ideas, Policy and National Culture
A Comparison of Three Market Economies
Edited by Eelke de Jong

Political Economy of Contemporary Italy
The Economic Crisis and State Intervention
Nicolò Giangrande

For more information about this series, please visit: www.routledge.com/Routledge-Frontiers-of-Political-Economy/book-series/SE0345

Economic Ideas, Policy and National Culture

A Comparison of Three Market Economies

Edited by Eelke de Jong

Routledge
Taylor & Francis Group
LONDON AND NEW YORK

First published 2022
by Routledge
2 Park Square, Milton Park, Abingdon, Oxon OX14 4RN

and by Routledge
605 Third Avenue, New York, NY 10158

Routledge is an imprint of the Taylor & Francis Group, an informa business

British Library Cataloguing-in-Publication Data
A catalogue record for this book is available from the British Library

Library of Congress Cataloging-in-Publication Data
Names: Jong, Eelke de, 1955-editor.
Title: Economic ideas, policy and national culture: a comparison of three market economies/edited by Eelke de Jong.
Description: Milton Park, Abingdon, Oxon; New York, NY: Routledge, 2022. |
Series: Routledge frontiers of political economy | Includes bibliographical references and index.
Identifiers: LCCN 2021025092 (print) | LCCN 2021025093 (ebook) | ISBN 9781032077291 (hardback) | ISBN 9781032077307 (paperback) | ISBN 9781003208549 (ebook)
Subjects: LCSH: Comparative economics. | United States–Economic policy. | France–Economic policy. | Germany–Economic policy.
Classification: LCC HB90 .E273 2022 (print) | LCC HB90 (ebook) | DDC 330–dc23
LC record available at https://lccn.loc.gov/2021025092
LC ebook record available at https://lccn.loc.gov/2021025093

ISBN: 978-1-032-07729-1 (hbk)
ISBN: 978-1-032-07730-7 (pbk)
ISBN: 978-1-003-20854-9 (ebk)

DOI: 10.4324/9781003208549

Typeset in Bembo
by Deanta Global Publishing Services, Chennai, India

Contents

Contributors

Ivan Boldyrev is currently Assistant Professor of History and Philosophy of Economics at the Radboud University, Nijmegen, the Netherlands. He is a philosopher and an historian of ideas with wide-ranging interests including the history and philosophy of recent economics, German idealism, and critical theory. Representative recent publications include the collections *Economic Knowledge in Socialism, 1945–1989*, co-edited with Till Düppe; and *Enacting Dismal Science: New Studies on the Performativity of Economics*, co-edited with Ekaterina Svetlova (Palgrave, 2016); and two books: *Hegel, Institutions and Economics* (with Carsten Herrmann-Pillath) and *Ernst Bloch and His Contemporaries.*
ORCID: https://orcid.org/0000-0003-4009-6708

Iwan Bos is an Associate Professor of Industrial Organisation at the Maastricht University School of Business and Economics, the Netherlands. He obtained his PhD degree from the University of Amsterdam in 2009. His dissertation deals with cartel theory and competition policy, and he has continued conducting research in these areas. Recently, he broadened his research agenda to oligopoly theory and law and economics.
ORCID: https://orcid.org/0000-0001-8389-7228

Rosolino Candela is a Director of Academic and Student Programs and a Senior Fellow with the F. A. Hayek Program for Advanced Study in Philosophy, Politics, and Economics at the Mercatus Center at George Mason University. Prior to George Mason University, Candela taught in the Department of Economics at Brown University, where he was also a postdoctoral research associate in the Political Theory Project. He was also a visiting professor of economics at Universidad Francisco Marroquin and a visiting fellow in the Department of Political and Social Sciences at the European University Institute. He currently serves as the book review editor of *The Review of Austrian Economics.*
ORCID: https://orcid.org/0000-0003-3129-1624

Lei Delsen is a retired Associate Professor of Socio-Economic Policy at the Department of Economics of the Nijmegen School of Management, Radboud University, Nijmegen. He joined the department in 1987. He studied economics at the Rijksuniversiteit Groningen. He received his PhD from the University of Maastricht in 1995. From 1984 to 1987, he was a research fellow at the European Centre for Work and Society in Maastricht. He has published numerous articles in scientific and professional journals and written and edited several scientific volumes, covering topics such as social security, labour economics, and welfare economics.

ORCID: https://orcid.org/0000-0001-5861-8450

Roland Fritz studied sociology and socio-economics in Graz, Vienna, and Geneva and is currently a research assistant and doctoral candidate in economics at the University of Siegen, Germany. He was also a two-time holder of the Adam Smith Fellowship at George Mason University. His dissertation deals with the provision of social services in (quasi-)markets and potential cultural resistance to market use in these sectors. He is also interested in the Austrian School of Economics, institutional economics, as well as the history of economic thought.

ORCID: https://orcid.org/0000-0002-5918-740X

Nils Goldschmidt is Professor of Contextual Economics and Economic Education at the University of Siegen. In addition, he is director of the ASM-Alliance for the Social Market Economy, Tübingen, board member of the Wilhelm-Röpke-Institute, Erfurt, and the Goerres Society, Bonn, as well as Affiliated Fellow at the Walter Eucken Institute, Freiburg. He is co-editor of the *Journal of Contextual Economics* (Schmollers Jahrbuch), *ORDO Yearbook of Economic and Social Order*, and the *Journal for Politics* (Zeitschrift für Politik). Goldschmidt studied Catholic theology as well as economics. He finished his PhD in economics in 2001 and his habiliation in 2008, both at the University of Freiburg.

ORCID: https://orcid.org/0000-0003-3261-3779.

Eelke de Jong is Professor of International Economics at the Radboud University, Nijmegen, The Netherlands. His research has dealt with various issues in the field of international monetary economics. Since 2000, the focus has changed to the relationship between culture, in the sense of norms and values, formal institutions, and economic behaviour. He has published 11 books and several articles in national and international journals, among which the *European Economic Review, European Journal of Political Economy, Economics of Transition*, and *World Development*. De Jong has obtained research grants from several national and European funds, among which the Dutch National Science Foundation and the Templeton World Charity Foundation.

ORCID: https://orcid.org/0000-0002-4947-0199

Annemiek Schilpzand holds degrees in international economics and European law. Her interests lie in the field of cultural and institutional economics and their overlap with law. She is currently a PhD candidate at the Nijmegen School of Management of the Radboud University.

ORCID: https://orcid.org/0000-0003-3428-7575

Preface

During the second half of the 1990s, the relation between an independent central bank and low inflation was an important topic for both monetary policy and economic research. The premise was that an independent central bank would lead to a low rate of inflation. I did not understand the causality of this relation and sought a third factor that might explain both the degree of central bank independence and the level of inflation. During this period, I came across the work of Geert Hofstede on the consequences of cultural differences. These cultural dimensions could partly solve the problems I had with understanding the relation between central bank independence and inflation. From then onwards, the relation between culture, in the sense of norms and values, and economic phenomena became an important topic of my research agenda.

After about ten years, I did not feel at ease with this approach of culture and economics. Studies on the role of culture assume that people's cognitive abilities are limited and that they therefore rely on heuristics and traits. Researchers assume that a group of people, often a nation, shares these traits. In this practice, the researcher acts as the external independent observer. However, researchers (economists) are people. If national traits influence people's views, then logically these traits will also influence economists' opinion and thus the dominant economic theory in the country concerned.

From the moment I realized that national culture determines economists' ideas, I sought the opportunity to collaborate with a scholar in the field of the history of economic thought in order to join forces on a project on economic ideas, policy, and national culture. This opportunity came when Govert Buijs and Johan Graafland asked me to join their project on the morality of markets. My former colleague, Floris Heukelom, was willing to take responsibility for the chapters on the history of economic thought. However, at the time of the start of the project, he decided to leave academia and became an entrepreneur. Fortunately, his successor, Ivan Boldyrev, was willing to take over the responsibilities. He arranged the contacts with Rosolino Candela, Roland Fritz, and Nils Goldschmidt. Preliminary drafts of all chapters of the present volume were discussed during a workshop on May 9 and 10, 2019.

I would like to seize this opportunity to thank the contributors to this volume for their willingness to write a chapter or be a co-author of one of the chapters. In particular, I thank Ivan Boldyrev for his efforts to find authors in the field of the history of economic thought and Annemiek Schilpzand for her support during all activities of my part in the morality and markets project. I thank Govert Buijs and Johan Graafland for inviting me to join their project and Eefje de Gelder for her administrative and organizational support during the project and for organizing the workshop in Nijmegen in May 2019. Finally, I thank the Templeton World Charity Foundation for financing the research for this book and the May 2019 workshop as part of the project "What Good Markets Are Good For: Towards a Moral Justification of Free Markets in Europe" grant number 0141/AB91.

Eelke de Jong
Malden, The Netherlands
April 2021

Abbreviations

ABC	Allied Banking Commission
ADC	Aid to Dependent Children
AFDC	Aid to Families with Dependent Children
ASM	Aktionsgemeinschaft Soziale Marktwirtscht
BdL	Bank deutscher Länder
CDC	Caisse des Dépôts et Consignations
CDU	Christlich Demokratische Union
CETA	Comprehensive Employment and Training Act
CRA	Community Reinvestment Act
DDR	Deutsche Demokratische Republik
DSGV	Deutscher Sparkassen- und Giroverband
ECB	European Central Bank
EEC	European Economic Community
ECSC	European Coal and Steel Community
EdF	Électricité de France
EITC	Earned Income Tax Credit
EMS	European Monetary System
EMU	Economic and Monetary Union
ENA	Ecole National d'Administration
ERISA	Employee Retirement Income Security Act
ESC	Economic and Social Council
EVS	European Values Study
FED	Federal Reserve System
FLSA	Fair Labor Standards Act
FOMC	Federal Open Market Committee
FTC	Federal Trade Commission
GDP	Gross Domestic Product
GLBA	Gramm–Leach–Bliley Act
GPS	Global Preference Survey
GSE	Government Sponsored Enterprise
HDI	Human Development Index
HFCS	Household Finance and Consumption Survey
IKB	Industrie Kredit Bank

IMF	International Monetary Fund
INSEE	Institut National de la Statistique et des Études Économiques
INSM	Initiative Neue Soziale Marktwirtschaft
IPO	initial public offering
JTPA	Job Training Partnership Act
KfW	Kreditanstalt für Wiederafbau
LTV	Loan-to-value
MMMF	Money Market Mutual Fund
NIRA	National Industrial Recovery Act
NLRA	National Labor Relations Act
OASDI	Old-Age, Survivors, and Disability Insurance
OASI	Old Age and Survivors Insurance
OECD	Organization for Economic Co-operation and Development
OSHA	Occupational Safety and Health Administration
PAP	Prêts en accession a la propriété
PTZ	Prêts a taux zéro
RMI	Revenu Minimum d'Insertion
SCF	Survey of Consumers Finances
SGP	Stability and Growth Pact
SPD	Social Democratic Party
SMIC	Salaire Minimum Interprofessionnel de Croissance
SMIG	Salaire Minimum National Interprofessionnel Garanti
SMP	Securities Market Programme
SNAP	Supplemental Nutrition Assistance Program
TANF	Temporary Assistance for Needy Families
USA	United States of America
WIA	Workforce Investment Act
WVS	World Values Survey

Part I

Setting the stage

1 Introduction and motivation

Eelke de Jong

1.1 Introduction

The fall of the Berlin Wall marked a fundamental change for many: first, of course, for the inhabitants of the countries on the eastern side of the Iron Curtain. Many hoped for a better life, freedom, and improved material conditions such as better products and housing. Second, the fall of the Berlin Wall had consequences for the debate about the best economic and political system. Many were of the view that the rivalry between the different economic and political systems had been settled in favour of the democratic free market system. The best-known representative of this view is Fukuyama, who in 1989 had already written, 'The triumph of the West, of the Western idea, is evident first of all in the total exhaustion of viable systematic alternatives to Western liberalism' (Fukuyama 1989: 3).[1] Consequently, those involved in policy advice to the governments of formerly centrally planned economies were of the view that implementing the right institutions would be the best way to go forward. At first, this discussion was about the speed at which new institutions had to be installed. Some wanted to implement a shock therapy (see, among others, Blanchard *et al.* 1994). Others, Murrell (1995) for example, thought a gradual introduction would be wise because people have to get used to new rules. In a later stage, questions about the characteristics of a market economy became more prominent.

The questions about the best or most appropriate market economy, provoked by the fall of the Berlin Wall, had a significant impact on economic theory. The formerly centrally planned countries had to reform their economies into market economies. It appeared that the market economy was not as universal as claimed by some; almost every industrialized country had its own approach. This stimulated the literature on varieties of capitalism and comparative economics (Albert 1993; Amable 2003; and Hall and Soskice 2001). This literature discusses the differences between economies in terms of institutions and performance. Questions considered are whether subsystems (labour markets, educational systems, financial systems) are complementary, and how historical events have led to the present national systems.

DOI: 10.4324/9781003208549-1

In order to explain the differences between countries, mainstream economists developed an interest in the role of formal institutions as well as the dominant norms and values of a country, region, or group (Alesina and Guiliano 2015; Beugelsdijk and Maseland 2011; and de Jong 2002 and 2009). These dominant norms and values, deemed culture, can be an important factor in explaining the success and failure of countries and of the transition to a market economy (see, e.g., Pejovich 2003). In conclusion, the fall of the Berlin Wall, along with other events such as the Asian values debate and the failure of the International Monetary Fund's structural reform programmes (see de Jong 2009: Chapter 3), triggered an interest in extending the traditional economic model to include formal institutions and culture in the sense of norms and values.[2]

Although these developments extended economic models by including non-material elements, they did not affect the position of the academic economist as an impartial observer. One implicitly assumed that economic behaviour is context dependent but did not pay attention to the likelihood that economists' interpretation of facts might also depend on the situation in which they live and the education they were exposed to. There are those who think that economics as a scientific discipline should stick to the notion of Pareto efficiency. Dani Rodrik, for example, states that:

> All that an economist can claim about a market [...] is that it yields an efficient allocation of resources in a precise sense: there is no feasible way to make some people richer without making others poorer. Any economist who makes a broader argument about the fairness, justice, or moral worth of markets that is based on economics proper is simply engaged in malpractice.
>
> (Rodrik 2014: 105)

In this book, we take the contrary position and argue that 'the economic way of thinking is just as value-laden as any other way of thinking about society' (Foley 2006: xiv). In particular, we study the interaction between economic ideas and the national environment the economists concerned are living in. For this, we investigate the connection between the views on free markets and state intervention held by a country's dominant economic school, its population, and its politicians. These views on (free) markets will show what these actors value, and what human flourishing entails. As will become clear in the following chapters, the views on markets and on the role of the state are related to the view on values, virtues, and human flourishing. For example, if one expects that each individual is autonomous, i.e., that human beings flourish if they can make decisions for themselves, then free markets will be held in high regard and state intervention is not appreciated.

The set-up of this chapter is as follows. In the next section, we describe the concepts of human flourishing, values, virtues, markets, and state intervention. Human flourishing represents the aim of the economic process. Markets and state intervention are instruments for arriving at the economies' goals. Values and virtues are core elements of economic ideas and culture. Section 1.3 describes this book's aim, and Section 1.4 the methodological approach chosen. The chapter concludes by explaining the structure of the book.

1.2 Human flourishing, values, virtues, markets, and state intervention

The aim of an economy is to enhance people's life; to enable them to realize the goals they have set for themselves. All people have more or less the same basic needs: health, food, shelter, and safety. Although these needs are universal, the importance attached to each will depend on the degree to which these needs are already fulfilled. In addition to these basic needs, individuals can strive for immaterial items such as self-expression. The priorities can change over time. Immaterial goals will be 'emphasized *after* people have attained material security, and *because* they have attained material security' (Inglehart 1997: 35). Finally, people think differently about the preferred way of achieving certain goals. Should individuals try to attain goals by themselves or are others also responsible for achieving a better situation?

Opinions of the population and academics differ on the preferred way of organizing a society so that the inhabitants can realize the goals they have set for themselves. As we will see in the rest of the book, views differ on aspects such as the role of markets, virtues, and state intervention. Are markets the best way to coordinate economic activities or are they just one possibility among many others? Must market participants have certain values and virtues in order for a market to function properly, or does the market teach us how to behave? Finally, many agree that the state should guarantee property rights and ensure access to courts. Opinions differ on the degree to which a state should actively participate in firms. Can a state be the owner, or one of the owners, of a company, and if so, only temporarily? As we will see in this book, even within a group of wealthy nations, the dominant views on these matters differ greatly. Before proceeding, we provide some definitions of the key concepts, namely human flourishing, (free) markets, state intervention, and virtues.

Human flourishing consists in those things that characterize human life that is thriving, including freedoms as well as achievements, and including society-level features as well as qualities that pertain to individual lives. It can refer to both the material and non-material aspects of a person's life. At the individual level, this refers to elements of life through which people flourish, by which they obtain enough food, are healthy, have a home, are safe, and are able to express themselves in the way they prefer. At the macro level, income per capita, the employment rate and the human development index are frequently used measures. The latter includes income per capita, life expectancy, and education. In recent academic literature, human flourishing is often measured by subjective well-being, which has two dimensions: happiness and life satisfaction. These two dimensions can also be labelled as 'feeling good' and 'functioning well' (Huppert and So 2013). Another, more recently developed, indicator is the Better Life Index, developed by the Organization for Economic Co-operation and Development (OECD).

Values form the central part of culture, which is the 'collective programming of the mind' (Hofstede 2001: 9) of a group. A *value* is 'an enduring belief that a specific mode of conduct or end-state of existence is personally or socially preferable to an opposite or converse mode of conduct or end-state of existence' Rokeach (1973: 159 and 160). Virtues are closely related to values. A virtue is an acquired character trait or disposition that is judged to be good (Bruni and Sudgen 2013). Similarly, Velasquez (1998) defines (moral) virtues as an acquired disposition that is socially valued as part of the character of a morally good human being and exhibited in the person's habitual behaviour. Therefore, values refer to relatively abstract and generally held desired states, whereas virtues refer to a person's behaviour. In classical philosophy and early Christian thinking, the four cardinal virtues were prudence, courage, temperance, and justice (see, e.g., McCloskey 2007). A virtuous person is someone who can naturally find the right balance. Consequently, the acts of a virtuous person are dependent on the situation at hand. A free market economy asks for other virtues than a centrally planned economy, for example. Both theoretical and empirical studies in economics scarcely pay attention to virtues but do consider values and norms.[3]

The market consists of voluntary exchanges of goods and services. Legal rules support these transactions and are intended to protect the weaker partner, and an arrangement for settling conflicts exists. The way disputes are solved can differ. One can, for example, aim for a cooperative solution or directly follow the legal route and bring the counterparty to court: 'I sue you.'

The state provides the legal framework within which agents, and therefore markets, operate. Traditions differ in their view on an active role of the state. According to some, the state should refrain from active intervention in the economy. Others are of the opinion that a state can own a company and can act in markets alongside private competitors.

Views differ with respect to the exact content of the different concepts and with respect to the relationship between them. For example, is state intervention good or bad for economic flourishing? Does competition, and thus a free market, enhance the quality of people's lives or does it undermine the possibility of them earning a decent wage and thus limit the possibility of them having a good life? Finally, some are of the opinion that people should have acquired certain skills, including moral standards, before they are allowed to act in markets. Others think that these skills are no prerequisite, but that acting in a market will teach people how to behave.

1.3 The aim of this book

This book's basic assumption is that human beings live in a complex world in which individuals must make sense of other people's reactions. People's cognitive capabilities are limited in such a way that considering a broad set of relevant factors in order to interpret events is not possible. It simply takes too much time. Consequently, people use frames and look at the reactions of others to make up their minds.[4] People use cognitive frames to interpret actions and interactions in this complex world.[5] These cognitive frames are built during a person's formative years, when parents and teachers are important in forming a person's mental frame (Hofstede *et al.* 2010: 5–10). These educators transmit to the next generation norms, values, virtues, and habits. What exactly they transmit depends on their own education and experience.[6] The mental frame that children construct will depend on the intergenerationally transmitted morality and on their own experience. Consequently, a person's cognitive frame depends on *vertical* and *horizontal* transmission of values, norms, and virtues (Bisin and Verdier 2011: 341). The former concerns the transmission from generation to generation and the latter the influence of the environment. This environment can be close friends, the village, the neighbourhood in a city, and, at a greater distance, the nation. Each person also influences others and, as a group, they form their surroundings. These interaction processes between generations and between the individual and the group result in dominant ideas of preferred behaviour.

The processes described above lead to a way of thinking that involves mental models. These mental models refer to broad ideas about the way the world works and the individual's place in it. Mental models are shared by a group and include 'categories, concepts, identities, prototypes, stereotypes, causal narratives, and worldviews' (World Bank 2015: 62). Shared mental models are necessary for people to develop institutions and solve collective action problems. These mental models correspond with the concept of culture as described before and play a dominant role in this volume.

Thinking in mental models holds for all human beings, lay people, and experts such as academic economists and policymakers alike. In this volume, we focus on these agents' views on markets, state intervention, virtues, and human flourishing and we claim that these views (mental models) differ between countries. Within a country, however, one can find a strong correlation between the views of academics, decision-makers such as politicians, and the population at large. All three groups use the same or a very similar mental model. Consequently, within a country, people, academics, and politicians have a common understanding of the free market, its relationship with values and virtues, and whether it contributes to human flourishing.

The aim of the book is to show that academic researchers, the population, and politicians have a common view on markets, state intervention, virtues, and human flourishing. Moreover, within a country all three types of agents have a similar idea about the relations between the concepts and whether a certain relationship has to be valued as positive or negative,[7] for example, whether state intervention such as nationalization is in principle good or bad.[8]

The framework of the present study is represented in Figure 1.1, which shows similarities with the culture as preferences approach developed in de

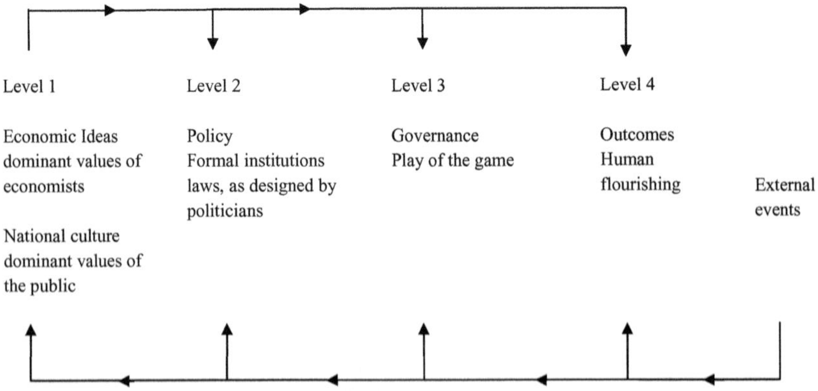

Figure 1.1 Theoretical framework.

Jong (2009: 34–38). Economic ideas and national culture reflect the values of dominant economists and the public at large. Policy is the process by which formal rules are developed and implemented. Governance concerns the way the game is played: whether in case of conflicts one seeks consensus or goes to court. Outcomes refer to economic outcomes, such as income, consumption unemployment, and inflation and are thus part of human flourishing. The arrows indicate that the four levels interact. Dominant ideas will influence legislation, which leads to certain outcomes. Ideas and culture can change because of certain outcomes, e.g., hyperinflation can change the attitude towards uncertainty (arrows at the bottom). The national economy is not a closed system but is part of worldwide developments. The box 'External events' reflects this and the arrows directed from there to the other parts of the figure.

1.4 The method used

In order to be able to show that opinions differ between different nations, we have opted for a comparative case study. Such a set-up allows us to thoroughly investigate the positions of academic economists, the population, and political decision-makers. Each of the countries selected for this comparative case study represents a different type of market economy. We focus our research on three Western countries: the United States of America, Germany, and France. These countries are selected because market institutions have been prevalent here for a long time, so that differences cannot be ascribed to transition problems, but are likely a reflection of deeply rooted differences. In addition, these three countries are at a similar stage of development, so that differences in attitude and beliefs cannot be ascribed to differences in the level of economic development.[9] Finally, each of them represents a different type of market economy: the free, also known as liberal, market economy, the coordinated market economy, and the hierarchical market economy. This typology corresponds with the categorization used in the Varieties of Capitalism (VoC) literature (Hall and Soskice 2001). This literature focuses on the free market economy and coordinated market economy. In 2009, Schneider and Soskice extended this categorization with the category of hierarchical market economies, which, in their article, refers to Latin American countries (Schneider 2009; and Schneider and Soskice 2009). In the present study, the hierarchical market economy refers to Latin European countries, in particular France. The countries associated with the liberal and the coordinated market economy are the same as in the VoC literature.[10] The categorization of countries is also in accordance with that of other authors, for example Schmidt (2003) and Witt *et al.* (2018).[11]

The economic ideas are studied by investigating the writings of dominant economists in the countries concerned. The view of the public is derived from large surveys, such as the European Values Study and the World Values Survey and Hofstede's ground-breaking book *Culture's Consequences*. The views of politicians come to the fore in the descriptions of the history of certain policy areas in the three countries concerned. These descriptions do not merely list facts but focus on the arguments for choosing a certain trajectory. These arguments reveal the values of politicians and, in some cases, those of the population or academics. The topics covered are the labour market, financial systems, competition policy, and monetary policy.

This study relates to many different types of studies. The first type consists of studies that investigate how different countries, cultures, deal with the same phenomenon. Sheikh (2017), for example, investigates the way different cultures have dealt with modernity. The core of modernity is a 'sphere of human living shaped by a technical approach or *way of relating* to the world and to humanity' (Sheikh 2017: 12, italics in original). He then shows how different traditions, cultures we would say, have dealt with modernity in a way that connects to their history; modernity is embedded in the countries' traditions. In a similar manner, Brunnermeier *et al.* (2016) show how the differences between German and French economic ideas have prevented a swift and robust solution to the European sovereign debt crisis. This type of reasoning also forms part of our discussion of central bank independence and monetary policy in Chapter 9. These two studies start with an external development or event and then show how differences in culture or economic ideas influence the way by which countries deal with these developments or shocks. Some start with a particular economic idea and then investigate how differences in culture or economic circumstances can explain the degree of acceptance of these ideas. The authors in Hall (1989) take this route. They study how Keynesian ideas have found their way in different countries: the United States, Britain, Germany, France, Japan, and Scandinavia. The comparative analysis allows for finding factors that have enhanced or hampered the reception of Keynesian ideas. Another route related to our approach is to argue that economic ideas are influencing the analysis of a situation and thus policymakers' decisions. This influence of economic ideas is in particular relevant in crises, when uncertainty is that high that the interpretation of the circumstances is greatly influenced by ideas (Blyth 2002).[12] In a similar way, the chapters in Part III of this volume illustrate how economic ideas have shaped policy in the three countries concerned.

The present study distinguishes itself from the previous ones in at least two ways. First, it is not confined to one particular economic idea or external event. Three different economic ideas and cultures are considered over a period of at least 50 years. During these years, different shocks have hit the countries concerned, which enables us to investigate the way economic ideas and culture influence decisions and the manner by which economic outcomes influence national culture and economic ideas. Second, this is the only study which explicitly considers culture as represented by respondents' answers in national representative questionnaires.

1.5 Structure of the book

This book consists of four parts. Part I sets the stage. It contains the present introduction in which we explain the reasons for our study, relate it to existing literature, and explain our approach. Chapter 2 is devoted to national culture as the opinion of the populations in the respective countries. It starts with a brief description of the history of each country, providing the historical roots of the dominant values in each population. The values and virtues themselves are derived from large surveys, such as the World Values Survey and the European Values Study. These surveys are organized from 1990 onwards, and cover views held during the last three decades. In addition, some relevant cultural dimensions developed by Hofstede are described. The original data for these dimensions were collected at the end of the 1960s and the beginning of the 1970s. Finally, a study by van Oudenhoven and co-authors reveals the dominant virtues in the three countries.

Part II is devoted to economic ideas as the views of dominant academic economists. This part begins with the free market tradition according to which markets consist of voluntary exchanges that benefit both parties. A free market economy is an economy in which an authority enforces exchangeable private property rights. Chapter 3 argues that the institutional structure of a free market economy enables firms to compete against each other successfully for the benefit of others, namely by offering goods and services that consumers value. Competition under the rule of law liberates the individual from being confined to their natural condition of race, ethnicity etc. The other two traditions are less positive about the consequences of the market. The ordoliberal view, discussed in Chapter 4, shares with the free market tradition the appraisal of market processes but emphasizes the embeddedness of the market arrangements in a social and cultural context. It emerged as a reaction to the centralization of the German economy under the Nazis and shares with the German Historical School the emphasis on the cultural embeddedness of economic activities. In the ordoliberal tradition, the market is part of the ordering of society and acts as a counterbalance against the state. Chapter 5 is devoted to the French school of economic engineers as this (re)emerged after the Second World War. In this tradition, the market is not an existing phenomenon in real life but a theoretical construct of competition that can be modelled. These models are used to help the state in setting prices in such a way that the economy fulfils the criteria of efficiency.

Part III investigates the sense in which the traditions of economic thought, the economic ideas, along with the values of the population as described in Chapter 2, play a role in different fields of economic policy in the three types of market economies. This part describes the practices in different policy fields for each of the three types of market economy. Two chapters refer to the organization and functioning of markets for production factors, namely labour (Chapter 6) and finance (Chapter 7). These markets are of importance for the functioning of an economy as such.[13] In addition, the labour market generates the primary distribution of income and wealth and thus the material part of human flourishing. Thereafter, two essential fields of economic policy are discussed, namely competition policy (Chapter 8) and monetary policy and the independence of central banks (Chapter 9).

When describing the evolution of the policies, we refer to the economic ideas of the academics as these have been described in Part II and to the values of the population as these are presented in Chapter 2. In this manner, we link the views of the population, academia, and politicians on these matters. Competition policy and monetary policy are chosen as fields of economic policy because they are important in themselves and have direct consequences for relationships with other countries. Therefore, potentially, these policies can lead to conflict between countries, not only because of different interests but also because of a different understanding of reality: different mental models. These potential conflicts resulting from different mental models reflected in different economic ideas are particularly important for France and Germany who both participate in the Economic and Monetary Union. In the chapters on competition and monetary policy, we illustrate how the different traditions described in the previous chapters come to the fore when these two countries have to cooperate at the European level.

The last part of the book consists of one chapter (Chapter 10) in which we draw the main lessons from our endeavour and sketch directions for future research.

Notes

1 In his view, the turn towards a liberal market economy would also lead to a demand for a democratic political system (idem: 13 and 14).

2 Douglass C. North has introduced the distinction between formal institutions and informal institutions. The formal institutions are rules that human beings devise and the informal ones are conventions and codes of behaviour (see North 1990: 4). These informal institutions correspond with our notion of culture.

3 McCloskey (2007) being the exception that proves the rule.

4 The use of frames is called automatic thinking or using System 1. Deliberative or reflexive thinking refers to System 2. The phenomenon of people coordinating their opinions

and actions with that of others is called thinking socially, see Kahneman (2011) and World Bank (2015).

5 A similar reasoning can be found in the Critical Political Economy (CPE).

> A key argument of CPE is that no individual or collective agent can ever comprehend the totality of all economic (and economically relevant) activities in all its complexity – let alone in real time. This is why it focuses on economic imaginaries as enforced efforts to reduce the complexity as a condition of going on in the world … CPE interprets culture as sense- and meaning making.
>
> (Kutter and Jessop 2015: 66)

6 Chwieroth (2010) shows how the education of the members of staff of the International Monetary Fund has shaped the staff's advice on freeing international capital flows.

7 Caplan (2007) argues that opinions differ between the public and economists. Note that he studies the opinions of persons living in the same country, whereas we study the relation between opinions from persons living in different countries. In Chapter 2, we will discuss the relation with Caplan's work in more detail.

8 In many aspects, our approach is similar to Piketty's view that ideas and ideologies count in history. He writes that the conceptual definitions people choose to work with 'are shaped by each society's conception of social justice and economic fairness and by relative political and ideological power of contending groups and discourses. Importantly, this relative power is not exclusively material; it is intellectual and ideological' (Piketty 2020: 7).

9 In principle, the central theme of the present volume, namely that the economic ideas, national culture, and policy are correlated, can also be studied by investigating other groups, such as the Nordic, Mediterranean, or some Asian countries. However, such an investigation should take care of the different phases of development of the countries concerned. Ideas and culture can also reflect one's economic situation. Moreover, including more countries also implies including more chapters about economic ideas, which would only increase the book's length without contributing to its main message.

10 In the VoC literature, liberal market economies are the United States, United Kingdom, Canada, Australia, New Zealand, and Ireland. The coordinated market economies are Germany, the Netherlands, Austria, Denmark, Finland, Norway, Sweden, and Switzerland (Schneider and Soskice 2009, Table 1: 21). Within the group of OECD countries, Hall and Soskice (2001: 21) have six countries with an ambiguous position (France, Italy, Spain, Portugal, Greece, and Turkey).

11 Vivien Schmidt distinguishes market capitalism (Great Britain, although United States is the ideal type), managed capitalism (Germany; cooperative), and state capitalism (France).

12 These are situations of Knightian uncertainty when agents do not know the outcome of a process nor its distribution, see Knight (1921).

13 In addition, van Bavel (2016) argues that the organization of these two markets is of crucial importance for distinguishing a market economy from another type of economy. In all types of economies, final products and many services are exchanged via markets. However, a market economy stands out as the society in which production factors are also traded by means of markets.

References

Albert, M. (1993) *Capitalism versus Capitalism: How America's Obsession with Individual Achievement and Short-Term Profit Has Led It to the Brink of Collapse*, New York: Four Wall Eight Windows.

Alesina, A. and P. Giuliano (2015) Culture and institutions, *Journal of Economic Literature* 53(4): 898–944.

Amable, B. (2003) *The Diversity of Modern Capitalism*, Oxford: Oxford University Press.
Beugelsdijk, S. and R. Maseland (2011) *Culture in Economics: History, Methodological Reflections and Contemporary Applications*, Cambridge: Cambridge University Press.
Bisin, A. and T. Verdier (2011) The economics of cultural transmission and socialization. In J. Benhabib, A. Bisin and M. O. Jackson (eds.), *Handbook of Social Economics* (Vol. 1A), Amsterdam: North Holland: 339–416.
Blanchard, O. J., K. A. Froot and J. D. Sachs (eds.) (1994) *The Transition in Eastern Europe, Vol. 1 Country Studies and Vol. 2 Restructuring*, Chicago, IL and London: University of Chicago Press.
Blyth, M. (2002) *Great Transformations: Economic Ideas and Institutional Change in the Twentieth Century*, Cambridge: Cambridge University Press.
Bruni, L. and R. Sugden (2013) Reclaiming virtue ethics for economics, *Journal of Economic Perspectives* 27(4): 141–164.
Brunnermeier, M. K., H. James and J.-P. Landau (2016) *The Euro and the Battle of Ideas*, Princeton, NJ: Princeton University Press.
Caplan, B. (2007) *The Myth of the Rational Voter: Why Democracies Choose Bad Policies*, Princeton, NJ: Princeton University Press.
Chwieroth, J. M. (2010) *Capital Ideas: The IMF and the Rise of Financial Liberalization*, Princeton, NJ.: Princeton University Press.
De Jong, E. (2002) Why are price stability and statutory independence of central banks negatively correlated?: The role of culture, *European Journal of Political Economy* 18: 675–694.
De Jong, E. (2009) *Culture and Economics: On Values, Economics and International Business*, New York: Routledge.
Foley D. K. (2006) *Adam's Fallacy. A Guide to Economic Theology*, Cambridge, MA: Harvard University Press.
Fukuyama, F. (1989) The end of history?, *The National Interest* 16(Summer 1989): 3–18.
Hall, P. A. (ed.) (1989) *The Political Power of Economic Ideas: Keynesianism across Nations*, Princeton NJ: Princeton University Press.
Hall, P. A. and D. Soskice (eds.) (2001) *Varieties of Capitalism: The Institutional Foundations of Comparative Advantage*, Oxford: Oxford University Press.
Hofstede, G. (2001) *Culture's Consequences: Comparing Values, Behaviors, Institutions and Organizations Across Nations*, Thousand Oaks, CA: Sage.
Hofstede, G., G. J. Hofstede and M. Minkov (2010) *Cultures and Organization: Software of the Mind*, New York: McGrawHill.
Huppert, F. A. and T. T. C. So (2013) Flourishing across Europe: Application of a new conceptual framework for defining well-being, *Social Indicators Research* 110(3): 837–861.
Inglehart, R. (1997) *Modernization and Postmodernization: Cultural, Economic, and Political Change in 43 Societies*, Princeton NJ: Princeton University Press.
Kahneman, D. (2011) *Thinking, Fast and Slow*, London: Allen Lane.
Knight, F. H. (1921) *Risk, Uncertainty and Profit*, Chicago, IL: University of Chicago Press.
Kutter, A. and B. Jessop (2015) Culture as a discursive practice: Combining cultural political economy and discursive political studies in investigations of the financial crisis. In B. Jessop, B. Young and C. Scherrer (eds.) *Financial Cultures and Crisis Dynamics*, New York: Routledge: 64–82.
McCloskey, D. N. (2007) *The Bourgeois Virtues: Ethics for an Age of Commerce*, Chicago, IL: The University of Chicago Press.
Murrell, P. (1995) The transition according to Cambridge, Mass., *Journal of Economic Literature* 32(March): 164–178.

North, D. C. (1990) *Institutions, Institutional Change and Economic Performance*, Cambridge: Cambridge University Press.

Pejovich, S. (2003) Understanding the transaction costs of transition: It's the culture, stupid, *The Review of Austrian Economics* 16(4): 347–361.

Piketty, T. (2020) *Capital and Ideology*, Cambridge MA.: The Belknap Press of Harvard University Press.

Rodrik, D. (2014) *Economics Rules: The Rights and Wrongs of the Dismal Science*, New York: W.W. Norton.

Rokeach, M. (1973) *The Nature of Human Values*, New York: Free Press.

Schneider, B. R. (2009) Hierarchical market economies and varieties of capitalism in Latin America, *Journal of Latin American Studies* 41: 553–575.

Schneider, B. R. and D. Soskice (2009) Inequality in developed countries and Latin America: Coordinated, liberal and hierarchical systems, *Economy and Society* 38(1): 17–52.

Schmidt, V. (2003) French capitalism-transformed, yet still a third variety of capitalism, *Economy and Society* 32(4): 526–554.

Sheikh, H. (2017) *Embedding Technopolis: Turning Modernity into a Home*, Amsterdam: Boom Publishers.

Van Bavel, B. (2016) *The Invisible Hand?: How Market Economies have Emerged and Declined since AD 500*, Oxford: Oxford University Press.

Velasquez, M. G. (1998) *Business Ethics, Cases and Concepts*, 4th Edition, Upper Saddle River, NJ: Prentice Hall.

Witt, M. A., L. R. Kabbach de Castro, K. Amaeshi, S. Mahroum, D.Bohle and L. Saez (2018) Mapping the business systems of 61 major economies: A taxonomy and implications for varieties of capitalism and business systems research, *Socio-Economic Review* 16(1): 5–38.

World Bank (2015) *Mind, Society and Behavior, World Development Report 2015*, Washington, DC: The World Bank.

2 National culture in the three types of market economies

Eelke de Jong and Annemiek Schilpzand

2.1 Introduction

This chapter presents some indicators that summarize the public attitude towards values and virtues in the selected (and related) countries. In addition, a few indicators of the dominant attitude towards governance in each country are presented. The chapter begins with a brief description of each country's history as this can be related to the indicators that will be presented later.

Various datasets are used for measuring the dominant attitudes or cultural dimensions. The European Values Study (EVS) and the World Values Survey (WVS) are representative questionnaires for the national level and data have been taken from waves 2–4 for the EVS and waves 2–6 for the WVS, covering the years 1990–2014. In the 1980s, Hofstede developed cultural dimensions (Hofstede 2001, and Hofstede *et al.* 2010). The original cultural dimensions were derived from a survey among employees of IBM at the end of the 1960s and the beginning of the 1970s. The most recent versions make use of the answers to questions in the WVS.

Recently, the results of the Global Preferences Survey (GPS) have been released (Falk *et al.* 2018). This survey contains questions based on an ex-ante experimental validation procedure (Falk *et al.* 2016). The data were collected in 2012 as part of the Gallup World Poll, which contains representative samples for each country concerned. The measures refer to time preference, risk preference, altruism, positive reciprocity, negative reciprocity, and trust. Rieger *et al.* (2015) have used a similar method to that of the GPS for deriving measures of risk aversion and ambiguity aversion. They use the so-called matched samples consisting of undergraduate students.[1]

Empirical studies asking respondents for their views on the most important virtues are scarce. The only cross-country empirical study we know of is van Oudenhoven *et al.* (2014). The authors surveyed 2,908 university students from 14 nations and asked respondents, 'What do you find are important personal characteristics which you would like to bring into practice in daily life?'

The data for GPS and the survey by van Oudenhoven and co-authors were collected only once. Several waves of the WVS and the EVS have been organized over the period 1980–2014, while Hofstede's dimensions

DOI: 10.4324/9781003208549-2

are derived from data collected at the end of the 1960s and the beginning of the 1970s. Scores that are more recent are based on the data of the World Values Survey. Since observations for different years are available for the WVS and EVS, it is possible to study the stability of the country scores over time. In addition, Beugelsdijk and co-authors have studied the stability of the national scores on Hofstede's dimensions by means of the WVS (Beugelsdijk *et al.* 2015).

The evolution over time in the WVS scores has been a central theme in Inglehart's work. He claims that value patterns change as economic prosperity increases. The wealthier nations are, the more their inhabitants value the immaterial elements of life; this marks the transition from the modernization phase to the post-modernization phase (Inglehart 1997). With this goes an increase in individualism (Hofstede 2001: 255). Such a movement over time does not necessarily imply that countries' relative positions change. A study of the EVS' scores for the 1981, 1990, and 1999/2000 waves revealed 'that cohort differences are more important than period effects. In most cases the differences between observation years are smaller than the differences of two consecutive cohorts' (Arts *et al.* 2003: 40). Beugelsdijk *et al.* (2015) confirm this conclusion of the relative stability of scores between countries for Hofstede's dimensions. The authors construct scores on the indices for two cohorts: those born between 1902 and 1958 (cohort 1) and those born after 1958 (cohort 2). Their main result is that the scores can change but that each country's relative position remains almost the same, as is reflected by the high correlation (higher than 0.96) between the scores of cohort 1 and cohort 2. Consequently, cultural differences between country pairs (i.e., cultural distances) are generally stable. From the results presented in this paragraph, we conclude that, within the period considered, the scores on the indices for culture and values are stable.

This chapter is structured as follows. The next section provides a brief historical overview per country that can be regarded as relevant for understanding how the different scores are arrived at. The remaining sections deal first with values and virtues and then with the preferred way of governance. The aspects discussed are the position of the individual versus the group, the attitude towards uncertainty and risk, the acceptance of concentration of power and wealth, and time preference. Indicators of the way governance is executed and of the preferred style of governance are presented in Section 2.4. Section 2.5 concludes and also provides a bridge to Part II.

2.2 Historical roots of value differences

Before we present the three countries' scores on different cultural dimensions in Sections 2.3 and 2.4, this section provides a historical background. Of course, the description of the countries' history is very concise. We focus on those aspects that might be relevant for the discussion on the importance of markets, which is the central theme of this volume.

2.2.1 United States of America[2]

The present culture in the United States is dominated by the influence of those who migrated to the country from the sixteenth century onwards. The first wave of migrants fled the European countries because of religious intolerance. Later waves, for example the influx in the first half of the nineteenth century and that at the beginning of the twentieth century, came for economic reasons. The first settlers lived in small independent settlements where they worked in small-scale enterprises. When they fought for independence from Great Britain, they developed a unique American culture, characterized by, amongst other things, freedom from oppression and a deep belief in government by the people. A system of checks and balances should prevent one group from dominating another. The immigrants who settled in the West developed a kind of frontier mentality, involving hard work and individual independence. During 1815–1850 approximately, a notion of the 'common man' emerged. This 'common man' had to be protected against the might of the government and the rich. From 1850 onwards, large corporations developed, which led to a widening of inequalities between the rich and the poor and a concentration of power in the hands of a few firms (see also Chapter 8). This trend undermined the social fabric, but the success of some also reinforced the image of a land of abundance and opportunity. From the seventeenth century onwards, successful settlers propagated this image in order to induce further migration from Europe. At times, political forces pushed teachers towards this view (Alesina and Glaeser 2004: 199 and 204). Since the 1930s, the United States has developed into a super power. First politically and militarily, later as an economic power.

One can easily understand that such a history leads to a preference for the individual, independence, a high degree of accepting uncertainty and risk, and an aversion against the concentration of power. However, striving for the realization of any one of these values can be at the cost of another, which leads to tensions. Hoppe and Bhagat (2007: Table 14.1) mention 12 recurrent themes and tensions in US culture. We will encounter some of these in the next chapters.

A tension that is relevant for the present book is that between liberty (free markets) and equality; between equality in opportunity and equality in outcome. A dominant inclination is to stress the importance of the equality of opportunity. 'No one justly may deny the equality of opportunity which made us what we are', according to President Harding in his inaugural address of 1921. However, the equality of opportunity offered by free markets can lead to a concentration of power and wealth in the hands of a few. Many, still, will argue in favour of offering more opportunities rather than taxing the rich for helping the poor.[3] When the concentration of power and wealth undermines the common man too much (a subjective judgement of course), actions to protect the latter have been taken. We will see in Chapter 8 that this has been a motivation for competition policy.

A related theme concerns the concentration of power. The American attitude towards the concentration of power is nicely illustrated by a quote from former president John Quincy Adams, who wrote: 'Power for good, is power for evil, even in the hand of Omnipotence' (cited in Timberlake 1993: 39). This aversion to the concentration of power is so strong that Americans try to avoid centralization of power, even in cases where it is self-evident to outsiders that some concentration would be more than welcome (see Chapter 9). It also explains why banks were small for a long period of time (Chapter 7).

2.2.2 Germany[4]

Germany is a relatively young nation. It was founded in 1871 when most of the German states unified into the Prussian-dominated German Empire. This new nation has experienced a turbulent history. It was a central player in both the First and Second World War and it was defeated in both cases. Political unrest, hyperinflation, recession, and the coming to power of the Nazis characterized the 1920s and 1930s. After the Second World War, the country was first occupied and thereafter divided into two independent nations, and finally reunited in 1990.

Largely, this recent history of war and divide can be considered a continuation of the events before the establishment of Das Deutsche Reich. The geographical area of what is now Germany had been torn apart several times and contained many divisions. The first division was that between civilization and barbarism. The Limes – a wall that the Romans built to keep the barbarian Germans out – went through the middle of what is now Germany. A similar division existed between the eastern and western states. Most western states followed the ideas of the French Revolution and democracy. The eastern states were less influenced by these ideas and idealized the state.

Another division in Germany is between adherents of Catholicism and Protestantism. After the Reformation many states became Protestant, a decision made by the ruler of the state. In 1618, the Thirty Years' War began between Protestants and Catholics. Although armies from different countries took part in this war, it was almost exclusively fought on the soil of what is now Germany. The states most affected by this war suffered huge losses. Famines, killings, looting, and the plague killed about one-third of the population. One can imagine that these events could result in German angst (anxiety). The hyperinflation of the 1920s has also been brought forward as a reason for German's aversion to uncertainty (Issing 2005). It is possible that these experiences have produced a longing for stability (Stabilitätskultur) and a tendency towards conservatism.

After the Thirty Years' War, the German land mass consisted of many (about 300) sovereign states. Each individual state was powerless against the outside world. During the eighteenth century, this situation inspired administrators (cameralists) and academics from several middle-sized principalities to investigate systematically how best to manage their relatively small and land-locked economies. Their answer was a strong central government and an efficient and effective bureaucracy that could react quickly to new situations. The sovereignties were very diverse, which triggered a competition between them in such fields as music and theatre. German national unity in 1872 was enforced by the Prussians and not achieved by a popular revolt. The late foundation of the German state meant that as a state Germany came too late to get its rightful place among the European powers. For example, at the beginning of the twentieth century, much smaller states such as The Netherlands and Portugal had extensive and rich colonies, whereas Germany had almost none. This also led to a feeling of uncertainty.[5]

After the Second World War, the Allied forces occupied the country and the Americans succeeded in implementing a decentralized, federal system (see also Chapters 8 and 9). Against the background of a long history of rule by local authorities, dukes, and princes, this federal structure was thought to fit the German population better than a very centralized one.

2.2.3 France[6]

Of the three countries considered in this book, France has by far the longest history as an independent state. This does not imply that this long time of a common history led to a uniform culture. Perhaps it even led to the opposite. France is full of paradoxes, which, according to some, might be explained by the fact that it is a large country (Braudel 1990: 305–307). Ernest Labrousse notes that that part of France which is open to foreign influences is confronted with a France that is strongly inward looking. According to him, the latter consists of the rural areas including small and medium-sized towns (see quote in Braudel 1990: 297). An important paradox is that between authority, freedom, and related values.

> Since the Middle Ages and the Counter Reformation, centralized government and industry, submission to hierarchy, lack of autonomy, and a strong civil service have remained French features. However, this style clashes with the values of freedom and fraternity, originally expressed in the French Revolution.
>
> (Castel *et al.* 2008: 549)

During the last centuries, France has continued to maintain 'two contrasting traditions; first the aura of elitist aristocratic values, elegance, and grandeur associated with pre-1789 France, and second, the continuation of egalitarian and radical values associated with the French revolution' (idem: 549).

Throughout their history, the French developed the idea that their national view was not only good for their own civilization but had universal validity. French people have an ambivalent attitude towards authority and employers. When in need, employees turn to their employer and the government. These paternalistic tendencies originate in the *pater familias* way of organizing a group (society) so characteristic of the Middle Ages (Siedentop 2014). The national political elite is the highest elite. Since employers often decide things without extensive consultation with the employees, the latter will eventually challenge the authority of the employers (see Section 2.4.2 on cooperation). Trade unions were legalized in 1884. However, for many years both the state and employers neglected trade unions.

Intellectuals have always held a special place in French society. They have quite an abstract mindset and prefer more general and abstract plans for reform than their Anglo-Saxon counterparts. Prestigious higher education is not provided by universities but by the *Grandes écoles*. Students have to take a competitive entrance exam. Emphasis is on mathematics and logical and abstract thinking. The graduates of these schools play an important part in society, both in the civil service and in the private sector (see Chapters 5 and 9). This extremely hierarchical nature of the educational system reinforces the existing social cleavages (Piketty 2020: 757).[7] Family-owned businesses are an important characteristic of French business. In 1992, 25 out of the 100 leading companies were family controlled.

Louis XIII and Napoleon Bonaparte made France an operative state. The state was actively involved in economic life (*dirigisme*) due to the weakness of the private industrial sector. The state was both an owner of firms and a model for the business community: in many companies it was the largest shareholder. Today, there is an active exchange of top positions between the civil service and industry. These top managers are often alumni from the *Grandes écoles*. The appointment of top civil servants as heads of major private companies or public sector enterprises is known as 'parachuting.'

This brief review reveals a paternalist society in which the government is intensely involved in economic affairs. The separation of power required for a well-functioning free market is not guaranteed upfront. More importantly, that is also not what the French want.

2.3 Values and virtues

Economic activities can be coordinated in different ways: by means of free markets in which agents only meet once for the exchange of goods or services or by means of an arrangement based on a more long-lasting relationship. Often the latter forms contain an implicit commitment to other transactions, which constrains the individual. In a free market economy, the individual is very important, much more so than in the hierarchical one. The coordinated market economy is in the middle. Another aspect concerns the role of risk and uncertainty. In a free market economy, the individual fully bears the consequences of his action. Social security has a less significant role than in the other types. This implies that the attitude towards uncertainty and risk is expected to be different between the three types of societies. A third aspect on which the ideal types differ is the role of the elite, if any exists. In the hierarchical type, an elite is important and part of society's ideal frame. The coordinated and free market economies do not differentiate the layers of society. In the previous section, we have represented in broad brush strokes the history of the three countries concerned to get at the roots of present attitudes. In this and the following section, we present measures of these attitudes, as they have been collected over the last 40 years. We deal consecutively with the view on the position of the individual, the attitude towards uncertainty and risk, and that towards differences in power.

2.3.1 Individualism

The free market tradition emphasizes the role of the individual. The individual should be allowed to act independently and to act on their own initiative. The other two traditions, and in particular the hierarchical one, put much less emphasis on the freedom of the individual. The cultural dimension of Individualism versus Collectivism measures the relationship between the individual and the group. A higher score on this dimension corresponds with the view that the individual is more important than the group. Hofstede (2001: Exhibit 5.1) finds the highest score (91) for the United States and the lowest for Guatemala. The mean over 53 countries is 43. France and Germany have a score of 71 and 67, respectively (see Table 2.1, first row). Therefore, from a worldwide perspective all three countries concerned are individualistic. As expected, the United States scores higher than the other two countries whose scores do not differ much.

2.3.2 Uncertainty and risk

Uncertainty is a basic feature of life that results from the fact that time goes only one way. We are caught in a present that is just an infinitesimal borderline between past and future. We have to live with a future that moves away as fast as we try to approach it, but into which we project our present hopes and fears (Hofstede 2001: 145 and 146).

Uncertainty is associated with anxiety. Uncertainty differs from risk. In both cases, the outcome is unknown; however, under uncertainty the outcome's probability distribution is unknown, whereas it is known under risk. A distribution can be unknown because a certain type of event, a crisis for example, happens very rarely. On the other hand, for events that occur frequently one can calculate a distribution for the outcomes of these events. A distribution can also be obtained if physical circumstances enforce it, for example, the chance that throwing a die will deliver a certain integral number. Emotionally, uncertainty and risk are very different. Uncertainty is related to anxiety and both are diffuse feelings. Risk is related to fear and both risk and fear are focused on something specific. This difference implies that in the case of risk, agents have the feeling that they have some control over the outcome, whereas that is not the case for uncertainty.[8]

Hofstede (2001: Ch. 4) has developed the cultural dimension of Uncertainty Avoidance, which measures the attitude of the inhabitants of a country towards

Table 2.1 Scores on values and virtues

	United States	Rank	*Germany*	Rank	*France*	Rank
Individualism[a]	91	*1*	67	*21*	71	*15*
Uncertainty Avoidance[a]	46	*66*	65	*45*	86	*20*
Rieger: Ambiguity Aversion[b]	42%	*51*	47%	*47*	54%	*35*
Power Distance[a]	40	*60*	35	*67*	68	*27*
Child qualities differences high versus low SES[c]						
Thrift	–0.112		–1.007***		–0.959***	
Manners	–0.432**		–0.450***		–0.848***	
Tolerance	0.342***		1.201***		0.306*	
Determination	0.768***		0.567***		1.107***	
Obedience	–0.480***		–1.561***		–1.301***	
Unselfish	0.108		–0.148		0.491***	
Hard-working	0.0236		–0.472***		–0.685***	
Independence	–0.0160		0.461***		0.882***	
Responsible	0.233*		1.151***		0.596***	
Imagination	0.796***		0.907***		1.327***	
Faith	–0.153		0.0416		0.191	
Long-Term Orientation[a]	26	*53*	83	*5*	63	*18*
Trust[d]	41%	*19*	36%	*24*	23%	*54*
Cooperation in Labour[e] Relations	5.0	*30*	5.1	*25*	3.9	*110*
Willingness to Delegate Authority[e]	5.2	*9*	4.9	*19*	3.9	*51*

[a] Scores on Hofstede dimensions generally range between 0 and 100. The ranking is based on a sample of 78 countries, except for Long-Term Orientation, which is based on a sample of 66 countries. As an example, the United States' score of 91 on Individualism is high and this is the highest in the group, represented by rank 1. A high score on Uncertainty Avoidance indicates that inhabitants of the country concerned have a high aversion to uncertainty. Similarly, a high score on Long-Term Orientation indicates that a country's inhabitants attach a high value to long-term consequences. Source: Hofstede *et al.* (2010).

[b] Ambiguity Aversion by Rieger *et al.* (2015) is the proportion of ambiguity-averse participants. In their sample, it ranges from 0.39 (Austria) to 0.82 (India) in a sample of 53 countries.

[c] Each child quality item is estimated for either the United States, Germany, or France using data from the World Values Survey and European Values Study. The estimation is a logit analysis including controls for survey wave, age, age-squared, trust, religiosity, and gender. The coefficient in the table denotes the dummy that is constructed as 1 for the two highest education categories ('some university' and 'university') and 0 for the two lowest education categories ('no' and 'elementary'). *t* statistics in parentheses and * $p < 0.1$, ** $p < 0.05$, ***$p < 0.01$.

[d] Trust is measured as the percentage of the respondents in a country answering 'most people can be trusted', from the WVS and EVS in waves 1–6. Ranking is based on 105 countries.

[e] Item scores range from 0 to 10. A score of 10 implies high cooperation and willingness to delegate authority. Source: Global Economic Forum, World Competitiveness Report 2016.

uncertainty. The higher a country's score on this dimension, the more uncertainty-averse the people in that country are. This dimension ranges from 8 (Singapore) to 112 in Greece. Its mean is 65, which corresponds to the score for Germany. France scores higher, 86, and the United States lower, 46 (Table 2.1, row 2). The ranks illustrate that on this cultural dimension the differences between the three countries are quite large. The inhabitants of the United States accept uncertainty much more easily than those of Germany and France.

Rieger *et al.* (2015) use an Ellsberg type of question to measure the degree of ambiguity aversion, which can be regarded as equivalent to uncertainty.[9] This type of question asks the respondents to make a choice between drawing a ball of a particular colour from an urn in which one knows the percentage of balls of that colour compared to one where this percentage is not known. The percentage of respondents choosing to draw from an urn with known distribution is taken as a measure of ambiguity aversion. Ambiguity corresponds in this terminology with uncertainty. The order is the same as in Hofstede's Uncertainty Avoidance (Table 2.1).

Human beings tend to dislike uncertainty. The measures of uncertainty aversion and ambiguity aversion presented above indicate the extent to which people in different countries dislike uncertainty. Many people want to avoid uncertainty. The manner in which they try to diminish it differs between persons and between groups. Some persons and groups see uncertainty more as a challenge than as a threat, whereas the opposite holds for others. The ways in which one can cope with uncertainty depend on the source of uncertainty (Hofstede 2001: 146). Technology has helped humanity deal with uncertainty caused by nature. Religion is an activity by which people can deal with uncertainties against which human beings cannot defend themselves. One can cope with uncertainty resulting from the behaviour of others by adhering to rules and laws, and by concentrating power in the hands of an authority.[10] As will be discussed in the rest of the book, it can be argued that the inhabitants of the United States tend to accept uncertainty; Germans prefer to stick to rules; and the French to delegate power to an authority. That inhabitants of the United States accept uncertainty more than those of the other two countries is reflected by the higher proportion of shares and equity in the US households' portfolio of financial assets.[11] The prominent authority of rules in Germany is reflected in the German expression *Befehl ist Befehl*, which reflects that the authority is derived from the position a person occupies, not the person themself. The French expression *bon plaisir*, which literally means 'good pleasure', describes the arbitrary will of the ruler in the seventeenth century, and reflects the high authority the French ascribe to a person (Hofstede 2001: 147). A study on subordinate–superior relations in production plants in France, the United States, and the Netherlands[12] reveals an *honour* relationship in France and a *fair contract* relationship in the United States. Social classes are important in France and thus also in French companies. This results in a hierarchy of different classes, white-collar workers versus blue-collar workers, and, within classes, skilled workers versus production workers. The interaction between the classes is governed by the respect for the honour concomitant to each class. This restricts the kind of orders a superior can give to a subordinate. In the United States everybody is supposed to be equal. The relationships are contractual so that a superior can ask anything within the limits of the contract. This can imply that they can ask more from subordinates than is possible in the French case.

2.3.3 The attitude towards concentration of power

The hierarchical market economy distinguishes itself from the other two types in that the society's design explicitly makes a difference between the ruler and the subordinates. In these societies, a hierarchical system is in place in which an elite (the state, in France) has to take care of the other members. In practice, this means a concentration of power and wealth in the hands of a few. Such a system can only operate if the majority in society accepts the role of the elite. An implicit social contract has to be in force by which the population allows power to rule (see Rousseau's famous *Du Contract Social* (2001 [1762])).

Hofstede's cultural dimension Power Distance measures the extent to which less powerful members of a society accept and expect that power and wealth is distributed unequally. The scores range from 11 (Austria) to 104 (Malaysia), with a mean of 57. Of the three countries concerned, France scores 68, the United States 40, and Germany (Federal Republic) 35 (Table 2.1). These scores indicate that, indeed, in France the acceptance of differences in power is higher than in the two other countries.

The study by van Oudenhoven *et al.* (2014) finds that French respondents are the only ones who mention generosity among the ten most important virtues (see Table 2.2). Generosity appears to be the most important one. This could indicate that according to the French the better-off have to be generous to their fellow citizens, a character trait, which could be important for the elite to show.

The ideal type of the hierarchical market economy explicitly singles out a group of persons, the elite, from the rest of the population. The other two types do not at first hand make a distinction between the different groups in society. Since the French elite is formed by design, one would expect that, due to their privileged position, members of the elite would also have different values and that the virtues they select as important would be different from those of the population at large. One would not expect such a difference between the social classes in the other two countries. If such differences are present there too, then we expect them to be less significant than in France.

In order to investigate these differences, we created social economic classes with data from the WVS based on the highest level of education attained by respondents. There are eight levels of education ranging from no education to a university-level degree. The answers to questions about which qualities are to be encouraged in children are used as indicators for preferred character traits. These questions read as follows: 'Here is a list of qualities that children can be encouraged to learn at home. Which, if any, do you consider to be especially important? Please choose

Table 2.2 Rank order (1–10) of the freely mentioned virtues in 14 nations, frequencies are indicated below the virtue

Rank order *Nation*	*1*	*2*	*3*	*4*	*5*	*6*	*7*	*8*	*9*	*10*
Austria	Honesty	Helpfulness	Kindness	Reliability	Openness	Punctuality	Tolerance	Ambition	Resolution	Humour
N = 276	169	80	79	68	47	45	42	29	27	27
France	Generosity	Courage	Honesty	Kindness	Respect	Empathy	Patience	Altruism	Smartness	Openness
N = 213	55	52	52	41	38	30	28	21	20	16
Great Britain	Kindness	Honesty	Humour	Happiness	Respect	Resolution	Patience	Helpfulness	Empathy	Openness/ Trust
N = 149	68	34	34	26	24	19	18	17	17	16
Germany	Honesty	Openness	Reliability	Respect	Tolerance	Kindness	Helpfulness	Humour	Punctuality	Justice/Joy
N = 220	157	80	67	66	63	58	50	32	30	25
Netherlands	Respect	Kindness	Honesty	Helpfulness	Social	Openness	Joy	Tolerance	Reliability	Responsibility
N = 6601	203	201	175	129	77	64	58	58	57	56
Norway	Openness	Empathy	Kindness	Honesty	Optimism	Humour	Social	Consideration	Patience	Helpfulness/ Caring
N = 190	72	55	52	48	44	32	31	30	23	23
Spain	Respect	Love	Honesty	Friendship	Happiness	Joy	Justice	Solidarity	Tolerance	Trust
N = 203	86	44	38	32	23	17	15	14	13	13
United States	Honesty	Kindness	Caring	Respect	Empathy	Patience	Openness	Modesty	Love	Humour/ Diligence
N = 191	105	57	36	31	28	26	24	22	21	20
	55%	30%	19%	16%	15%	14%	13%	12%	11%	10%

Note: The numbers are free listed virtues. They denote the rank orders of the ten most frequently mentioned virtues in each nation. Source: van Oudenhoven *et al.* (2014: 12).

up to five.' The respondent can then choose between thrift, good manners, tolerance and respect for other people, determination and perseverance, obedience, unselfishness, being hard-working, independence, being responsible, imagination, and religious faith. For each of the three countries, we estimate the individual score per child quality item. The estimation is conducted using a logit analysis that includes the two highest educational categories and the two lowest as an explanatory variable.[13] Then we investigated whether the scores of the two highest classes, encompassing 'some university and university categories', significantly differ from those of the two lowest classes, which include 'no education' and 'elementary school.' The results are summarized in the middle of Table 2.1. The most apparent result is that for the United States, the differences between the education classes are low; in seven out of ten cases, there is no significant difference and for the remaining three the difference is less significant than for one of the other two countries. The difference between the lowest and highest education groups is most significant for France in the case of thrift and obedience. The lower classes find it more important to teach their children thrift and obedience than do the more highly educated French. This confirms the idea that in France, the lower classes are more submissive and accept differences between classes, as is suggested by the high score on Power Distance. The highest difference is found for Germany in the case of imagination, determination, and hard-working. The higher educated in Germany score higher on imagination and determination and lower on hard-working.[14]

2.3.4 Time preference

Transactions on free markets are often between anonymous persons and are one-time events. Due to these characteristics of market transactions, the agents regard the transaction as such and do not consider the consequences for the future. This is less so for transactions that take place between people who know each other or who belong to the same network. Then, they are more likely to consider the consequences of their behaviour for their future position in the network. In accordance with this, firms in a network society appear to strive to increase the firm's values for all stakeholders, whereas in free market societies, shareholder value is more prominent. With this goes managers' preferences for continuity of the firm versus short-term profits. In sum, differences in time preference are likely to be a distinguishing cultural value between different types of market economies.

Hofstede's Long Term Orientation measures the relative importance attached to the future over the present. This dimension was not part of Hofstede's original analysis but has been added after the Chinese Connection Group found a dimension that they first called Confucianism. A high score on Long-Term Orientation means that the country's inhabitants attach a high value to future consequences. Germany is very much at the high end of the scale, scoring 83, and the United States, scoring 26, at the low end with France in between (see Table 2.1). The score for the United States suggests that US inhabitants are oriented towards the short term, a finding that is in accordance with studies on firm managers' goals (see, e.g., Hofstede *et al.* 2002).

2.4 Governance

Governance refers to the way people interact. Interactions between people are much easier if the different partners trust each other. Transaction costs are expected to be lower in such a case. A high degree of willingness to cooperate is expected to have similar effects. We therefore present scores on trust and on the willingness to cooperate.

2.4.1 Trust

Trust is a frequently used cultural variable. It is measured by the dichotomous item whether 'most people can be trusted or whether you cannot be too careful' from the World Values Survey. Table 2.1 shows the percentages of people answering yes to the question. Trust appears to be highest in the United States and the lowest in France. The German score is closer to the United States' score than to the French score. The Global Preferences Survey measures trust by means of the question: 'I assume that people have only the best intentions.' The order of these scores is similar to the WVS measure. Only Germany has a lower rank than in the WVS measure.

2.4.2 Cooperation

Whether differences in opinion or interest lead to a conflict depends on whether one is willing to cooperate instead of seeking confrontation. The business leaders' opinions on the degree of cooperation in labour employment relations are used as an indicator of willingness to cooperate. It appears that the United States and Germany have a relatively high degree of cooperation in labour relations (Table 2.1 at the bottom). For France, however, cooperation is much less. Labour relations there are often very conflictive and violent. A good example is a board meeting of Air France on October 5, 2015. The board discussed the need to cut costs. During the board's discussions, a group of angry employees stormed the fence and took control of the board room where the managers were meeting. [...] a short time later it was clear that some managers had been physically assaulted. Human resources manager Xavier Broseta was in a particularly bad way, losing not only his glasses but also his jacket and shirt. He escaped his attackers by fleeing and scaling a fence, still wearing his tie but minus his shirt. One union leader later said that Broseta had 'narrowly escaped being lynched.' (van Laer 2020: 25)

During the financial crisis of 2008, similar scenes were observed. In some cases, employees locked managers in their offices, blaming the latter for factories having to be closed or for employees being fired because of financial problems. The protests by the Yellow Vests in 2018 and 2019 are evidence of the same phenomenon. Van Laer (2020: 24–29) ascribes this cleavage between managers and employees to the fact that managers in large French companies are recruited from the alumni of the *Grandes écoles* (see also Piketty 2020: 757, and Chapters 5 and 7). This is a group of in-crowds, who pass jobs to each other without any serious investigation of the qualifications needed.

Arriving at a deal can also be facilitated if leaders are willing to delegate authority to subordinates. This can increase the speed by which a solution can be found; more people can work towards finding a solution. In addition, a solution offered is more easily accepted if the various parties involved have had a say in the process. Once again France stands out as the country where, according to business leaders, the willingness to cooperate is relatively low (Table 2.1).

2.4.3 Views on market mechanisms

The different waves of the World Values Survey contain questions directly referring to the organization or possible outcomes (distribution of income and wealth) of a market economy. The three countries' scores on each of these indicators are presented in Table 2.3. As expected, the United States' scores

Table 2.3 How a market should function

	United States	*Germany*	*France*
Competition: harmful (1) or good (10)[i]	7.68	7.46	6.27
Income inequality: more equal (1) or larger (10)[ii]	6.00	5.22	5.08
Ownership of businesses: state-owned (1) or private (10)[iii]	7.60	6.54	6.61
Responsibility: government (1) or people (10)[iv]	6.83	5.95	6.58
Luck and connections (1) or hard work brings success (10)[v]	7.35	6.53	6.58
Enough for all (1) or wealth at expense of others(10)[vi]	4.61	4.39	4.94

Note: All items are included in waves 2–6 of the World Value Survey, except for the items referring to hard work and wealth at the expense of others. These latter two items were not included in wave 4. Respondents are asked to score the following items on a scale from 1 to 10:

(i) Competition is good because it stimulates people to work hard and develop new ideas, or competition is harmful because it brings out the worst in people;
(ii) Income inequality: incomes should be made more equal or we need larger income differences as an incentive;
(iii) Private or government ownership of businesses should be increased;
(iv) The government should take more responsibility that everyone is provided for, or whether people should do that themselves;
(v) In the long run, hard work usually brings a better life or hard work doesn't generally bring success—it's more a matter of luck and connections; and
(vi) People can only get rich at the expense of others or whether wealth can grow so there's enough for everyone.

indicate a preference for competition, private ownership, and responsibility taken by the people themselves. Consistent with these scores, hard work is considered important for success. These scores reflect the high degree of individualism in the United States and the belief that people are responsible for their own success (see also Alesina and Glaeser 2004). Of the three countries concerned, the inhabitants of Germany are most in favour of the government owning firms and taking responsibility. The respondents in the United States care less than those in Germany and France for equality in income. French respondents are most inclined to think that one can only get rich at the expense of others.

2.5 Concluding remarks

In this chapter, we have sketched each of the three countries' history and their scores on measures of dominant values of the population at large. From the information thus provided, we conclude that the culture of the United States stimulates individual initiative and accepts uncertainty. German culture favours competition less but still accepts it. Uncertainty is a phenomenon the Germans dislike to a great extent. France is a hierarchical country. The elite is expected to behave in a different way from the common people and their scores differ on many items from those of lower classes. The low level of willingness to cooperate combined with the hierarchical approach can easily set the scene for conflicts. This is one of France's paradoxes: employees expect help from employers but distrust them too.

This chapter brings Part I of this book to an end: the stage is set. This part has described the developments in economics motivated by, amongst other things, the fall of the Berlin Wall. It noted that these developments have increased interest in the place of norms and values in the functioning of an economy, but that at the same time the position of the economist has remained that of an impartial observer. The aim of this book is to show the relationship between values and norms in economic theories, the population at large, and the consequences for the functioning of economies. Chapter 2 has provided an overview of the dominant views of the population and brief descriptions of historical events that may have inculcated these values. Part II will discuss in more detail the positions of the three schools of economic thought associated with each country, namely the free market tradition (Chapter 3), the ordoliberal school in Germany (Chapter 4), and the French school of economic engineers (Chapter 6). Where appropriate, we will link these descriptions to the population's values as presented in the present chapter.

Notes

1 Representative samples represent the structure of a country's population. It is well known that values can be different because respondents differ on birth year (cohort effect), age, gender, or occupation. Consequently, using representative samples in

order to investigate differences in values between inhabitants of different countries can deliver biased results in cases where the structure of the populations differ. It is therefore recommended that matched samples be used in order to study cultural differences. Two matched samples differ only in that the respondents are from different countries or organizations. The age, gender, and occupation structure of the samples is the same.

2 Unless indicated otherwise, this section is based on Hoppe and Bhagat (2007).

3 See the following quote from the inaugural address of Calvin Coolidge: 'The wise and correct course [...] is not to destroy those who have already secured success but to create conditions under which everyone will have a better chance to be successful.'

4 This section is largely based on Brodbeck and Frese (2008).

5 In 2002, *The Economist* published a report on Germany entitled 'The Uncertain Giant.'

6 Much of this section is from Castel *et al.* (2008).

7 The critique on the privileged background of these schools' students has inspired president Macron to announce a reform of the system and to close the École Nationale d'Adminstration (ENA), see Abboud (2021).

8 Knight (1921) has introduced this distinction between uncertainty and risk in economics.

9 The concept known as uncertainty in economics is equivalent to ambiguity in the psychological literature. In psychology, the term 'uncertainty' encompasses both ambiguity and risk.

10 Hofstede argues that, in general, this process of accepting that others take the decisions is not related to uncertainty but to the degree to which the lower classes in society accept that the elite has more power and wealth. He also notes that within Europe and the Western world these two are highly correlated so that one cannot distinguish between the two (see Hofstede, 2001: 150). Since we confine our analysis to Western countries, we feel free to regard delegating power to an authority as a valid way of reducing uncertainty.

11 Over the period 2008–2017, this share is about 30% in the United States, 20% in France, and 10% in Germany (see OECD, 2019, Household financial assets [indicator]. doi: 10.1787/7519b9dc-en, accessed on 30 July, 2019).

12 This study is carried out by Phillipe d'Iribane and referred to in Hofstede (2001: 118 and 119).

13 Other variables used in the estimation are survey wave, age, age-squared, trust, religiosity and gender.

14 For the United States of America, Caplan (2007) studies the difference in opinion on economic issues between economists, the public, and the enlightened public. The latter is a person with average income, average job satisfaction, etc., except for being an economist. The opinion of the enlightened public is often between the public and the economists but closer to the economists' view. For our study, it is most important to notice that opinions can differ between different layers within the same society but that across societies there is a correlation between the opinions of different classes. This can imply, as in the case of France, that all classes agree that each class has its own role, which is different from that of others.

References

Abboud, L. (2021) Macron to close training school of France elite, *Financial Times*, April 8, 2021.

Alesina, A. and E. L. Glaeser (2004) *Fighting Poverty in the US and Europe: A World of Difference*, Oxford: Oxford University Press.

Arts, W., J. Hagenaars and G. Moors (2003) Exploring Europe's basic value map. In W. Arts, J. Hagenaars and L. Halman (eds.), *The Cultural Diversity of European Unity: Findings,*

Explanations and Reflections from the European Values Study, Leiden and Boston, MA: Brill: 23–58.

Beugelsdijk, S., R. Maseland and A. van Hoorn (2015) Are scores on Hofstede's dimensions of national culture stable over time?, *Global Strategy Journal* 5: 223–240.

Braudel, F. (1990) *Beschaving, Economie en kapitalisme (15de – 18de eeuw): Deel III De tijd van de wereld (Civilization, Economics and Capitalism (15th – 18th Century): The Time of the World)*, Amsterdam: Uitgeverij Contact.

Brodbeck, F. C. and M. Frese (2008) Societal culture and leadership in Germany. In J. S. Chhokar, F. C. Brodbeck and R. J. House (eds.), *Culture and Leadership Across the World: The GLOBE BOOK of In-depth Studies of 25 Societies*, New York: Lawrence Erlbaum Associates Publishers: 147–214.

Caplan, B. (2007) *The Myth of the Rational Voter: Why Democracies Choose Bad Policies*, Princeton, NJ: Princeton University Press.

Castel, P., M. Deneire, A. Kurc, M.-F. Lacassagne and C. A. Leeds (2008) Universalism and exceptionalism: French business leadership. In J. S. Chhokar, F. C. Brodbeck and R. J. House (eds.), *Culture and Leadership Across the World: The GLOBE BOOK of In-depth Studies of 25 Societies*, New York: Lawrence Erlbaum Associates Publishers: 547–581.

Coolidge, C. (1925) Inaugural address, March 4, 1925.

Falk, A., A. Becker, T. Dohmen, B. Enke, D. Huffman and U. Sunde (2016) *The preference survey module: A validated instrument for measuring risk time and social preferences*, IZA Discussion Paper 9674, Bonn: IZA Institute of Labor Economics.

Falk, A., A. Becker, T. Dohmen, B. Enke, D. Huffman, U. Sunde (2018) Global evidence on economic preferences, *The Quarterly Journal of Economics* 133(4): 1645–1692.

Hofstede, G. (2001) *Culture's Consequences: Comparing Values, Behaviors, Institutions and Organizations across Nations*, Thousand Oaks, CA: Sage Publications.

Hofstede, G., C. A. van Deusen, C. B. Mueller and T. A. Charles (2002) What goals do business leaders pursue? A study in fifteen countries, *Journal of International Business Studies* 33(4): 785–803.

Hofstede, G., G. J. Hofstede and M. Minkov (2010) *Cultures and Organizations: Software of the Mind*, New York: McGraw-Hill.

Hoppe, M. H. and R. S. Bhagat (2007) Leadership in the United States of America: The leader as cultural hero. In J. S. Chhokar, F. C. Brodbeck and R. J. House (eds.), *Culture and Leadership Across the World: The GLOBE BOOK of In-depth Studies of 25 Societies*, New York: Lawrence Erlbaum Associates Publishers: 475–546.

Inglehart, R. (1997) *Modernization and Postmodernization: Cultural, Economic and Political Change in 43 Societies*, Princeton, NJ: Princeton University Press.

Issing, O. (2005) Why did the great inflation not happen in Germany?, *Federal Reserve Bank of St. Louis Review* 87(2): 329–336.

Knight, F. H. (1921) *Risk, Uncertainty and Profit*, Boston, MA, and New York: Houghton Mifflin Company.

Piketty, T. (2020) *Capital and Ideology*, Cambridge, MA: The Belknap Press of Harvard University Press.

Rieger, M., M. Wang and T. Hens (2015) Risk preferences around the world, *Management Science* 61(3): 637–648.

Rousseau, J. J. (2001 [1762]) *Du Contact Social*, Paris: Flammarion.

Siedentop, L. (2014) *Inventing the Individual: The Origins of Western Liberalism*, Cambridge, MA: The Belknap Press of Harvard University Press.

Timberlake, R. H. (1993) *Monetary Policy in the United States: An Intellectual and Institutional History*, Chicago, IL: The University of Chicago Press.

Van Laer, E. (2020) *The Desperate Union: What Is Going Wrong in the European Union?*, London: Union Bridge Books.

Van Oudenhoven, J. P., B. de Raad, M. E. Timmerman, F. Askevis-Leherpeux, P. Boski, C. Carmona, …, M. Yik (2014) Are virtues national, supranational, or universal? *SpringerPlus* 3(1), 223. doi:10.1186/2193-1801-3-223.

Part II

Economic ideas

3 The morality of the market process and the normative implications of catallactic competition

Rosolino A. Candela

3.1 Introduction

The most incredible fact in recent economic history is the rapid decline of extreme poverty throughout the developing world. According to the World Bank, the world's population currently living on less than two dollars per day has fallen from roughly 2 billion people in 1990 to 700 million in 2015 (Cruz *et al.* 2015). This dramatic reduction in poverty has occurred in spite of an increase in the world's population of about 2 billion during that same time. This 'Great Escape', as Angus Deaton has termed it, has been due to an *institutional* turn from central economic planning towards the market, specifically an institutional framework of private property and freedom of contract under the rule of law, particularly in countries such as China and India (Deaton 2013: 44). Moreover, the proportion of the world's population living in extreme poverty is the lowest it has been in recorded history. As of the end of 2015, the percentage of individuals living on less than two dollars per day has fallen to less than 10% of the world's population. Life expectancy has increased and the incidence of infant mortality has plummeted. Human beings are living healthier, wealthier, and more productive lives than ever. These astonishing facts remind us, as Robert Lucas has stated, that 'once one starts to think about them, it is hard to think about anything else' (1988: 5). In spite of this 'Great Fact' of economic history, as Deidre McCloskey puts it (2006, 2010, 2016), the market process is regarded, at best, as being orthogonal to questions of distributive justice and morality (see Heath 2018), and at worst, generating the conditions for atomistic greed, crass consumerism, or other social interaction that crowds out the scope for human flourishing.[1]

This raises the central question of this chapter: do the same institutional conditions that frame the market process also make the conditions for moral action *possible*? To answer this question, I will develop the normative implications of competition in the market process. As a value-free science, positive economics illustrates the economic consequences of different forms of competitive behaviour for resource allocation and income distribution. I explore the normative implications of competition under alternative institutional arrangements. In doing so, I distinguish between catallactic competition, based upon

DOI: 10.4324/9781003208549-3

an individual's willingness and ability to pay for resources generated through trade and productive specialization, and non-catallactic competition, based upon legal status and privilege generated through political exchange. I argue that the normative implications of substituting market, or catallactic, competition for non-market, or non-catallactic, competition is that the conditions for human flourishing are made possible. Whereas catallactic competition tends to *liberate* the individual from arbitrary assignments of resources and income based on creed, gender, race, or legal status, non-cattalactic competition tends to *confine* an individual's potential for self-actualization to such arbitrary assignments.

3.2 The free market tradition: A critical assessment

In the wake of the collapse of centrally planned economies in Central and Eastern Europe, one of the most well-respected and outspoken socialists of his time, Robert Heilbroner, wrote in *The New Yorker* that capitalism had been triumphant over socialism (1989). He later declared that Ludwig von Mises, the great Austrian economist of the twentieth century, 'had been right' in his assessment of the inefficiency of socialism (Heilbroner 1990). As early as 1920, Mises had argued that economic calculation under socialism would be impossible. By abolishing private property in the means of production, exchange ratios in the form of money prices would not emerge to calculate the scarcity of capital goods relative to their alternative consumer uses. Therefore, socialism would be unable to organize production more efficiently compared to capitalism (Mises 1920 [1975], 1922 [1951], 1949 [1966]).

Though the debate over economic calculation under socialism has been settled, Mises had also been right about something else: 'A social system, however beneficial, cannot work if it is not supported by public opinion' (1949[1966]: 865). It is because capitalism is still regarded as being inherently unjust[2] that it has not yet been fully vindicated (Kirzner 1989 [2016]: 5). For example, in a recent article, philosopher Joseph Heath has declared the following: 'The one thing that can be said with certainty, however, is that the way wages are set in a market economy strikes most people as morally counterintuitive, if not positively unjust' (Heath 2018: 3).

Indeed, Mises' critique of socialism was *neither* a normative critique of the declared ends of socialism (1920 [1975]: 120), nor a normative defence of the moral superiority of capitalism. Rather, it was a positive critique regarding the internal consistency between the stated end of socialism, namely, to deliver advanced material production to the benefit of the least advantaged in society, and the means by which to achieve this end, namely, to abolish private property in the means of production. Mises had been trying to illustrate that socialism would fail on its own terms, no matter how benevolent or motivated central planners would be about meeting their stated ends. That said, it would be false to conclude that either Mises or the broader free market tradition of which he was part, were silent or otherwise bereft of sympathy towards the economic and social conditions of the poor working class of society. If anything, free market economists from at least the time of Adam Smith have consistently *shared* the same ends as its critics, including the elimination of exploitation of the poor and least advantaged in society. Smith went so far as to argue that the economic *and* moral superiority of capitalism was *dependent* upon eliminating artificial barriers that prevented the least advantaged in society from realizing their full potential.

> The liberal reward of labour, therefore, as it is the necessary effect, so it is the natural symptom of increasing national wealth. The scanty maintenance of the labouring poor, on the other hand, is the natural symptom that things are at a stand, and their starving condition that they are going fast backwards.
>
> (Smith 1776 [1981]: 75)

> No society can surely be flourishing and happy, of which the far greater part of the members are poor and miserable. It is but equity, besides, that they who feed, clothe and lodge the whole body of the people, should have such a share of the produce of their own labour as to be themselves tolerably well fed, clothed and lodged.
>
> (Smith 1776 [1981]: 96)

Building on Adam Smith, the founder of the Austrian school of economics and one of the pioneers of the Marginal Revolution, Carl Menger, writes the following:

> The economic policy of classical political economy was precisely dedicated to the most immediate and urgent needs of the time in which it came into being, a time full of unjust class privileges and detrimental restrictions on the poor and weak, full of irrational and self-interested over-regulation. Smith and his disciples recognized the needs of *Social-Politik* in their time very precisely when they first pressed for the abolition of the harmful restrictions on workers and when they opposed the state interventions in the economy detrimental to the poor.
>
> (emphasis original, Menger 1891 [2016]: 482)

This statement by Menger is evidenced not only in the quotes from Adam Smith, but as I show below, also among early neoclassicals, such as Alfred Marshall, running throughout the twentieth century to free-market economists of the Chicago School, including Milton Friedman and George Stigler. For example, Marshall clearly shared the same concern as Smith and Menger with the injustice of inequality, particularly when it came at the expense of the least advantaged in society:

> The drift of economic science during many generations has been with increasing force towards the belief that there is no real necessity, and

> therefore no moral justification for extreme poverty side by side with great wealth. The inequalities of wealth, though less than they are often represented to be, are a serious flaw in our economic organization. Any diminution of them which can be attained by means that would not sap the springs of free initiative and strength of character, and would not therefore materially check the growth of the national dividend, would seem to be a clear social gain.
>
> (emphasis added, 1920 [2013]: 594)

This consistent attention to the welfare of the least advantaged in society had led George Stigler to argue that '[e]conomists as a class have *always been opposed* to inequality of income' (emphasis added, 1949: 1). Building on this point, Friedman states that there 'is a clear justification for social action of a very different kind than taxation to affect the distribution of income', namely by adjusting

> the rules of the game so as to eliminate these sources of inequality. For example, special monopoly privileges granted by government, tariffs, and other legal enactments benefiting particular groups, are a source of inequality. The removal of these, the liberal will welcome.
>
> (Friedman 1962 [2002]: 176)

Therefore, the question amongst free-market economists has never been whether or not less inequality is a desirable end. The relevant inquiry, rather, has been regarding the most effective means to reduce income inequality. For classical political economists, and market-oriented neoclassical economists, income inequality is a consequence of a more fundamental injustice related to restrictions on economic and social mobility. 'The lesson of history, *explained by classical economic analysis*', according to William Hutt, 'is that disinterested market pressures, under the profit-seeking inducement, provide the *only* objective, systematic discipline that would dissolve traditional barriers and offer opportunities irrespective of race or colour' or other inherited attributes of individuals (emphasis added, Hutt 1964: 73). Therefore, labour market restrictions are regarded as immoral not because of their effect on the distribution of income per se, but rather because they cause disproportionate harm to the least advantaged in society. We will return to this latter point in greater detail in Section 3.4.

In spite of the fact that, from Adam Smith onwards, economists identified as defenders of the free market have consistently and persistently upheld the welfare of the least advantaged in society as the normative benchmark by which to assess the performance of markets, this message has become lost in translation. Why, then, has it been the case that free markets have come to be regarded as unjust, immoral, and deaf to the cries of the least advantaged in society? For the purposes of the point being made here, namely that the same institutional conditions that make free markets possible are also the same institutional conditions that make moral action possible, I shall offer two explanations.

The first explanation is one suggested by Walter Lippmann in *The Good Society* (1937 [2005]). Lipmann gives 1870 as the year from which liberalism coincidentally entered into an intellectual crisis of its own construction. The irony is that the classical political economists predating the Marginal Revolution, who had explicitly outlined the institutional conditions necessary for the free market as well as liberalism, had come to be identified with extreme laissez faire, which seemed unable to address the realities of monopoly power, of inherent instability caused by the speculative behaviour of financial capital, and of the inequalities and injustice that resulted from concentrations of wealth. The new liberals of the progressive left, though, in their effort to respond to this earlier intellectual weakness, moved too easily into collectivism. There is a modicum of truth to this argument, but not due to any moral callousness, lack of concern for the poor, or indifference to income inequality among defenders of a market economy. Rather, the association of the free markets with laissez faire is indicative of a misunderstanding of the proper institutional conditions framing a market economy.

This misunderstanding was borne out of a *methodological* transition in early neoclassical economics and the equilibrium paradigm that was later adopted by neoclassical economists, who did so to rectify the deficiencies left by classical political economists, including the 'failure to work out the theory of the effects of competition on the distribution of income' (Stigler 1957: 5). For example, in attempting to illustrate that the outcome of the market process resulted in income distributions that were not exploitative, John Bates Clark (1899) and Phillip Wicksteed (1894) based their analysis upon an application of Euler's theorem to the distribution of income. Euler's theorem states that, under the assumption of constant returns to scale, the separate marginal value products of each factor of production exhaust the total value of output. The exhaustion of payments from total output to factors of production had both positive and normative implications. Positively speaking, Euler's theorem illustrated mathematically that the share of total output accrued to owners of capital is derived from its marginal contribution to output. Normatively speaking, this implies that the redistribution of income is unjustified, since the income paid to capitalists is not a result of exploitation or theft of labour income. Moreover, to the extent that modern defenders or critics of Adam Smith have focused on the allocative efficiency of the free market understood as an outcome of the invisible hand, this has been filtered through an equilibrium paradigm. Therefore, it is more appropriate to claim that early neoclassicals, at best, illustrated that the distribution of income by free markets was *not unjust*, rather than claiming they illustrate that it is just, since an equilibrium analysis of free markets cannot justify the residual payments, such as profits to entrepreneurs. By neglecting the role of competition and entrepreneurship, and leaving undefended the role of entrepreneurial profits in the market process, ironically, early neoclassicals adopted the same normative implications regarding the justice of the market process as those held by the early Marxists against whom they were defending the distributive justice of the free market. Given that neoclassical economists took equilibrium as their theoretical point of analytical departure, defining entrepreneurial profits out of existence, the presence of firms selling goods above opportunity costs not only implies monopoly power, but even worse, the presence of 'unearned' rents to capitalists (see Boettke, Candela, and Woltz 2018, 2021; Kirzner 2019).

Thus, an equilibrium paradigm, by definition, excludes from its analysis not only the appropriate institutional conditions upon which free markets, but also moral agency, are based. That is, in a world in which all the gains from trade have already been exhausted, as is the case in equilibrium, the *process* by which such gains become created, become realized, and become exhausted by human agency within alternative sets of institutions becomes irrelevant to the positive as well as the normative analysis of markets. The irony is that the so-called 'free market' in this model, one that is populated by *homo economicus*, who maximizes passively to constraints, is a model that is devoid of free human agency, upon which moral action, and markets, are based. To be free implies responsibility for one's actions, which in turn presupposes human moral agency. But instinctual response to constraints, as is the case with *homo economicus*, is inconsistent with human agency. Moreover, in a world of equilibrium, one in which transaction costs are zero, markets are unnecessary and redundant, since resources have already been allocated to their most valued uses. In the words of the nineteenth-century French political economist, Frédéric Bastiat, one of the most eloquent defenders of the market process, 'the worst thing that can happen to a good cause is, not to be skilfully attacked, but to be ineptly defended' (1996: 107).

This raises the second explanation, which is fundamentally the basis for the first as well. As I have argued elsewhere (see Boettke and Candela 2017, 2019), early neoclassical economists had a common understanding of the proper institutional context undergirding a liberal market order. However, the Marginal Revolution had begun a tendency that relegated such a common understanding to the background of analysis. What emerged into the foreground was a growing emphasis on analyzing markets as equilibrium states rather than processes. The twin analytical revolutions of subjective utility theory and marginal analysis would repair most of the serious difficulties in the economist theories of value, cost, exchange, production, and distribution during the 1870–1930 period. However, the institutions that frame a liberal market order were taken as given, so much so that their role in providing the rules governing a market economy, which critics of liberalism claimed to be lacking, had become relatively neglected, resulting in the notion that markets operated in an institutional vacuum.

The resulting association of liberalism with *laissez faire*, therefore, required a rearticulation and restatement of the role that institutions play in the operation of a liberal market order. Among the economists at the forefront of this intellectual effort was Lionel Robbins of the London School of Economics. In

The Theory of Economic Policy in English Classical Political Economy (1952), a book written during the 1930s, but not published until after the Second World War, Robbins argued that critics of economics were wrong to suggest that classical political economists from Adam Smith to J. S. Mill treated economic actors as asocial beings devoid of any historical and institutional context. Quite the contrary, classical political economy always saw commercial activity embedded within legal, political, and moral contexts.

> The English Classical Economists never conceived the system of economic freedom as arising *in vacuo* or functioning in a system of law and order so simple and so minimal as to be capable of being written down on a limited table of stone (or a revolutionary handbill) and restricted to the functions of the night watchman. Nothing less than the whole complex of the Benthamite codes – Civil, Penal and Constitutional – was an adequate framework for their system.
>
> (emphasis original, 1952: 188)

It was only by resurrecting an analysis of the institutional preconditions of a market economy that the moral content of the market process could be reintroduced by its defenders, and its normative implications analyzed.

3.3 Cattalactic vs. non-catallactic competition

Before turning to the normative implications of competition in the market process, it is first important to provide a positive analysis of the *institutional* basis for the market process as well as its consequences. I use the word 'institutional' to emphasize that the distinguishing characteristic of the market process is *not* competition based on *laissez-faire*. While this statement may seem controversial, a simple 'unpacking' of the words 'competition' and '*laissez-faire*' will lead us to understand, first, why such a characterization is highly misleading, and, second, what distinguishes the market process from other forms of economic and social interaction.

First, competition, at its most fundamental level, is nothing more than *a process of conflict resolution*, and, therefore, is a universal attribute of all human interaction across time and place. Given the fundamental pervasiveness of scarcity, *every* form of economic and social interaction is inherently competitive in that individuals must resolve how to fulfil their own individual ends, which are always greater than the means to achieve such ends (Alchian 1965; Alchian and Allen 1972). No economic or social system, such as capitalism, communism, or fascism, can abolish scarcity, and therefore cannot eliminate competition. While competition is ubiquitous, the manner in which competition manifests itself is *institutionally contingent* (Boettke 2012). Therefore, to characterize a free market economy as a 'competitive system' implies nothing about the unique *manifestation* of competition in the market process.

Secondly, this brings us the distinguishing *institutional* characteristic of a free market economy, which is *catallactic competition* within a legal framework of well-defined and well-enforced exchangeable private property rights. To argue that a free market economy is a *laissez-faire* economy implies that markets operate within an institutional vacuum, without any account of the rules governing what forms of competition are sanctioned and those that are prohibited by formal and informal rules.[3] As F. A. Hayek has stated on this point:

> a government that is comparatively inactive but does the wrong things may do much more to cripple the forces of a market economy than one that is more concerned with economic affairs but confines itself to actions which assist the spontaneous forces of the economy.
>
> (1960: 222)

That is, the distinguishing characteristic of a free market economy is one in which a governing authority enforces *exchangeable private property rights*. Property rights, broadly speaking, refer to a set of sanctioned social relationships that define one's expectations regarding the utilization of scarce resources (Furubotn and Pejovich 1972: 1139 see also Barzel 1997).

Private property rights refer not to rights to an object *per se*, but a set of rights to *action*, including the right to exclude, use, and exchange resources. Secure private property rights imply that individuals have the ability to exclude resources from both private and public predation, including one's own labour. Excludability of resources assigns residual claimancy over the costs and benefits of an action initiated by an individual. Without private ownership, when a person uses resources, they impose costs involuntarily onto third parties, also known as externalities. Therefore, private property rights provide accountability over the costs and benefits of an individual's actions through the internalization of positive and negative externalities (Demsetz 1967: 350). Through such internalization, private property rights promote social responsibility since the decision-maker of a particular action must bear the full cost of his action. From this perspective, if 'market failures' associated with business cycles, externalities, monopoly power, or public goods are systematic and pervasive, this implies a government failure to enforce private property rights, or the preclusion of entrepreneurs from bearing the full costs and benefits of their decision-making. The right to use resources implies that individuals have the ability to use resources for direct consumption, deferred consumption (i.e., savings and investment), and *indirect* consumption via productive specialization and trade. It is the distinct ability to use one's land, labour, and capital to *compete* by productively specializing in one's comparative advantage and trading resources that distinguish the right to private property from other forms of property, such as public property or communal property. It is in this sense that Ludwig von Mises (1949 [1966]: 274), F. A. Hayek (1976: 108–109), and James Buchanan (1964: 216–217) referred to such competition in the market process as *catallactic*.

The term 'catallactics' was first used by Reverend Richard Whatley in 1831 to suggest a replacement for the word 'economics', which is derived from the Greek word *oikonomia*, meaning 'household management.' Such a term misleadingly implies that economic science is about the deliberate allocation of resources via the conscious direction of given means and given ends. The term 'catallactics' is derived from the Greek verb *katallattein* (or *katallassein*), which means 'to exchange', and 'to admit into the community', as well as 'to change from enemy into friend' (see Hayek 1976: 108–109). Mises, Hayek, and Buchanan revived this term in the twentieth century to emphasize a broader point about the market process, which is to say that productive specialization and exchange is a *peaceful* and *cooperative* form of competition, the conditions of which also provide the *possibility* of human flourishing. How this possibility is realized by individuals will be discussed in greater detail in Section 3.4. Suffice it to say, a free market economy provides the institutional context for this possibility, since the security of private property establishes the conditions for moral agency and, by its very definition, must prohibit individuals from competing for resources through the utilization of violence, either directly through private predation or indirectly through public predation. Therefore, a free market economy implies that private property rights are secure *under the rule of law*.

The rule of law refers to the absence of political or legal privilege among market actors *and* the absence of arbitrary discretion among political actors. It is a political–legal principle, whereby the governing authority of a particular society is restricted to enforcing laws applied equally to all and not intended to benefit one particular party at the expense of another. Any violation of the rule of law implies that political or legal privileges cannot be granted without simultaneously granting discretionary power to those political actors who are in the position to grant such privileges. Therefore, the presence, or lack thereof, of the rule of law determines whether human interaction will be positive-sum or negative-sum in nature (Candela and Piano 2018).

Without the rule of law, catallactic competition will degenerate into non-catallactic competition, namely the indirect use of violence to compete for resources. Such competition manifests itself in entrepreneurs courting the favour of those in power in order to obtain tariffs, monopoly privileges, or other regulations that protect them from competition in the market place, a competitive process known as rent-seeking (Tullock 1967). The opposition to government intervention into the market process by proponents of the free market is not due to an objection to government enforcement of 'the rules of the game.' Rather, from Adam Smith to Vernon Smith, the opposition among free market economists to government intervention is due to the fact that government intervention fundamentally changes the rules by which the game is played by entrepreneurs. Because in a free market entrepreneurs are barred from rent-seeking, the rules of the game dictate that they can only compete against each other successfully by benefiting others, namely by offering goods and services that consumers value. Government intervention, by its very nature, introduces political and legal discretion, which represents a profit opportunity for entrepreneurs to capture for their own private benefit at the expense of other producers in the market process, to say nothing about consumers (Stigler 1971). Therefore, government intervention tends to redirect the allocation of entrepreneurial talent from productive and catallactic activities to unproductive and non-catallactic activities.

3.4 Natural and artifactual man: The morality of the market process

In the previous section, we discussed the positive implications of catallactic and non-catallactic competition, the purpose of which was to establish a positive basis for the normative implications of such forms of competition. This positive basis for the morality of the market process can be summarized as follows: *there exist mutual gains from productive specialization and trade*. In doing so, I illustrate how the institutional conditions of the market process also provide the context within which moral action is made possible, and how interventions into the market process tend to create the possibility of immoral action.

In order to understand the non-normative basis for the normative implications of the market process, we must first begin by stating that, going back to Adam Smith, a consistent analytical approach to positive theorizing has existed among proponents of the free market (though it is not exclusive to them), dubbed by economists Sandra Peart and David Levy as 'analytical egalitarianism' (2008). According to this approach, the analytical thrust in explaining differences in economic outcomes across place and time is placed on differences in institutions. Analytical egalitarianism abstracts away from any inherent or observed differences among individuals by treating them, from an analytical standpoint, as natural equals, in order to illustrate how alternative institutional arrangements filter through different manifestations of competition, and as a by-product of such purposive behaviour, different economic, political, and social outcomes. James Buchanan summarizes this approach quite nicely in the following statement: same players, under different rules, generate different games (Buchanan 2008). From an analytically egalitarian standpoint, all individuals are striving to actualize their own potential under the given circumstances they face, and therefore, whether or not they realize this potential will depend upon the free exercise of their agency.

At first blush, analytical egalitarianism may seem to be a highly unrealistic theoretical approach, but in order to further unpack this idea, and illustrate its positive explanatory power for our normative purpose here, let us incorporate James Buchanan's distinction between 'natural' and 'artifactual' man (Buchanan 1979). According to Buchanan, self-actualization and human flourishing are defined in the process of one's own choices through time. The ability of individuals to imagine and become something different from what they already are is a categorical feature of being human. Human flourishing, therefore, is not defined by a set of constraints but is realized in the process of actualizing one's potential. That being said, this does not deny that individuals are born into a particular historical context, not of their own choosing, defined by inherited physical or biological traits, including race, creed, and gender, but also by the evolved cultural and legal norms into which the individual is born. This inherited aspect of an individual that constrains one's choice set is the 'natural' part of man. This natural aspect of man, however, does not predefine one's ability to lead a flourishing life but *becomes a part of what individuals will become*. Within these limits, therefore, by virtue of the fact that individuals must exercise their agency, there is an artifactual aspect of man that is dependent on the freedom to pursue one's human flourishing.

Thus, the point of employing analytical egalitarianism, for our purposes here, is both positive and normative. It is of course the case that individuals are different with respect to their 'natural' differences. However, from an analytical egalitarian standpoint, the relevant differences between individuals, namely those that explain income differences *across societies*, are *by-products* of productive specialization and social cooperation under the division of labour; such differences are not explained by innate traits or talents. Moreover, such large-scale productive specialization can only be realized under an individual framework of private property and freedom of contract under the rule of law. Therefore, the explanatory variable regarding differences in human progress are *differences in institutions, not differences in individuals*. Normatively speaking, by focusing on the universal attribute of all individuals and abstracting from one's natural characteristics, the moral justification for a market economy under the rule of law is that it *liberates* the individual from their human flourishing being confined to their natural self, and expands the scope for the artifactual creation of possible selves. Because this creative process cannot be defined independently of one's choice, the attenuation of private property and the rule of law is immoral in the sense that it introduces political and legal discretion that tends to confine one's flourishing to their natural self.

That the actualization of one's human nature has both universal qualities and qualities that are particular to each individual is not only consistent but also the source of the creativity and innovation required for a prospering liberal market order. In his recent book, *Mass Flourishing*, Edmund Phelps, Nobel Laureate in economics, argues that an institutional framework that protects private property rights, enforces contracts, and upholds the rule of law is a necessary condition for the emergence of the informal norms and values, such as creativity, risk-taking, and innovation, that drive economic growth. Normatively speaking, he states that the 'good' economy is one that provides the institutional conditions that protect the possibility of human flourishing among individuals (2013: 288). Employing an Aristotelian notion of human flourishing, Phelps recognizes universality in human nature that

> includes—at the highest level—a desire to express creativity, a relish for challenge, an enjoyment of problem solving, a delight in novelty, and the restless need to explore and to tinker. The pursuit and experience of these

> 'highest goods' is the way to human fulfilment—and to 'becoming,' which is a large part of it.
>
> (2013: 297)

Besides the universal nature of human flourishing, it is the unique and particular manifestation of one's self-actualization that is made possible by a liberal market order. As Phelps continues, an individual's

> *freedom to act* (or not to act) on their unique knowledge, judgement, and intuition may be indispensable to people's sense of self-sufficiency and thus self-worth. In this view, the freedom to take charge of one's own heading and make one's own mistakes is a primary good itself, one of huge importance.
>
> (emphasis original, 2013: 59)

However, human flourishing, although individualized, cannot manifest itself in isolation; man is inherently a social animal.

Not only does human cooperation under the division of labour expand the possibility of human flourishing; it is ultimately also an expression of human flourishing (Kline 2008: 152). Human flourishing is not reduced to a single end but is also inclusive and constitutive of a series of intermediate ends spread over one's lifetime (Rasmussen and Den Uyl 2005: 129–132). From an economic perspective, trade is simply an alternative form of production, an intermediate step in a larger structure of production. Taken from a bird's eye view, what is regarded as a means to an end – exchange activity – at a snapshot in time is simply an intermediate end integral to the exercise of one's self-direction during their lifetime. For example, working as a waiter might be regarded as antithetical to realizing one's end of becoming a professor. Exchanging waiting services for money, at the moment of time, may be regarded as corrupting this pursuit, since such means are not intrinsically consistent with one's stated end. This conclusion, however, disregards the intrinsic worth of actualizing another good, such as self-responsibility, which is an end in itself, not only constituent to the more final ends, but also integral to the process of living a worthy life.

Should individuals wish to live peaceful lives as Robinson Crusoes, living independently from each other, this is of course consistent with a liberal market order based on non-coercion. But these would not be flourishing lives. Human flourishing is a radically social yet radically individualized activity, in that trade contributes to one's own self-actualization, and, as a by-product, contributes to that of others. 'Trading is an objective good' not only because it is inherent in our nature to truck, barter, and exchange, but also because 'it serves our biocentric need for physical survival that is fundamentally human' (Kline 2008: 152). Moreover, the fundamental importance of economic growth that is promulgated by human cooperation under the division of labour is not merely an increased level of material prosperity. As Deirdre McCloskey has written, economic progress is not merely about consuming more stuff. As she puts it, '[m]odern economic growth gives the scope to do much more, whether or not the opportunity has been fully seized by everybody' (2010: 65). In this sense, an expanded scope for catallactic competition expands the possible scope of human flourishing by expanding that *range* of options available to actualize their artifactual selves (emphasis added, Alchian 1967: 372). As Phelps adds, 'an increased general level of wages is liberating: it enables persons confined to the lower reaches of the available wages—unskilled workers, in the usual terminology—to move from work they previously could not afford to reject work that is more desirable' (2013: 47). Therefore, the extension of the division of labour not only increases productivity but also allows individuals the possibility of pursuing enterprises and of realizing productive possibilities that otherwise might not have been afforded to them.

This brings us to the connection between catallactic competition discussed in Section 3.3, artifactual man, and human flourishing. It is indeed the case that a free market economy has delivered economic growth and prosperity wherever the private property rights and freedom of contract under the rule of law have been secure. Critics of the market, however, argue that social interaction in the marketplace 'crowds out' the need for individuals to behave morally. This is not an unmerited claim, as even defenders of the morality of free markets unintentionally slip into language that might imply (though not necessarily so) that moral action is not necessary for markets to operate. For example, as Clark and Lee argue:

> It is our view that the most effective way to make a moral case for markets requires accepting the dominant view of moral behavior as a legitimate one, while recognizing that the superiority of markets is the result of their ability to generate desirable outcomes without relying on what is widely seen as moral behavior. This leads us to argue that markets are essential for decent and humane social order because they can be substituted for the morality of caring that is necessary for decent and humane relationships.
>
> (Clark and Lee 2011: 2)

However, I do not wish to imply that it is the market process itself that *guarantees* or *makes* individuals act morally. Rather, the market process is a social and moral *space* (Storr 2008, 2009), or a framework within which moral action is made *possible*.

That said, catallactic competition increases the *scope* for human flourishing, while interventions into the market process create a tendency towards non-catallactic completion, and hence increase the scope for immoral action, specifically by stifling the creative process of one's artifactual self. While 'the free market does not make people moral, it raises the cost of unethical behavior' (Pejovich 1990: 16). Where, then, does the moral content of the market process reside? Indeed, there exists a common theme among free market economists across the twentieth century, including Armen Alchian, Gary Becker (1957), Harold Demsetz (1965), William Hutt (1964), Ludwig von

Mises (1927 [2005]), and Walter Williams (1982, 1989). This common theme is that *the market process tends to discriminate on margins that contribute to one's monetary preferences and tends not to discriminate on margins that contribute to one's non-monetary preferences.* The distinction between monetary and non-monetary preferences runs parallel to the distinction between artifactual and natural man, respectively. A restatement of this point then goes as follows: *the market process tends to discriminate on margins that realize one's artifactual potential and tends not to discriminate on one's natural margins.*

In making this distinction, my point here is twofold. First, to the extent that critics of the free market argue that decision making based on the profit motive is immoral, positive economics illustrates that this claim is *inconsistent* with also holding the normative claim that discrimination based in terms of race, creed, gender or other 'natural' characteristics is morally undesirable (Alchian and Kessel 1962: 175). Secondly, and normatively speaking, to the extent that private property rights are secure under the rule of law, the morality of the market process is based on protecting the possibility of individuals realizing their artifactual self through peaceful social cooperation and productive specialization under the division of labour.

In its broadest sense, discrimination, from an economic perspective, is an act of choice with scarce information (Williams 1982: 25). 'Discrimination, competition, and scarcity are three inseparable concepts' (Alchian 1965: 816), but the margin on which markets discriminate is *institutionally contingent.* Therefore, to the extent that private property rights are secure in a market economy, implying that individuals are bearing the costs and benefits of their decision-making, the possibility of an individual accruing greater wealth is not based primarily on their natural characteristics, but is a by-product of their artifactual creation of productive skills and talents. Conversely, when the exercise of legal discretion intervenes in the market process, the immoral implication is the tendency for individuals to be precluded from developing their artifactual self, thereby reducing the scope for human flourishing.

To illustrate this point, let us take the example of construction workers. By rational, I do not mean an egotistical sense of pure self-interest; I simply imply that the construction workers, like anyone else, prefer more of whatever they desire rather than less. They desire more income, but also may have aspirations that go beyond a pure monetary motive, including the ability to realize a better life for themselves and their families, or obtain a college education to engage in a more fulfilling form of employment. Suppose in their natural characteristics that the individuals are relatively equal in their productive capacity. However, the noticeable personal characteristic that distinguishes the two construction workers from each other is their skin colour. Suppose also that their present employer has a greater preference for workers with white skin. In this case, the total income of the owner of the construction firm includes not only the monetary profits that can be taken as disposable income but also non-monetary 'profits' taken as income 'spent' within the firm, in this case hiring workers to indulge their racial preferences.

By itself, the institutional conditions of a free market will not eliminate such preferences. However, our point here is that alternative institutional arrangements will affect how employers negotiate the trade-off between monetary and non-monetary income. This trade-off can be restated as follows: *as legal discretion becomes more effective against an employer accruing monetary income, the more likely it becomes that an employer will compensate for such legal discretion by accruing greater non-monetary income.* Therefore, government intervention into the market process, in the form of price controls, monopoly privileges, or other regulations, is immoral precisely because the cost of such coercion in the form of legal discretion is borne arbitrarily by individuals on margins for which they made no choice, namely their natural and personal characteristics.

To modify the previous example, let us suppose now that the construction workers are granted a special legal privilege, namely an exemption from antitrust laws (as is the case in the United States). This violation of the rule of law allows the construction workers to form a labour union and restrict the entrance of workers into the construction labour market. Restricting the supply of construction workers bids up their real monetary wages. To the extent that unionized construction workers are protected from competition by excluding non-unionized construction workers from the labour market, they will not bear the full cost in terms of foregone productivity by engaging in racial discrimination when choosing their members. It is therefore no accident that minimum wage laws, labour unions, and occupational licensing in countries such as the United States and South Africa were established not for the purpose of benefiting the least advantaged in society, but the exact opposite (see Hutt 1964; Williams 1982, 1989). 'The leading lights of American economic reform' during the Progressive Era of the early twentieth century, according to Thomas Leonard:

> advocated regulation of workers' wages and hours to bar or remove the unemployable from employment, on the grounds that their inferior nationality, race, gender, or intelligence made their economic competition a threat to the American working man and to Anglo-Saxon racial integrity.
>
> (2016: xii)

The immorality of such government intervention into the free market can be summarized in a twofold manner. First, the cost of legally assigning special privileges to particular interest groups is borne disproportionately by individuals with natural characteristics over which they had no choice. Second, legal discretion, by its very nature is a coercive transfer of resources, namely by granting a political official the power to grant special privileges to one party that cannot occur without simultaneously disadvantaging another party. When such discretion falls disproportionately on individuals with undesirable natural characteristics, namely by precluding them from freely contracting with other individuals or otherwise engaging in voluntary association, it reduces the scope for human flourishing. It therefore not only undermines an individual's ability to engage in productive specialization under a division of labour but also to develop their artifactual self.

3.5 Liberty and human flourishing

In the previous section, we emphasized the ethical implications of the market process as well as interventions in that process. These implications suggest that ethical primacy in the defence of a liberal market order must be grounded in the self-directed nature of human flourishing. In this section, I develop the political and social manifestations of that argument. I argue that liberty is a necessary condition for self-direction, and therefore paramount in protecting the possibility of human flourishing. In a political/legal framework that protects individual rights, markets are processes of moral discovery (Powell and Candela 2014). Markets can and do emerge in contexts outside of liberalism (Storr 2009: 290). However, only where the moral agency is protected from coercion can the possibility of human flourishing be fully realized. Therefore, the liberal market order is the institutional manifestation of self-direction.

In their most recent book, *The Perfectionist Turn* (2016), Rasmussen and Den Uyl argue that the 'moral hero' of ethical theorizing is not a merely rule-following agent, but the insightful entrepreneur. Entrepreneurship in the marketplace overlaps quite well with the self-directed nature of human flourishing. They are not synonymous with Robbinsian maximizing, but with the open-ended discovery of the means and ends required for a worthwhile life. In the *Nichomachean Ethics*, Aristotle elaborates on his definition of moral virtue in a manner that embodies entrepreneurial characteristics. Exercising moral virtues properly in the context of action means 'to have them at the right time, about the right things, towards the right people, for the right end, and in the right way, is the mean and best; and this is the business of virtue' (2000: 30). What this suggests is that human flourishing is a discovery process that integrates particular and contingent knowledge not only through self-reflection but also in association with other individuals, much like the Kirznerian entrepreneur.

Where private property rights are well-defined and enforced, profit-making in the marketplace is an extension of human flourishing. 'The central idea, for an understanding of individual liberty', Kirzner argues, 'lies in the individual's freedom to identify for himself what the opportunities are which he may endeavour to grasp' (1992: 66). As Rasmussen and Den Uyl argue, the

> analog here in ethics may equally be a recognition of a need for course-correction of one's action. One might notice, for example, some version of 'working too hard,' to the neglect of other important factors of one's life, such as family, friends, civic responsibilities, or even such things as one's own talents or the care with which one undertakes any of these.
> (2016: 293)

The rules of the game in a liberal market order structure one's ethical conduct. They give us the guidelines on how to 'play' the game. However, within the context of rules, entrepreneurship has moral significance precisely because its effect is to create information by which other individuals *learn* how to play the game *well*. This ethical content can only be substantiated at the entrepreneurial moment of choice, and cannot be built into the rules prior to playing the game. Human flourishing is an entrepreneurial discovery process, primarily of ourselves, but also of our relationship with others.

Without self-direction, self-interest can never be regarded beyond the instrumental role of passive utility maximization, analogous to *homo economicus* of neoclassical equilibrium models. By disregarding the role of self-direction, self-interest cannot be tied to excellent moral and intellectual development that is required for acting, adapting, and achieving virtue under uncertainty. An institutional framework that protects liberty as the paramount value allows for the possibilities of other values and allows individuals to discover what it means for them to be virtuous in order to achieve human flourishing. The argument in this section should not be regarded as a rejection of deontological or consequentialist modes of ethical theorizing; rather, the claim here is that such modes of ethical theorizing account for the rules required to facilitate social order (Candela 2018). Yet, such rules, and the generalized norms upon which they are based, must be derived from a deeper ethical foundation consistent with protecting human flourishing, and its economic counterpart, entrepreneurship. Private property provides the moral space for individual liberty, not merely because it minimizes coercion, but fundamentally so that individuals can *learn* what it means to be free. The exploitation of opportunities is a part of our human nature, and freedom can only be understood in terms of the individual expression of one's human flourishing.

3.6. Conclusion

Ultimately, the very same institutional foundations for the market process also provide the *possibility* of human flourishing. The institutional foundations of a free market cannot guarantee that individuals will self-actualize their potential and behave morally, since liberty and responsibility are inseparable. Though liberty implies that individuals are free to behave immorally, it does place costs on such behaviour by disproportionately increasing the gains from the catallactic competition and therefore increasing the scope of human flourishing. The violation of liberty, however, introduces coercion in the form of legal discretion. Such legal discretion is immoral not only because it increases the gains from non-catallactic competition. It is also immoral because the costs of discretion are disproportionately borne by individuals who possess non-preferred natural characteristics, over which they have no choice. The costs come in the form of forgone opportunities, not only to participate in voluntary association with other individuals but also the forgone opportunity to realize their artifactual self.

Notes

1 Though not unrelated, but beyond the scope of this chapter, are criticisms of the market process based on the existence of market failures associated with externalities, monopoly power, public goods, business cycles, and inequality.

2 Following the classical liberal economist William Hutt (1964: 9), I attribute economic injustice to any set of economic policies or institutional arrangements, which is intended to perpetuate, through arbitrary legal status, the inferior economic and social conditions of a group of people based upon inherited or otherwise accidental attributes, including creed, gender, nationality, or race. My focus on the *institutional nature* of economic injustices is not out of indifference to human failings associated with racism or sexism, but rather, taking such human failings as given, to understand the institutional arrangements that erode or exacerbate the indulgence of such preferences.

3 As Leeson and Harris (forthcoming) state, the current association of neoliberalism with the imposition of a 'free-market fundamentalism' takes out of context where the term 'neoliberalism' was coined, namely at the 1938 Walter Lippmann Colloquium, a precursor to the Mont Pelerin Society organized by Louis Rougier. Liberal scholars, including Hayek, Wilhelm Röpke, and Ludwig von Mises, gathered at the colloquium to discuss a 'new liberalism', and the perceived misunderstanding of the institutional conditions governing a market economy.

References

Alchian, A. A. (1965) Some economics of property rights, *Il Politico* 30(4): 816–829.

Alchian, A. A. and R. A. Kessel (1962) Competition, monopoly, and the pursuit of money. In *Aspects of Labor Economics*, Princeton, NJ: Princeton University Press: 157–183. https://www.nber.org/system/files/chapters/c0605/c0605.pdf; https://www.amazon.com/Aspects-Economics-National-Economic-Research/dp/0691041628

Alchian, A. A. (1967) How should prices be set?, *Il Politico* 32(2): 369–382.

Alchian, A. A. and W. R. Allen (1972) *University Economics: Elements of Inquiry*, 3rd Edition, Belmont, CA: Wadsworth.

Aristotle. (2000) Nicomachean ethics. In R. Crisp (ed.), *Cambridge Texts in the History of Philosophy*, New York: Cambridge University Press.

Barzel, Y. (1997) *Economic Analysis of Property Rights*, 2nd Edition, New York: Cambridge University Press.

Bastiat, F. (1996) *Economic Sophisms*, Translated and edited by Arthur Goddard. Irvington-on-Hudson, NY: Foundation for Economic Education.

Becker, G. S. (1957) *The Economics of Discrimination*, Chicago, IL: University of Chicago Press.

Boettke, P. J. (2012) *Living Economics: Yesterday, Today, and Tomorrow*, Oakland, CA: The Independent Institute.

Boettke, P. J. and R. A. Candela (2017) Price theory as prophylactic against popular fallacies, *Journal of Institutional Economics* 13(3): 725–752.

Boettke, P. J. and R. A. Candela (2019) Liberalism in crisis and the promise of a reconstructed liberalism, *Journal of Contextual Economics – Schmollers Jahrbuch* 139(2–4): 189–212.

Boettke, P. J., R. A. Candela and K. Woltz (2018) Is the market wage the just wage? A reassessment of factor pricing and distributive justice, *Erasmus Journal for Philosophy and Economics* 11(2): 124–143.

Boettke, P. J., R. A. Candela and K. Woltz (2021) The institutional justice of the market process: Entrepreneurship, increasing returns, and income distribution. In G. P. Manish and S. C. Miller (eds.), *Capitalism and Inequality: The Role of the State and Market*, New York: Routledge: 43–60.

Buchanan, J. M. (1964) What should economists do?, *Southern Economic Journal* 30(3): 213–222.

Buchanan, J. M. (1979) *What Should Economists Do?*, Indianapolis, IN: Liberty Fund.

Buchanan, J. M. (2008) Same players, different game: How better rules make better politics, *Constitutional Political Economy* 19(3): 171–179.

Candela, R. A. (2018) The socialist calculation debate and its normative implications, *Advances in Austrian Economics* 23: 29–44.

Candela, R. A. and E. E. Piano (2018) Rule of law. In A. Marciano and G. Ramello (eds.), *Encyclopedia of Law and Economics*, New York: Springer.

Clark, J. B. (1899) *The Distribution of Wealth: A Theory of Wages, Interest and Profits*, New York: Macmillan.

Clark, J. R. and D. R. Lee (2011) Markets and morality, *Cato Journal* 31(1): 1–25.

Cruz, M., J. Foster, B. Quilla and P. Schellekens (2015) *Ending Extreme Poverty and Sharing Prosperity: Progress and Policies*, Policy Research Note; PRN/15/03. Washington, DC: World Bank Group.

Deaton, A. (2013) *The Great Escape: Health, Wealth, and the Origins of Inequality*, Princeton, NJ: Princeton University Press.

Demsetz, H. (1965) Minorities in the marketplace, *North Carolina Law Review* 43(2): 271–297.

Demsetz, H. (1967) Toward a theory of property rights, *The American Economic Review* 57(2): 347–359.

Den Uyl, D. J. and D. B. Rasmussen (2016) *The Perfectionist Turn: From Metanorms to Metaphysics*, Edinburgh, UK: Edinburgh University Press.

Friedman, M. (1962 [2002]) *Capitalism and Freedom, Fortieth Anniversary Edition*, Chicago, IL: University of Chicago Press.

Furubotn, E. G. and S. Pejovich (1972) Property rights and economic theory: A survey of recent literature, *Journal of Economic Literature* 10(4): 1137–1162.

Hayek, F. A. (1960) *The Constitution of Liberty*, Chicago, IL: University of Chicago Press.

Hayek, F. A. (1976) *Law, Legislation, and Liberty, Vol. II: The Mirage of Social Justice*, Chicago, IL: University of Chicago Press.

Heath, J. (2018) On the very idea of a just wage, *Erasmus Journal for Philosophy and Economics* 11(2): 1–33.

Heilbroner, R. (1989) The triumph of capitalism, *The New Yorker*, January 23, 64(49): 98– 109.

Heilbroner, R. (1990) Reflections after communism, *The New Yorker*, September 10, 60(30): 91–100.

Hutt, W.H. (1964) *The Economics of the Colour Bar: A Study of the Economic Origins and Consequences of Racial Segregation in South Africa*, London: Andre Deutsch.

Kline, W. (2008) Flourishing through trade. In A. J. Skoble (ed.), *Reading Rasmussen and Den Uyl: Critical Essays on Norms of Liberty*, Lanham, MD: Lexington: 149–164.

Kirzner, I. M. (1992) *The Meaning of the Market Process: Essays in the Development of Modern Austrian Economics*, New York, NY: Routledge.

Kirzner, I. M. (1989 [2016]) Discovery, capitalism, and distributive justice. In P. J. Boettke and F. Sautet (eds.), *The Collected Works of Israel M. Kirzner*. Indianapolis, IN: Liberty Fund.

Kirzner, I. M. (2019) The ethics of pure entrepreneurship: An Austrian economics perspective, *The Review of Austrian Economics* 32(2): 89–99.

Leeson, P. T. and C. Harris (forthcoming) Hayek, neoliberalism, and the Washington Consensus. In R. A. Candela (ed.), *A Companion to F.A. Hayek*, Guatemala City: Universidad Francisco Marroquin.

Leonard, T. C. (2016) *Illiberal Reformers: Race, Eugenics & American Economics in the Progressive Era*, Princeton NJ: Princeton University Press.

Lippman, W. (1937 [2005]) *The Good Society: With an Introduction by Gary Dean Best*, London: Routledge.

Lucas, Jr., R. E. (1988) On the mechanics of economic development, *Journal of Monetary Economics* 22(1): 3–42.

Marshall, A. (1920 [2013]) *Principles of Economics*, 8th Edition, New York: Palgrave Macmillan.

McCloskey, D. N. (2006) *The Bourgeois Virtues: Ethics for an Age of Commerce*, Chicago, IL: University of Chicago Press.

McCloskey, D. N. (2010) *Bourgeois Dignity: Why Economics Can't Explain the Modern World*, Chicago, IL: University of Chicago Press.

McCloskey, D. N. (2016) *Bourgeois Equality: How Ideas, Not Capital or Institutions, Enriched the World*, Chicago, IL: University of Chicago Press.

Menger, C. (1891 [2016]) The social theories of classical political economy and modern economic policy, Translated by E. Dekker and S. Kolev, *Econ Journal Watch* 13(3): 467–489.

Mises, L. Von. (1920 [1975]) Economic calculation in the socialist commonwealth. In F. A. Hayek (ed.), *Collectivist Economic Planning*, Clifton: August M. Kelley: 87–130.

Mises, L. von. (1922 [1951]) *Socialism: An Economic and Sociological Analysis*, New Haven, CT: Yale University Press.

Mises, L. von. (1927 [2005]) *Liberalism: The Classical Tradition*, Indianapolis, IN: Liberty Fund.

Mises, L. (1949 [1966]) *Human Action: A Treatise on Economics*, 3rd Edition, Chicago IL: Henry Regnery.

Peart, S. J. and D. M. Levy (eds.) (2008) *The Street Porter and the Philosopher: Conversations on Analytical Egalitarianism*, Ann Arbor, MI: University of Michigan Press.

Pejovich, S. (1990) *The Economics of Property Rights: Towards a Theory of Comparative Systems*, Boston, MA: Kluwer.

Phelps, E. (2013) *Mass Flourishing: How Grassroots Innovation Created Jobs, Challenge, and Change*, Princeton, NJ: Princeton University Press.

Powell, B. and R. Candela (2014) Markets as processes of moral discovery, *Studies in Emergent Order* 7: 258–272.

Rasmussen, D. B. and D. J. Den Uyl (2005) *Norms of Liberty: A Perfectionist Basis for Non-Perfectionist Politics*, Pennsylvania: Pennsylvania State University Press.

Robbins, L. (1952) *The Theory of Economic Policy in English Classical Political Economy*, London: Macmillan.

Smith, A. (1776 [1981]) *An Inquiry into the Nature and Causes of the Wealth of Nations*, Indianapolis, IN: Liberty Fund.

Stigler, G. J. (1949) *Five Lectures on Economic Problems*, London: Longman, Green, and Co.

Stigler, G. J. (1957) Perfect competition, historically contemplated, *Journal of Political Economy* 65(1): 1–17.

Stigler, G. J. (1971) The theory of economic regulation, *The Bell Journal of Economics and Management Science* 2(1): 3–21.

Storr, V. H. (2008) The market as a social space: On the meaningful extra economic conversations that can occur in markets, *The Review of Austrian Economics* 21(2–3): 135–150.

Storr, V. H. (2009) Why the market? Markets as social and moral spaces, *Journal of Markets & Morality* 12(2): 277–296.

Tullock, G. (1967) The welfare costs of tariffs, monopolies, and theft, *Western Economic Journal* 5(3): 224–232.

Wicksteed, P. (1894) *An Essay on the Co-ordination of the Laws of Distribution, 1932 edition, Reprint No. 12*, London: London School of Economics.

Williams, W. E. (1982) *The State Against Blacks*, New York, NY: McGraw Hill.

Williams, W. E. (1989) *South Africa's War Against Capitalism*, New York, NY: Praeger.

4 Markets, morality, and human flourishing in the ordoliberal tradition

Roland Fritz and Nils Goldschmidt

4.1 Introduction and setting the stage

This volume aims at carving out the relationship between economic and normative thinking in different kinds of market economies. The present chapter is devoted to demonstrating this intricate interplay with regard to the school of German ordoliberalism. We highlight the normative and moral aspects of thinking about markets practised in the ordoliberal tradition in three ways. First, we draw on the historical genesis of the ordoliberal framework during the days of National Socialism and their practical implementation in Germany after the Second World War. Second, we describe ordoliberal thinking about the role of culture, social norms, and values for economic outcomes. Finally, we also link the latter aspects to current research in 'contextual economics.'

The chapter's set-up is as follows. After having given a (very) brief description of the main tenets of ordoliberalism, we use Section 4.3 to inquire into the historical emergence of ordoliberal ideas and thus review the role of the ordoliberal economists' experience during the Nazi dictatorship. We highlight the way in which the concept of freedom, and thus their self-conception as a liberal school of thought, gains importance for the ordoliberals during the dark days of National Socialism. In addition, we show how practical experiences led them to integrate mechanisms for the preservation of liberty into their frameworks for the successful ordering of social and economic structures. Section 4.4 deals with the time immediately following the Second World War and the implementation of ordoliberal ideas into practical policies: the emergence of the social market economy. This chapter shows how the ordoliberals attempted to adapt their vision of a well-ordered society to the particular problems and societal demands present in Germany at the time. We show how their responding to the particular circumstances resulted in an open-minded, non-dogmatic form of liberalism that does not understand itself as a fixed set of dogmas. Finally, Section 4.5 highlights another aspect where values, worldviews, and practices converge in the ordoliberal account, namely the conviction that many of the social problems experienced in modern societies are ultimately not economic, but reside in the area that 'lies beyond supply and demand', as Wilhelm Röpke (Röpke 1958 [2009]: 131) put it. With this conviction in

DOI: 10.4324/9781003208549-4

mind, the nature of ordoliberal proposals for policy reform, as well as the contemporary understanding of ordoliberalism as a contextual approach to economics, becomes understandable. Section 4.6 concludes.

4.2 A (very) brief introduction to ordoliberalism

For this project, ordoliberalism stands as a representation of a typical school of thought for the 'coordinated market tradition' prevalent in Germany. With all its peculiarities, ordoliberalism is commonly regarded as the German variety of neoliberalism (Riha 1986; Barry 1989; Kolev 2015; Gray 2009; Biebricher 2017). Ordoliberalism mostly dates back to an interdisciplinary research group of economists and legal scholars, the so-called Freiburger Schule (Freiburg School). It was founded at the University of Freiburg in the 1930s by the economist Walter Eucken (1881–1950) and two jurists, Franz Böhm (1895–1977) and Hans Großmann-Doerth (1894–1944). As the name implies, ordoliberalism emphasizes above all the necessity of basic principles for the establishment of an economic order, which must be created and maintained by the state as a legal framework in order to guarantee a free, prosperous, and humane society. Considering this to be the main characteristic of ordoliberalism and as a contrast to other liberal currents, further important scholars beyond the Freiburg School are: Alexander Rüstow (1885–1963), Wilhelm Röpke (1899–1966), Alfred Müller-Armack (1901–1978), and Ludwig Erhard (1897–1977).

While ordoliberalism as such had a rather little impact on the progress of economics as a scientific discipline in Germany after the Second World War, it nevertheless exerted considerable influence on policymaking (cf. Hesse 2010). It is particularly interesting to see that ordoliberal teachings were frequently 'merged' with and engrossed by other, sometimes quite different, approaches to political economy. Among these, Karl Schiller's[1] 'Globalsteuerung', which tried to harmonize the concerns of ordoliberalism with the Keynesian approach, is probably most prominent, even though the combination of 'Ordnungspolitik' and 'Prozesspolitik' must ultimately be seen as not having gained solid ground in Germany (cf. Hagemann 2017). But Helmut Kohl's chancellorship, too, around the time of German Unification was – at least as far as his rhetoric is concerned – very much influenced by the ordoliberal creed.[2] In more recent times, ordoliberally inspired arguments have helped legitimize Agenda 2010, one of the most comprehensive welfare state reforms ever undertaken in an industrialized country striving to embed social assistance, unemployment insurance, and activating labour market policies in a rules-based approach (Hien 2013). This illustrates the ordoliberal grounding of what is often referred to as 'the third way': a project of renewal for European Social Democracy initiated by the British Prime Minister Tony Blair and German Chancellor Gerhard Schröder in 1999 (cf. Blair and Schröder 1999). It sought to combine the advantages of a competitive market order with an efficient and functional welfare state by grounding the latter in a set of rules in order to ensure their compatibility. Lastly, the decisive ordoliberal underpinnings of the German take on monetary policy have also become visible during the Euro-crisis, of which Chapter 9 in this volume gives a brief account.

The ordoliberal thinkers, as such, always considered themselves to be liberals, but, as this chapter will point out, their liberalism differs in some important ways from other liberal currents. Among these is the detailed focus on the ways in which human flourishing might be attained by creating and improving the economic, legal, political, and social order of a society. In this endeavour, it is not only the state in its capacity as the provider of the legal order that is important but also the cultural environment under which economic activity takes place. In modern terminology, one would speak of an increased focus on informal institutions or culture (see Chapter 1). The ordoliberal's relationships with proponents of classical or 'Manchester-style' liberalism were always somewhat uneasy, as is evident from their role during the Colloque Walter Lippmann in 1938. For the purposes of the broader project of this book, this perfectly illustrates the differences and difficulties that proponents of and contributors to the 'coordinated market tradition' might have with the approach of the 'free market tradition.' These tensions were clearly felt during the debates of the Colloquium. Rüstow and Röpke oftentimes clashed with the 'paleoliberal' (Rüstow 1961) Ludwig von Mises (Reinhoudt and Audier 2018), against whom the ordoliberals put their own conception of a new liberalism, one that would be able to overcome the perceived shortcomings of classical liberalism.[3]

A chief difference is that for ordoliberalism the essence of liberalism is not so much the upholding of free exchange processes above everything else, but rather the peaceful coexistence of free individuals within a functional legal order (Broyer 1996: 13). Within this legal framework, the individual is free in the sense that rules guard their freedom and expand their scope for action, while the economic order ensures an efficient economy. The main argument that led the ordoliberals to this conviction was

> the question of private power in a free society. It necessarily leads to the question of how an order of the free economy is constituted. From there one arrives at the question of what types and possibilities there are at all, what role power plays in them, both the power of the government and the power of private individuals and private groups, and what disturbances of order occur when a different distribution of power develops within the state and society than that which is in conformity with the respective economic system.
>
> (Böhm 1957: 99)

This relative neglect of concentrations of economic and political power in free societies on the part of classical liberalism certainly is *the* starkest difference with ordoliberalism. The concentration of power should be checked and worked against; otherwise the very foundations of a free society could become shaky, according to the ordoliberals. This, however, does not mean that ordoliberalism is outside the 'liberal tradition' altogether, as is clearly shown by their strong involvement in the early- and mid-twentieth-century project of a redefinition of liberal principles and the search for institutions that would enable societies to preserve economic and civil liberties over time (Kolev, Goldschmidt, and Hesse 2019). Nevertheless, the ordoliberal thinkers were drawn to their liberal convictions in somewhat different ways, focusing on divergent strategies for achieving their vision of an optimally ordered and free society. The reasons for this become clear when one considers where the 'liberalism-part' of ordoliberalism actually stems from: their role in the resistance or as exiled persons during the days of the Nazi-regime.

4.3 The emergence of ordoliberalism during the dark days of National Socialism

As we have shown elsewhere (Fritz *et al.* 2021), ordoliberalism's roots are somewhat atypical for a self-styled 'liberal' approach to economics. While the single greatest influence in terms of economic thinking can be seen in the Younger German Historical School (Schefold 1995 and Häuser 1994) – hardly a contender in the competition for the most 'liberal' approach to political economy – the philosophical underpinnings of liberal thought also do not centre on the 'usual suspects' of liberal philosophy. Classics such as Locke or Hume are all but neglected in most of the ordoliberals' accounts,[4] while their philosophical roots can clearly be identified with phenomenology[5] and (neo-) Kantian approaches (Klump and Wörsdorfer 2009). If one adds to that the frequent and overly explicit delimitation to 'laissez faire-liberalism', other liberal economists and Adam Smith (Horn 2019), one might actually be tempted to ask whether ordoliberalism is indeed a liberal school of thought without liberal roots (Fritz *et al.* 2021). We answer the question about the ordoliberals' non-affiliation with liberalism in the negative, but point to the formative effect of the experiences of the ordoliberals during the time of the Nazi dictatorship. As such, ordoliberalism's founding and the search for rules for a harmonious and peaceful coexistence that is so characteristic of the ordoliberal approach both have their origin in highly normative and moral issues: the rejection of and fight against the Nazi dictatorship.

The issue can be illustrated with the ordoliberals' publication history: their early writing was clearly centred on narrow economic questions such as business cycle (Röpke 1929), trade theory (Rüstow 1925), or detailed descriptions of various business segments (Eucken 1914 and 1921), very much in the tradition of the German Historical School. However, their scope and aim changed in the 1930s and 40s and increasingly linked economic questions to matters of political organization and social philosophy.[6] In addition, the very concept of 'freedom' and clear statements about the desirability of its maintenance can only be found from this period onwards. The practical experiences with a very concrete loss of freedom lead to a deeper reflection about the prerequisites of an economic and social order that will reliably prevent such restraints in the future. The achievement of this aim requires extending the realm of analysis from merely economic topics to broader issues as is evident from the titles of their publications at the time: 'The Social Crisis of Our Time' (Röpke 1947a), 'Civitas Humana' (Röpke 1944 [1979]), 'Changes in State-Structures and the Crisis of Capitalism' (Eucken 1926), or 'Freedom and Domination: A Historical Critique of Civilization' (Rüstow 1980). These titles do not sound like titles of economics textbooks, and that is certainly not what they were.

This change of outlook and newly found appreciation of liberal social and economic orders can be directly linked to experiences with the Third Reich. Even though the experiences of Röpke and Rüstow (as forced emigrants) differ considerably from those of Eucken (who chose to stay in Germany), a meaningful effect can be shown in both cases. While Wilhelm Röpke's writings in the early 1930s are already soaked with pessimism about the future, the dire outlook (among which totalitarian tendencies were clearly included) is always seen as a consequence of faulty economic policies, especially with regards to money and trade (Röpke 1932 [2009]). Shortly after the takeover by the National Socialists, we already find much broader criticisms of the current state of affairs 'which is preparing to reforest the garden of culture and transform it back into the old jungle' (Röpke 1933 [2009]: 68). Also Alexander Rüstow, who was blacklisted shortly after the Nazis rose to power and was ultimately exiled to Istanbul, did not find kind words for the dictatorship in Germany:

> The whole mess came crawling out of its hiding places and rose like a cloud; its exhalations polluted the German air. […] Nietzsche's demand: 'The bad and the wrong shall come to light', had become daily reality in an undreamt-of way. To his longing question: 'Where are the barbarians of the nineteenth century?' the SS could answer with a harsh: 'Here!'
>
> (Rüstow 1957: 492)

As such, their activities during these dark times represented some sort of war effort for both of them, in which they used their pens and typewriters to fight against the regime in their very own way. Note how Röpke's and Rüstow's opposition is not targeted at particular policies or even the horrible treatment of certain groups of people in the Third Reich. What is at stake is nothing short of civilization as such. In this way, it is easy to see in which sense the experiences with a real-world dictatorship facilitated a deep reflection about the meaning and importance of freedom for human flourishing.

The case of the Freiburg School, in particular that of Walter Eucken, is perhaps even more instructive for these effects. Before these Freiburg economists had to endure losses of freedom in their private lives, they were sensitized to its value by the loss of freedom in the academic sphere. When Martin Heidegger was appointed as the rector of the University of Freiburg in 1933, the tune of academic life changed rapidly with Heidegger aiming to implement the 'Führerprinzip' in university life too. With that early experience in mind, the ordoliberals of the Freiburg School maintained their distance from the regime and gradually even became active in the resistance. Franz Böhm and Walter Eucken, for instance, were members of all of the three 'Freiburg Circles', which, coming from a strong church background, aimed at promoting a thorough criticism of and intellectual attack on the Nazi regime and, most importantly, devised plans for the post-war social and economic order.[7] Their role was most pronounced in the so-called 'Bonhoeffer Circle', whose members tried to discern what stance faithful Christians ought to take in the face of the gross inhumanity of the Nazi regime. The Circle produced a clandestine paper titled 'Politische Gemeinschaftsordnung. Ein Versuch zur Selbstbestimmung des christlichen Gewissens in den politischen Nöten unserer Zeit' ('Political and Communal Order: An Attempt at Self-Determination of the Christian Conscience in Our Politically Difficult Times'), which dealt with the question of how Christians ought to act in the face of the gross inhumanity of the Third Reich. More importantly, it also featured an essay written by Eucken and his two Freiburg colleagues Constantin von Dietze and Adolf Lampe, which included an appendix entitled the 'Wirtschafts- and Sozialordnung' ('Economic and Social Order') to be implemented after the war had ended. The appendix proposes an economic order for the post-war area that does not only focus on material aspects but also offers 'the strongest resistance possible to the power of evil' (Dietze, Eucken and Lampe 1943: 100). Throughout the text, the authors stress the ethical and religious pillars of a future economic order, at the heart of which stood the individual human as a free and moral being. The appendix also offers very concrete practical guidance for economic policy. For instance, the discussion of the promotion of competition and the avoidance of monopoly, which is characteristic of ordoliberalism, is found there along with an extensive treatment of the role of the state on the matter, given the necessity of embedding the economic order of a society in a safe and stable legal framework. In that sense, it is no surprise that the appendix has been described as 'containing the essence of ordoliberal thinking' (Horn 1996).

The ordoliberals' membership of the resistance also carried with it immediate practical consequences that placed their lives in severe danger. After the failed assassination attempt on Hitler on July 20, 1944, the endeavours of the Bonhoeffer Circle became known and its members frequent targets of police questionings and SS investigations. Some of its members, for instance Constantin von Dietze and Adolf Lampe, were sentenced to death, although the sentences were not carried out (Goldschmidt 2011).

In short, the experiences of the time period from 1933 to 1945 redefined the ordoliberals' stance on what human flourishing entails by ingraining in them the importance of individual freedom as a necessary value for the attainment of that goal. Even more so, the concept of 'order', which was already vaguely present before 1933, begins to emerge as the cornerstone of their outlook on social and economic life and the basis of their policy prescriptions. The strong normative commitment to personal freedom and the desirability of 'doing the right thing' under all circumstances, shaped and carved out during their 'battles' with National Socialism, finds its institutional manifestations in that overall order. This order aims to tackle economic and social problems on a society-wide level in order to prevent future catastrophes of the Nazi type.

4.4 The rise of the social market economy after the Second World War

While the moral underpinnings of ordoliberally inspired economic and social science stem from the practical experiences with an unfree political system and the failure of a democratic experiment (The Weimar Republic), the implementation of ordoliberal ideas after the war followed somewhat different values. Given the enormous success of the 'German Economic Miracle',[8] one is tempted to believe that the process unfolded without setbacks, opposition, or considerable efforts to push through the desired policies. This would be a grave misunderstanding of the matter, and the following section will thus demonstrate how the early efforts to implement ordoliberal ideas in practical policymaking were frequently met with resistance and thus often had to be, and were, tailored to fit certain popular beliefs and societal demands. The section will lay out in which sense not only economic thinking itself is influenced by moral values and social forces, but how the policy conclusions drawn from economic analysis need to be marketed, sold, and modified in political discourse and practice. The emergence of the social market economy in Germany post-Second World War represents a concise illustration of how policy changes may unfold in a coordinated market economy.

The colloquially told story about the birth of the social market economy and the German economic miracle goes something like this: the economy was in shambles after the war, there was an excessive money surplus, prices were controlled, and life was generally miserable. Out of all this came Ludwig Erhard, a hero-like figure, who single-handedly freed the economy from price controls when the Allied Powers introduced currency reform in 1948. From this moment onwards, everything went smoothly, Germans became rich and 'lived happily ever after.'

As the somewhat sarcastic tone of the first lines indicates, this account lacks nuance considerably: while the existence of an 'economic miracle' can be called into question, we will instead focus on the often-portrayed seamlessness of the process and instead demonstrate that a lot of 'convincing' was necessary before the social market economy could be introduced. Problems started soon after the lifting of price controls in June 1948, with the prices of some goods (particularly eggs) rising rapidly. This led to outrage and a rejection of the newly introduced market economy by wide segments of the population, casting doubt on the possibility of the implemented reforms being kept up in the long term. It sensitized the ordoliberals towards the prime importance of public opinion being favourable towards the idea of a market economy.

Consider Leonhard Miksch's[9] take on the matter:

> The fact is that in all European countries there is a broad stratum of officials who no longer understand the market economy and who do not want to understand it. That, and nothing else, is the real problem. Whether it

> is possible to cope with this society is decisive for the future of Western culture of personal freedom.
>
> (Miksch 1948)

In practice, this struggle for comprehension and acceptance of the 'new' system of market economy was orchestrated with social programmes aimed at alleviating cases of extreme hardship and promoting market access for most people. The most prominent example of this from the early days of the social market economy is the so-called 'Jedermann Programm' ('Everyman's Programme'), in the course of which certain important goods of daily use were produced, under the direct supervision of the government, to be sold at fixed prices. Private companies were incentivized to provide their facilities for the production of these goods by tying the supply of certain highly demanded resources to participation in the programme. While some interpreted this measure as a 'declaration of defeat' and a de facto return to fixed prices and a regulated economy, Ludwig Erhard himself made clear that 'The "Jedermann-Programm" is [...] not a sign of a new economic policy or a new economic form, it is an emergency measure. And it is a transitional measure' (Erhard 1948: 8). The 'thorough recovery' or the attainment of an 'economic equilibrium' could not be reached immediately in post-war Germany; hence, it made sense to him to temporarily 'leave out a market sector as a protected area for those whose incomes still need special social protection because of their lack of adaptability' (Erhard 1948: 8). Over the past 15 years, Erhard thought, the planned economy of the Nazi dictatorship had eroded the understanding of competition as a necessary and highly beneficial force for any economic system. He saw his task as a politician 'particularly in radiating peace, confidence and certainty that what is happening today is not a chaos that has slipped from our hands, from our conscious influence' (Erhard 1948: 8). As such, endeavours such as the 'Jedermann Programm' represented in these early days of the social market economy not a relapse into the old ways of organizing an economy but displayed the ordoliberals' fundamental conviction that economic policy needs to be adapted to the particular circumstances and social problems faced by a society at one point in time. If the times call for interventionist social policies, these can and should be implemented temporarily in order to insure the future acceptance of a market economy.

In a more institutionalized form, these measures were complemented by the definitional and practical efforts of Alfred Müller-Armack, who coined the term 'social market economy' and was also strongly engaged in defining its content. As such, asking 'how the diverging objectives of social security and economic freedom can be brought into a new balance' (Müller-Armack 1952: 236), became the yardstick and guideline for the social policy programme of the social market economy. In his efforts, Müller-Armack consciously combined 'a strong emphasis on a competitive market order as a programme of economic policy' with a system of 'market-compliant, but yet socially and socio-politically meaningful measures' (Müller-Armack 1965: 10).[10] This social concern of the social market economy can still be understood today as a genuinely ethical or normative goal. The market and competition within it are a means for shaping and improving society, but not goals in themselves. Instead, the goal is the construction of a humane order that serves the successful life of each individual. The ordoliberal position is also neatly summarized in the preface of the first edition of the *ORDO Yearbook for Economic and Social Order*, which is to this day an influential 'ordoliberally inspired' publication:

> Our demand is limited to the creation of an economic and social order in which economic performance and humane conditions of existence are equally guaranteed. Because competition can be made to serve this objective, which without it remains unattainable, we demand it. It is a means, not a final end.
>
> (Meyer and Lenel 1948: XI)

From this it clearly emerges that the social market economy has never been (and still is not) an unmovable doctrine, but a political project which is shaped and twisted by public opinion as well as by political necessities. While respect for the upholding and the stability of the ordering framework is of course crucially important, ordoliberalism, when properly understood, was and always is also aware of societal demands and social problems and does its best to accommodate these needs. Not only for the sake of granting the market economy additional legitimacy in the eyes of the populace but also because the alleviation and potential resolution of social problems is a legitimate concern in every society.[11]

A similar phenomenon at the same time can be observed in the form of a multitude of organizations set up to promote and create acceptance of the social market economy. These can be seen as a complementary measure to the social policies described above and served the goal of creating more acceptance of the social market economy. While their backgrounds and focal points differed, the existence of a large number of these bodies further illustrates our point about the necessary underpinnings of the social market economy in civil society (cf. Nicholls 2000). These think tanks organized, for instance, educational campaigns in schools and beyond. At times, advertisements for the market economy were even played in cinemas (see, e.g., Dörr and Kutzner [2017]) for the case of the Aktionsgemeinschaft Soziale Marktwirtscht [ASM] – The Alliance for the Social Market Economy). Another particularity of that time was the manifold partnerships that supporters of the social market economy were willing to enter into in order to achieve their aims. In the case of the early days, (again) the ASM had a somewhat puzzling partnership with the 'Freiwirtschaftsbewegung' (Association for a Free Economy), an association dedicated to the ideas of 'demurrage-money', as popularized by the German economist Silvio Gesell. While the idea of monetary units continuously losing purchasing power is not per se illiberal, an alliance between proponents of that type of thinking would have been almost unthinkable for members of other liberal schools of thought. This tendency to be open to different approaches to social science and economic policy and a rather consensual approach to social relations is still a characteristic of the ordoliberally inspired social market economy today. This also entails a certain theoretical openness to new developments in the real world and the willingness to adapt one's policy prescription and outlook on the social world in response to new insights.

The section will have sensitized the reader towards the necessity for economic orders to legitimize themselves and to adapt continuously to changing social conditions. It remains true to this day that market processes in Germany are closely embedded in a system of institutional and civil-society support that attempts to maintain a favourable public opinion about the social market economy. In this endeavour, bipartisan solutions are also usually preferred today.

We now leave behind the historical parts about the genesis of ordoliberalism and the social market economy and take a closer look at the interplay between markets, human flourishing, and notions of the good life in ordoliberalism. The reader may bear in mind, though, that parts of the ordoliberals' outlook on that topic (a) rest on their experiences with dictatorship described in Section 4.3 and (b) are always interrelated with their own efforts to implement their ideas in political practice.

4.5 Flourishing, virtue, and the good life in ordoliberalism

The chapter now turns to a thorough discussion of the normative and cultural underpinnings of economies, as viewed by the ordoliberals. We might best approach the matter by thinking through the relationship between markets, virtues, and the idea of a good life in ordoliberal thought. Chapter 3 has illustrated that in the free market tradition, markets are seen as promoters of virtues, which, if consistently applied and lived, will enable what can be dubbed 'the good life.' As we shall see, the ordoliberal view differs considerably from this. The notion of what constitutes a good life stands at the beginning of the ordoliberal analysis and is something to be defined by the analyzing economist, who for this purpose also has to be a sociologist or cultural critic. Therefore, markets are merely a way and not the source of achieving the goal of a good life for most people. However, their functioning, and thus also the degree to which they will be able to promote a good life for most people, is dependent on the presence of certain virtues to mediate market activities.[12] According to the ordoliberal account, the degree to which these virtues are present will determine the attainment of the good life for most.

4.5.1 Non-market prerequisites of the market

It has long been established that the focus on the surrounding frameworks of a market economy, the 'edges of the market', is one of the most pronounced characteristics of the ordoliberal approach. At the policy level, this chiefly comes down to a somewhat limited, but strong, state which guarantees the sustainability of the legal order and does not let itself be dominated by special interests.

Additionally, state institutions must actively prevent the formation of cartels and monopolies or, in the case that they already exist, attempt their break-up. In the presence of too much economic power influencing economic processes, a free and welfare-enhancing economic order cannot be realized. The most concise representation of this can be found in Eucken's seven 'constituting principles' and four 'regulating principles' of a market economy, according to which certain prerequisites (like private property, freedom to contract, or stable money) have to be met before economic activity can ever unfold on markets (Eucken 1952 [2004]). Once it is underway, principles such as 'monopoly control' or 'distribution of incomes' serve as the regulating principles.

However, it has often been overlooked that in the ordoliberals' estimation there also exist non-economic, we might say cultural or moral, prerequisites to successful market interaction, that can neither be created by the market itself nor always be provided by governments (though they can often help people to provide them). Among the elements where government action could potentially lead to conditions that are more favourable are equality of opportunity and some rudimentary knowledge about economic processes on the part of the general population, i.e., the promotion of economic education. With respect to the former, all ordoliberals take a stance that differs markedly from most other liberal approaches to economics, most drastically to what they themselves would refer to as 'paleoliberalism', i.e., Ludwig von Mises, for instance. For them, some form of material equality is seen as necessary for the beneficial functioning of a market economy and a prohibitively high inheritance tax as a prerequisite for successfully fighting the problem of economic concentration (Rüstow 1950 [2001]). However, they also viewed a more egalitarian distribution of incomes and wealth as morally superior to its more unequal counterpart. All in all, they thought that a society producing extremely non-egalitarian outcomes, and even more so starting positions, will, apart from being less desirable from a normative viewpoint, also create problems for the long-term viability of a market order and a free society. Additionally, the ordoliberals worried about widespread ignorance on the part of the people of their time about the economic order they were actually living in. Consider Eucken on the matter: 'The economic order remains unknown to man in essential traits - as decisive as it is for his existence' (Eucken 1952 [2004]: 194). While it would, of course, be unrealistic to make every citizen an informed expert about the economic order that they inhabit, the ordoliberals took seriously the 'social question' and in a way also the charges of 'alienation' in modern mass societies. Economic policy, they thought, can help to overcome these various deficiencies and provide the basis for the widespread use and acceptance of the market system.

The non-market prerequisites for market use also extend to purely cultural and sociological issues. Among them, the issue of 'massification' – people living in ever more crowded, consumerist, and homogenous conditions, and losing their individuality in the process[13] – is a theme that repeatedly shows up in the works of all ordoliberals (e.g., Eucken 1952 [2004]: 18). This massification is not so much a problem in itself, but it worried the ordoliberals mostly because of its consequences for the long-term upkeep of a free society. Alexander Rüstow put the matter most convincingly:

> if man so floats in emptiness, if he no longer has a tradition to trust and rely on, if he is to decide all questions of doubt himself, it is an intolerable situation, which must ultimately lead to a suffocating feeling of fear of the world [...] a suffocating feeling of world anxiety.
>
> (Rüstow 1957: 101f.)

This perceived alienation has, the ordoliberals believed, all sorts of negative consequences for human flourishing but can also pose dangers to the long-term efficacy of a liberal political order (Röpke 1951 [2009]: 256). For Röpke and Eucken, one necessary element for overcoming massification and the void felt by many contemporary people is constituted in a stronger and more widespread role for faith. While their discussion is nuanced, they are convinced that some form of transcendental belief is necessary to 'socially embed the uprooted man of today again' (Eucken 1952 [2004]: 348). Alexander Rüstow, a convinced atheist, who incidentally also had many positive things to say about the church, framed the issue more in terms of people's abilities to emancipate themselves from certain structural forces and decide most issues of their lives independently. This also pertains to the more practical organization of an economy, where he, like the other ordoliberals, favoured smaller and more independent production structures over large enterprises. For Rüstow, the ideal society was even mostly composed of vast amounts of independent farmers, who work on their own accounts and according to their own needs (Rüstow 1950 [2001]: 69). A decentralized, fragmented structure for the economy was seen by the ordoliberals not only as a prerequisite for the effective prevention of mono- and oligopolistic power but also as a highly desirable feature for promoting meaningful and fulfilled lives and an attractive feature of democracy.

In short, the ordoliberals believed that the market order rests on certain preconditions that it cannot produce by itself. As Wilhelm Röpke put it: 'the ultimate moral support of the market economy lies outside the market' (Röpke 1958 [2009]: 1), and only focusing on the implementation of markets without proper recourse to these framing elements could lead to severe negative outcomes. Instead, the answers to the question about what is really important, both in terms of what enables humans to have fulfilled lives and the methods of creating an order that will achieve this aim, lie 'at the edges of the market.'

4.5.2 The market economy and the good life

The preceding section will already have made clear that, for the ordoliberals, the important questions that will change the future of human societies for better or worse are not genuinely economic in nature. Consequently, the purely material dimension of human life is not regarded as decisive, and most liberal contributors are accused of overemphasizing the rank of the economy for human welfare (Rüstow 1950 [2001]: 103). As such, they objected to what would be termed 'economism' today; a notion that for them attributes far too much importance to the economic sphere within human life. In this way, competition in a free society (in the ordoliberal sense) will by no means have the function of 'stimulating performance' (Röpke 1958 [2009]: 136), but rather 'serve the control and order of the economic process' (Röpke 1958 [2009]: 136). Thus, one sees again the ordoliberals' conviction that markets are desired not necessarily because of their favourable effects on economic output, but more so because of their ability to order a society effectively. As Röpke put it, discussing the relative superiority of the capitalist vis-à-vis the socialist economic system:

> We can expect moral and spiritual resistance neither from the highest production of radio sets nor from their even distribution by the welfare state, but from the inner reflection of the West on the moral and spiritual values themselves, the defence of which gives meaning, nobility and impetus to the defensive struggle of the being. And if we thought we had to bribe the masses with butter and radios first, so that they would be prepared to defend the moral and spiritual values and goods, this endeavour is hopeless anyways.
>
> (Röpke 1955 [2009]: 393)

In other words, the great merit of the market economy is, according to the ordoliberals, not only its favourable effects on material economic production, but rather its execution of certain values that go along with its implementation and practice. Correspondingly, the ordoliberals also sharply criticized the related phenomenon of 'maximalism', which Alexander Rüstow decried as a 'cult of the colossal' (Rüstow 1957: 53). They saw the sole orientation on ever-increasing production and output without ever asking whether these will actually be able to contribute to human welfare as a cardinal sin of classical liberalism, which seemed to them to suffer from an 'emptiness of the senses.' In the ordoliberal reading, 'the market economy is not everything' (Röpke 1958 [2009]: 131). It derives its legitimacy not so much from the socially beneficial operation of markets, but mostly from the ordering framework, the surrounding institutions or, as they themselves called it, the 'edges of the market' which represent 'the actual domain of the humane, [and is] a hundred times more important than the market. The market itself merely has a serving function' (Rüstow 1961: 68). Correspondingly, ordoliberalism claims that 'society as a whole cannot be based on the law of supply and demand' (Röpke 1951 [2009]: 255) and that the market economy 'must be embedded in a higher overall context which cannot be based on supply and demand, free prices and competition' (Röpke 1958 [2009]: 131). Rüstow, who probably was the fiercest ordoliberal critic of classical liberals, specifically laments that self-interest is seen as the 'only motivation' in human interaction and thus actively promotes it (Rüstow 1950 [2001]: 27). Furthermore, classical liberalism would be guilty of *Soziologieblindheit* (blindness to sociology) (Rüstow 1950 [2001]: 61) and, correspondingly, the overlooking of institutional prerequisites and regulative forces of a market economy (Rüstow 1950 [2001]: 90–112), but would also advocate market structures for the wrong reasons.

What stood at the centre of economic inquiry for the ordoliberals was thus not the maximization of economic output, but finding out what actually makes human beings happy and then building institutions so that this desideratum could be reached. Market forces only have legitimacy for them to the degree that they help achieve this goal. The ordoliberals actually thought that markets had produced detrimental effects on community, family, and the conditions for small-scale agriculture that, to them, represented the best forms of life for humanity. Being convinced that a garden for personal use comes closest to the natural conditions of life for humanity for most of its history ('the proper living environment for the family' [Rüstow 1963: 287]), Rüstow advocates the promotion of gardens and their cultivation as one of the most important aspects of 'Vitalpolitik', his conception of social and public policy. In that sense, the socially desirable thing, a peaceful, rested, and self-determined life, might actually not be promoted by market use at all; to the contrary, its realization might depend on the effective curtailing or repelling of market forces.[14] The following quote best illustrates the central role of the garden as a symbol for a good, self-determined life for the ordoliberals, but even more so the differences in the evaluation of economic output as a societal goal compared with a more laissez-faire approach to liberalism:

> My friend Wilhelm Röpke once went to Holland with a colleague, through such a colony of small, private gardens, I can quietly betray the name of the colleague whom he concealed, it was the well-known and meritorious paleoliberal economist Ludwig von Mises, and Mr von Mises said: 'Unproductive way to produce vegetables!' - Röpke replied: 'Highly productive way of producing happiness!'
>
> (Rüstow 1963b: 286)

In a similar vein, and in addition to the objection of economic growth being a goal in its own right, the ordoliberals even opposed the reduction of working hours and corresponding gains in leisure time as a sufficient criterion for the formulation of public policy: if the spare time gained cannot be put to good and enriching use, what is the point of having it in the first place? Consider Rüstow on the matter:

> [W]hat is the advantage [of a quantitative shortening of working time], when the modern metropolitan proletarian does not know how to do anything meaningful with this leisure time, than to 'pass' or 'kill' it with the help of some industrialized kind of self-anaesthetization, with amusements

> and 'distractions', which are often no less agitated, unsatisfactory, and power-consuming than his work.
>
> (Rüstow 1957: 71)

The next section will describe how these differences in the valuation of market forces led to a vastly different outlook in their understanding of liberalism.

4.5.3 Liberalism as a cultural ideal

Their specific outlook on the relationship between markets and human happiness also led to a highly ambivalent assessment of liberalism. While they generally perceived themselves to be part of the broader liberal movement,[15] the ordoliberals' assessment of classical liberalism is rather negative. As such, classical liberalism is often associated by ordoliberals with the conception of laissez-faire and 'Manchesterism', which, as immanent features of the economic system, are seen as causing undesirable social phenomena, such as impoverishment and economic inequality, and are therefore downright counterproductive to the attainment of human flourishing. Liberalism's insistence on a 'weak state' (Rüstow 1942: 275) ultimately led to the fact that the actual economic policy prerequisites of a market economy – a 'pure efficiency competition' for performance (Rüstow 1942: 274) – could no longer be regarded as given, thus crowding out one of the crucially important prerequisites for market use. Their proposal for a new liberalism, a 'sociological liberalism', or a 'third way' is thus rooted in their conviction that the old liberalism was not fit to address the problems of the day. Accordingly, Röpke writes in his 'Civitas humana': 'The liberalism which we reach could be characterized as sociological, and against it the weapons which have been forged against the old, purely economic liberalism remain blunt' (Röpke 1944 [1979]: 51).

Eucken argues quite similarly in his *Grundsätze der Wirtschaftspolitik* (Principles of Economic Policy), demarcating ordoliberalism from classical liberalism by hinting at the great cultural tradition of which liberalism is part of:

> The principles outlined here are sometimes called 'liberal' or 'neoliberal'. But this term is often tendentious and not apt. [...] The liberals of the nineteenth century were mostly supporters of a policy of laissez-faire. They were based on a great tradition; but some of them were epigones. On the whole, the liberalism of that time is only a branch of the great tree of European culture which has been based on freedom ever since it existed, and which was threatened or decayed only when freedom decayed. The new historical context makes it necessary – and it is precisely this idea that has forced us to do so – to avert the massive threat to freedom posed by new, positive means.
>
> (Eucken 1952 [2004]: 374–375)

The ordoliberals' vision for a more encompassing liberalism is thus again rooted in the conviction that advocacy for markets per se is not necessarily liberal and that the most important questions for societies to answer are not economic in nature. And so, it is easy to see in which sense Röpke found it useful to distinguish between a fleeting [*vergänglich*] and lasting [unvergänglich] liberalism (Röpke 1947b: 12). The first one refers to the political and social movement of the nineteenth century that Röpke thought inadequate to solve the social and economic problems prevalent in the middle of the twentieth century. Lasting, true, or imperishable liberalism, however, fulfilled the 'cultural ideal' (Röpke 1947b: 1) of a liberalism consistent with certain values of Western civilization that is rooted in the Judaeo-Christian tradition (cf. also Goldschmidta and Dörr 2018). Without proper recourse to these cultural underpinnings of a liberal order, without the moral and spiritual prerequisites on the part of the inhabitants of a polity, the liberal ideal can never be realized. Lasting liberalism is not so much a set of policies that can be written down and wilfully transferred to other jurisdictions, but pertains much more to

> a cultural centre of strength, which has been effective in all periods of prosperity of Western culture and has been fed by the thoughts of the best of all time.
>
> (Röpke 1933 [1962]: 110)

It follows quite naturally from this that it is not strictly necessary for an ordoliberally understood liberalism to fully refrain from grounding their economic analyses in certain notions about the nature of some 'true' social goals to be achieved. Ordoliberalism certainly does not aim to prescribe an explicit and fixed idea of what a good life should mean to citizens via the political process. But it is nevertheless recognized that a useful economic framework conducive to human flourishing is based on immaterial prerequisites which can be objectively recognized and on which the activities of the liberal state should optimally be oriented.

Many of these prerequisites have already been discussed in the previous sections. However, it should not go unmentioned that this adherence to certain traditions, which have always served human life and will logically be able to do so in the future, also produces strange blossoms in Röpke's work. Even if the self-proclaimed 'angry old man' (Röpke 1964 [2009]: 431) did not see himself as culturally pessimistic or even reactionary (Röpke 1964 [2009]: 435), his late mourning of the Fraktur script (Röpke 1946 [2009]) or his criticism of central heating systems seems to be a little strange. The latter would favour the decay of the nuclear family and make people somewhat soft and non-resilient. On the other hand, statements according to which apartheid in South Africa could be justified by the fact that it would in any case be impossible for the black population to build up an effective state and a functional economic system (Röpke 1964) must be regarded as really problematic. The Western foundation of liberal political orders is, in Röpke's reading, carried out in clear demarcation from other cultural areas, for example. So, he considers it inappropriate, 'that we should surrender ourselves to state slavery, which has appeared to me more and more Asian-Russian than German' (Röpke 1932 [2009]: 66). Even though Röpke clearly assumes the 'pioneering role' in this regard, the adherence to and clear naming of non-market prerequisites for a market economy, and its defence, is nevertheless a fundamental concern of many ordoliberals, especially also for Alexander Rüstow. As in the case of the passages quoted from Röpke, his positions must sometimes be described as quite peculiar. For instance, in Rüstow (1950 [2001]), he argues that in liberal orders at least 50% of the population should be active in the agricultural sector and presents this hypothetical state as a kind of ideal state to be striven for. Here, too, of course, the search for establishing the non-market prerequisites of a market order and the inquiry into the ongoing, bidirectional interactions between a market order and its cultural underpinnings led some of the ordoliberals a bit astray at times.

4.5.4 Modern-day approaches: Contextual economics

Despite these occasional excesses in determining the appropriate market edge, we think that ordoliberal thoughts on the interplay of market activities and morality are still a useful source of inspiration for contemporary research. For example, the label 'Neue Ordnungsökonomik' links order economic approaches with contextual economics (Kolev, Goldschmidt and Zweynert 2019). The point here is not to understand economic action in the sense of an 'isolating economy', as is still common in mainstream economics. Rather, the aim is to look at economic action in its social, political, historical, and cultural contexts and to understand why economic facts are sometimes evaluated quite differently under different contextual conditions. Practical applications for contextual research programmes have been offered in recent years, for example, in development economics, in the explanation of economic system changes and their consequences, and in the field of social policy research (Goldschmidt *et al.* 2016). We posit that the ideas of ordoliberalism can be seen as a helpful starting point for further applied research in contextual economics.

The conviction of the ordoliberals that markets live from certain preconditions that they might not be able to create themselves is particularly striking here. On the one hand, the ordoliberal core concern with regards to power-free markets has clearly become a problem in recent years in the course of digitization. Perhaps it is thus not a coincidence that monopoly control in Germany has pioneered enriching traditional concepts for measuring market power with indicators that might be more helpful in a digitalized environment (market capitalization or user numbers instead of mere turnover, etc.).[16] Here it is also quite clear that, as was characteristic of the ordoliberals, there are no eternally valid laws, and that proposed solutions (e.g., those to avoid monopolies in the steel sector) cannot be applied arbitrarily to other industries or other periods. Additionally, contextual economists, inspired by the ordoliberal model, also open up interesting fields of research due to the non-market prerequisites of functional market economies. If 'true' liberalism is indeed so strongly based on its Judaeo-Christian heritage, what does this mean for social cohesion in Western societies in times of increased secularization and globalization? Can the moral–ethical underpinnings of market economies be easily maintained in pluralistic societies? Or: how will the enormous economic success of the Southeast Asian states affect their political structures in the long term if economic liberalization continues (so successfully) without appropriate cultural underpinning? Of course, it may turn out that Röpke and company were simply wrong about all these questions and that a Christian-centred understanding of liberalism is actually completely inappropriate – but at least these questions can still be used today as a basis for exciting research agendas that lie at the intersection of economics and other social sciences.

However, the 'neo-ordoliberal-contextual' research programme is much more topical and relevant to questions about the effects of market-economy activity. Of course, the environmental dimension plays a very special role here, since it represents both the character of a prerequisite and a variable potentially influenced (negatively) by economic activity. In the 1960s, when Röpke and Rüstow talked about the rapidly advancing destruction of the natural environment and a de-aestheticization of landscapes, this had to be seen as a 'fringe position.' In the meantime, however, environmental economic issues, and the search for state regulatory functions capable of combining economic activity with ecological sustainability, have clearly arrived in the mainstream. Moreover, of course, it is again a question of how economic activity on markets interacts with social values. In this sense, much can still be expected from the ordoliberal vision today for the formulation of questions about 'human flourishing.'

4.6 Conclusion

This chapter has demonstrated in which sense the ordoliberal approach to economic policy fits into the dichotomy of free-, coordinated, and regulated market systems. Special regard has been placed on uncovering the role of human flourishing and well-being in the thought of the ordoliberal theorists. We have shown in which sense even the genesis of ordoliberalism was not rooted in some genuinely new discoveries in the field of economics but instead was deeply rooted in the ordoliberals' role in the organized resistance against the Nazi regime in Germany between 1933 and 1945. As such, the practical efforts to implement ordoliberal ideas in post-war Germany in the form of the social market economy, through Ludwig Erhard and Alfred Müller-Armack, must also partially be seen in the light of enabling every citizen to have the biggest possible chance at a fulfilled and flourishing life. Furthermore, this chapter has also shown why ordoliberalism, unlike other strands of liberal thinking, has deemed it necessary to make temporary concessions to 'pure' economic or political liberal theory in order to gain widespread acceptance of a market order and thus increase the prospects of maintaining, over time, their desired free and humane social order. This undogmatic approach of ordoliberalism, which does not shy away from revising its advice on economic policy over time and does not take shame deviating from perceived 'first-best solutions' if societal conditions do not warrant their implementation, is still characteristic of its modern forms today (Goldschmidt 2018). Lastly, Section 4.5 has carved out in detail how the ordoliberals thought about the relationship between the market economy and human flourishing, focusing on cultural non-market prerequisites of market orders as well as the influence of market processes and economistic thinking on human flourishing. We will abstain from providing a summary of what has been said on the matter and instead let Alexander Rüstow summarize. In the following quote, he describes his concept of 'Vitalpolitik', which pertains to a social and economic policy that takes heed of the ordoliberals' reservations about 'economism', 'maximilism', and 'Soziologieblindheit.' To remedy this, Rüstow proposes to start with a clear notion in the mind of the analyzing economist as to which policies are actually desirable, not because of their effect on economic output, but because of their effect on overall human flourishing:

> [It is about a] Vitalpolitik, i.e. an economic and social policy that consciously does not strive for any records and top performances, does not strive for any curves of wage development or anything else to go up as steeply as possible, because after all one cannot live from upward sloping curves and not become happy, but which consciously asks the question what can be done to make the individual happy. This is a question that was despised by the 19th century's fanaticism of progress as 'Biedermeier', sentimental, etc., but which we should have the courage to defend again, for ultimately everything else depends on the answer to this question. Among these things, which, let us say calmly, as much as one has so far been in danger of making oneself ridiculous, are those which are decisive for the happiness of man, not least his social embeddedness.
>
> (Rüstow 1963: 182f)

Section 4.5.4 has also shown in which sense this ordoliberal search for the institutions that are conducive to human happiness and flourishing did not cease with Rüstow's and Röpke's passing. The ordoliberal research programme is alive and well and offers – especially in combination with contextual approaches to economics under the header of 'Neue Ordnungsökonomik' – vast prospects for better understanding the interrelation between markets and morality and thus, ultimately, also for contributing to greater amounts of human happiness.

Notes

1 Minister of economic affairs (1966–1972) and financial affairs (1971–1972) in West Germany.

2 The best illustration of this is the so-called 'Lambsdorff-Papier' (full name: Konzept für eine Politik zur Überwindung der Wachstumsschwäche und zur Bekämpfung der

Arbeitslosigkeit, cf. Bayerische Staatsbibliothek 2019) from 1982 that demands great fiscal discipline, deregulation, and supply-side policies. It led to a breakdown of the coalition between the German Social Democratic Party and the liberal FDP, thus paving the way for Kohl's chancellorship. For a more general description of the politics of the time, see Abelshauser (2016).

3 This is also the reason why Alexander Rüstow is credited with having first come up with the term 'neoliberalism' during the Colloque Walter Lippmann (Mirowski and Plehwe 2009: 12–13).

4 Rüstow (1980) may be viewed as a lone counterexample here, though it is also noteworthy that his assessment of the authors in question is not very favourable.

5 Especially in the case of Walter Eucken, see Goldschmidt (2013).

6 Blümle and Goldschmidt (2006) argue that the rise of dictatorship in Germany also taught the ordoliberals that attempting to solve small, technical problems of economic life might not be the way to go. While these could potentially not even be solved in isolation, their overall alignment could be attempted with the help of a well-ordered overall economic order.

7 Three Freiburg Circles must be distinguished: The *Freiburg Council* (First Freiburg Circle), the *Bonhoeffer Kreis* (Second Freiburg Circle), and the *Arbeitsgemeinschaft von Beckerath* (Working Group von Beckerath, Third Freiburg Circle). A detailed description of the members of the Freiburg School in all three circles can be found in Goldschmidt (2005). In this chapter, we will mostly use the Second Freiburg Circle for purposes of illustration.

8 For a critical review of that term, see Klump (1995) as well as Berger and Ritschl (1995). For Erhard's own take on the matter, cf. Erhard (1957).

9 A close associate of Ludwig Erhard, Miksch was responsible for preparing many of the post-war economic reforms in Germany (cf. Goldschmidt and Berndt 2005).

10 Here a striking similarity to Allais' approach of 'how to promote the greatest feasible economic efficiency while ensuring a distribution of income that would be generally acceptable' (as described in Section 5.4, Chapter 5) can be found.

11 For Eucken's treatment of the 'social question', cf. Eucken (1948).

12 Of course, the presence of some crucially important policy vehicles, such as monopoly control, is also important.

13 In this they were considerably influenced by Ortega y Gasset's (1932 [1994]) 'The Revolt of the Masses.'

14 This need not necessarily happen via policymaking, but most importantly through societal reflection about what matters most and thus with a return to the values held high by the ordoliberals themselves.

15 Their important role in the Mont Pelerin Society and the frequent discourse with other liberal scholars certainly strengthens this position.

16 Market capitalization or user numbers for an acquired platform, instead of mere turnover, as a criterion for determining whether a merger should be approved or not (cf. Monopolkommission 2015).

References

Abelshauser, W. (ed.) (2016) *Das Bundeswirtschaftsministerium in der Ära der Sozialen Marktwirtschaft. Der Deutsche Weg der Wirtschaftspolitik (= Wirtschaftspolitik in Deutschland 1917–1990, Band 4)*, Berlin: de Gruyter.

Barry, N. P. (1989) Political and economic thought of German neo-liberals. In A. Peacock and H. Willgerodt (eds.), *German Neo-liberals and the Social Market Economy*, London: Macmillan: 105–124.

Bayerische Staatsbibliothek (2019) Konzept für eine Politik zur Überwindung der Wachstumsschwäche und zur Bekämpfung der Arbeitslosigkeit, 9. September 1982. In: *100(0) Schlüsseldokumente zur deutschen Geschichte im 20. Jahrhundert.*

Berger, H. and A. Ritschl (1995) Die Rekonstruktion der Arbeitsteilung in Europa: eine neue Sicht des Marshallplans in Deutschland 1947–1951, *Vierteljahrshefte für Zeitgeschichte* 43: 473–519.

Biebricher, T. (2017) Ordoliberalism as a variety of neoliberalism. In J. Hien and C. Joerges (eds.), *Ordoliberalism, Law and the Rule of Economics*, Oxford/Portland: Hart Publishing: 103–113.

Blair, T. and G. Schröder (1999) *Europe: The Third Way/Die Neue Mitte*, Memento delivered in London on June 6th 1999. https://web.archive.org/web/19990819090124/http://www.labour.org.uk/views/items/00000053.html

Blümle, G. and N. Goldschmidt (2006) From economic stability to social order: the debate about business cycle theory in the 1920s and its relevance for the development of theories of social order by Lowe, Hayek and Eucken, *European Journal of the History of Economic Thought* 13(4): 543–570.

Böhm, F. (1957) Die Forschungs- und Lehrgemeinschaft zwischen Juristen und Volkswirten an der Universität Freiburg in den dreißiger und vierziger Jahren des 20. Jahrhunderts. (Das Recht der Ordnung der Wirtschaft). In H. J. Wolff (ed.), *Aus der Geschichte der Rechts- und Staatswissenschaften zu Freiburg i. Br.*, Freiburg: Albert: 95–113.

Broyer, S. (1996) The social market economy: Birth of an economic style, WZB Discussion Paper (96–308): 1–17.

Dietze, C. von, W. Eucken and A. Lampe (1943) Wirtschafts- und Sozialordnung. In N. Goldschmidt and M. Wohlgemuth (eds.), *Grundtexte zur Freiburger Tradition der Ordnungsökonomik*, Tübingen: Mohr Siebeck: 99–115.

Dörr, J. and M. Kutzner (2017) „Außerparlamentarischer Wachhund"? Die Entstehungsgeschichte der Aktionsgemeinschaft Soziale Marktwirtschaft und deren Aktivitäten zur Vermittlung der Wirtschaftsordnung in Deutschland, *Vierteljahrschrift für Sozial- und Wirtschaftsgeschichte* 104: 487–524.

Erhard, L. (1948) *Die Neue Marktwirtschaft*. Lecture given on December 16th 1948, https://www.ueberseeclub.de/resources/Server/pdf-Dateien/1922-1959/vortrag-1948-12-16 Professor%20Dr.%20Ludwig%20Erhard.pdf.

Erhard, L. (1957) *Wohlstand für Alle*, Düsseldorf: Econ-Verlag.

Eucken, W. (1914) *Die Verbandsbildung in der Seeschifffahrt*, München/Leipzig: Duncker & Humblot.

Eucken, W. (1921) *Die Stickstoffversorgung der Welt. Eine volkswirtschaftliche Untersuchung*, Stuttgart/Berlin: Deutsche Verlagsanstalt.

Eucken, W. (1926) Die geistige Krise und der Kapitalismus, *Die Tatwelt* 2: 13–16.

Eucken, W. (1948) Die soziale Frage. In E. Salin (ed.), *Synopsis. Festgabe für Alfred Weber*, Heidelberg: Lambert Schneider: 113–131.

Eucken, W. (1952 [2004]) *Grundsätze der Wirtschaftspolitik*, 7th Edition, Tübingen: Mohr Siebeck.

Fritz, R., N. Goldschmidt and M. Störring (2021) Contextual liberalism: The ordoliberal approach to private vices and public benefits, *Public Choice*, doi:10.1007/s11127-021-00879-w (online first).

Goldschmidt, N. (ed.) (2005) *Wirtschaft, Politik und Freiheit. Freiburger Wirtschaftswissenschaftler und der Widerstand*, Tübingen: Mohr Siebeck.

Goldschmidt, N. (2011) Planning for freedom. The repression and opposition of economists during the Nazi-regime in Germany on the example of the Freiburg circles. In *Subsidiarity and Institutional Polyarchy. Studies of Social Market Economy in Contemporary Democracies.* Centro Studi Tocqueville-Acton, Yearbook 2011. Soveria Mannelli: Rubbettino: 111–122.

Goldschmidt, N. (2013) Walter Eucken's place in the history of ideas, *Review of Austrian Economics* 26: 127–147.

Goldschmidt, N. and A. Berndt (2005) Leonhard Miksch (1901–1950): A forgotten member of the Freiburg School, *American Journal of Economics and Sociology* 64: 973–998.

Goldschmidt, N. and J. Dörr (2018) Wilhelm Röpke on liberalism, culture and development. In P. Commun and S. Kolev (eds.), *Wilhelm Röpke (1899–1966). A Liberal Political Economist and Conservative Social Philosopher*, Berlin: Springer: 203–217.

Goldschmidt, N., E. Grimmer-Solem and J. Zweynert (2016) On the purpose and aims of the Journal of Contextual Economics, *Schmoller's Jahrbuch. Journal of Contextual Economics* 136: 1–14.

Goldschmidt, N. (2018) Wirtschaft für den Menschen, *Frankfurter Allgemeine Zeitung*, June 1, 2018, Die Ordnung der Wirtschaft: 16.

Gray, J. (2009) *False Dawn – The Delusions of Global Capitalism*, London: Granta.

Hagemann, H. (2017) Ordoliberalism, the social-market economy, and Keynesianism in Germany, 1945–1974. In R. E. Backhouse, B.W. Bateman, T. Nishizawa and D. Plehwe (eds.), *Liberalism & the Welfare State: Economists & Arguments for the Welfare State*, Oxford: Oxford University Press: 57–74.

Häuser, K. (1994) Das Ende der Historischen Schule und die Ambiguität der deutschen Nationalökonomie in den Zwanziger Jahren. In K. W. Nörr, B. Schefold and F. Tenbruck (eds.), *Geisteswissenschaften zwischen Kaiserreich und Republik. Zur Entwicklung von Nationalökonomie, Rechtswissenschaft und Sozialwissenschaft im 20. Jahrhundert*, Stuttgart: Franz Steiner Verlag: 47–74.

Hesse, J.-O. (2010) *Wirtschafts als Wissenschaft. Die Volkswirtschaftslehre in der frühen Bundesrepublik*, Frankfurt: Campus Verlag.

Hien, J. (2013) The ordoliberalism that never was, *Contemporary Political Theory* 12(4): 349–358.

Horn, K. (1996) *Moral und Wirtschaft*, Tübingen: J.C.B. Mohr.

Horn, K. (2019) The difficult relationship between historical ordoliberalism and Adam Smith, *Freiburger Diskussionspapiere zur Ordnungsökonomik* 19/03.

Klump, R. (1995) Produktivitätslücken, Konvergenzprozesse und die Rolle der Wirtschaftsordnung: Anmerkungen zur "Catching up"-Hypothese, *Zeitschrift für Wirtschaftspolitik* 44: 29–44.

Klump, R. and M. Wörsdörfer (2009) Über die normativen Implikationen des Ordoliberalismus für die moderne Wirtschaftsethik (The ethical-normative implications of German Ordoliberalism), *Zeitschrift für Wirtschafts- und Unternehmensethik* 10(3): 332–340.

Kolev, S. (2015) Ordoliberalism and the Austrian School. In C. J. Coyne and P. J. Boettke (eds.), *The Oxford Handbook of Austrian Economics*, Oxford/ New York: Oxford University Press: 419–444.

Kolev, S., N. Goldschmidt and J. O. Hesse (2019) Debating liberalism: Walter Eucken, F. A. Hayek and the early history of the Mont Pèlerin Society, *Review of Austrian Economics*, online first: https://link.springer.com/article/10.1007%2Fs11138-019-0435-x.

Kolev, S., N. Goldschmidt, and J. Zweynert (2019) Neue Ordnungsökonomik. Zur Aktualität eines kontextualen Forschungsprogramms, *List Forum für Wirtschafts- und Finanzpolitik* 45(1): 646–660.

Meyer, F. W. and H. O. Lenel (1948) Vorwort – Die Aufgabe des Jahrbuchs, *ORDO – Yearbook for the Order of Economy and Society* 1: VII–XI.

Miksch, L. (1948) A diary entry of August 5 as archived in the Walter Eucken Institute in Freiburg.

Mirwoski, P. and D. Plehwe (2009) *The Road from Mont Pèlerin: The Making of the Neoliberal thought Collective*, Harvard: Harvard University Press.

Monopolkommission (2015) *Sondergutachten 68: Wettbewerbspolitik: Herausforderungen digitaler Märkte*. Sondergutachten der Monopolkommission gemäß § 44 Abs. 1 Satz 4 GWB.

Müller-Armack, A. (1952) *Stil und Ordnung der Marktwirtschaft*, Freiburg: Rombach.

Müller-Armack, A. (1965) *Wirtschaftsordnung und Wirtschaftspolitik: Studien und Konzepte zur Sozialen Marktwirtschaft und zur Europäischen Integration*, Freiburg: Rombach.

Nicholls, A. J. (2000) *Freedom with Responsibility: The Social Market Economy in Germany 1918–1963*, Oxford: Oxford University Press.

Ortega y Gasset, J. (1932 [1994]) *The Revolt of the Masses*, New York: W. W. Norton & Company.

Reinhoudt, J. and S. Audier (2018) *The Walter Lippmann Colloquium. The Birth of Neoliberalism*, Berlin: Springer.

Riha, T. J. F. (1986) Ordo – The German neoliberal model of economic order, *Economia Internazionale* 34: 31–47.

Röpke, W. (1929) *Die Theorie der Kapitalbildung*, Freiburg: Mohr Siebeck.

Röpke, W. (1932 [2009]) Die derzeitige Geld- und Finanzkrisis. In H. J. Hennecke (ed.), *Marktwirtschaft ist nicht genug. Gesammelte Aufsätze*, Bremen: Manuscriptum: 47–66.

Röpke, W. (1933 [1962]) Epochenwende? In W. Röpke (ed.), *Wirrnis und Wahrheit – Ausgewählte Schriften*, Erlenbach-Zürich: Ernst Rentsch Verlag: 105–124.

Röpke, W. (1933 [2009]) Grabrede auf Walter Troeltsch. In W. Röpke (ed.), *Marktwirtschaft ist nicht genug. Gesammelte Aufsätze*, Bremen: Manuscriptum: 67–68.

Röpke, W. (1944 [1979]) *Civitas humana. Grundfragen der Gesellschafts- und Wirtschaftsreform*, 4th Edition, Stuttgart: Paul Haupt Berne.

Röpke, W. (1946 [2009]) Freundlicher Nachruf auf die Fraktur. In H. J. Hennecke (ed.), *Marktwirtschaft ist nicht genug. Gesammelte Aufsätze*, Bremen: Manuscriptum: 361–366.

Röpke, W. (1947a) *The Social Crisis of Our Time*, Chicago, IL: University of Chicago Press.

Röpke, W. (1947b) *Das Kulturideal des Liberalismus*, Frankfurt am Main: G. Schulte-Bulmke.

Röpke, W. (1951 [2009]) Der Mensch, nicht der Eintopf. In H. J. Hennecke (ed.), *Marktwirtschaft ist nicht genug. Gesammelte Aufsätze*, Bremen: Manuscriptum: 253–257.

Röpke, W. (1955 [2009]) Gegenhaltung und Gegengesinnung der freien Welt. In H. J. Hennecke (ed.), *Marktwirtschaft ist nicht genug. Gesammelte Aufsätze*, Bremen: Manuscriptum: 374–399.

Röpke, W. (1958 [2009]) *Jenseits von Angebot und Nachfrage*, Düsseldorf: Verlagsanstalt Handwerk.

Röpke, W. (1964) Südafrika: Versuch einer Würdigung, *Schweizer Monatshefte* 44(2): 97–112.

Röpke, W. (1964 [2009]) Wir zornigen alten Männer, reprinted in: W. Röpke, H. J. Hennecke (eds), *Marktwirtschaft ist nicht genug: Gesammelte Aufsätze*, Waltrop: Manuscriptum 2009: 431–435.

Rüstow, A. (1925) *Schutzzoll oder Freihandel?* Frankfurt am Main: Frankfurter Societätsdruckerei GmbH.

Rüstow, A. (1942) General sociological causes of the economic disintegration and possibilities of reconstruction. Appendix to: W. Röpke, *International Economic Disintegration*, London/Edinburgh/Glasgow: Hodge: 267–283.

Rüstow, A. (1950 [2001]) *Das Versagen des Wirtschaftsliberalismus*, Marburg: Metropolis.

Rüstow, A. (1957) *Ortsbestimmung der Gegenwart. Eine universalgeschichtliche Kulturkritik, Band III: Herrschaft oder Freiheit*, Erlenbach-Zürich/Stuttgart: Rentsch Verlag.

Rüstow, A. (1961) Palöoliberalismus, Kommunismus und Neoliberalismus. In F. Geiß and F. W. Meyer (eds.), *Wirtschaft, Gesellschaft und Kultur. Festgabe für Alfred Müller-Armack (zum sechzigsten Geburtstag)*, Berlin: Duncker & Humblot: 61–70.

Rüstow, A. (1963a), Hat der Westen eine Idee?, reprinted in: A. Rüstow, *Rede und Antwort*, Ludwigsburg: Hoch.

Rüstow, A. (1963b) Garten und Familie, reprinted in: A. Rüstow, *Rede und Antwort*, Ludwigsburg: Hoch.

Rüstow, A. (1980) *Freedom and* Do*mination. A* Historical Critique of Civi*lization*. abbreviated translation from the German by S. Attanasio and D. A. Rustow, Princeton, NJ: Princeton University Press.

Schefold, B. (1995) Theoretische Ansätze für den Vergleich von Wirtschaftssystemen aus historischer Perspektive. In B. Schefold *et al.* (eds.) *Wandlungsprozesse in den Wirtschaftssystemen Westeuropas*, Marburg: Metropolis Verlag: 9–40.

5 The market in the hierarchical market tradition

The case of post-war French economic thought[1]

Ivan Boldyrev

5.1 Introduction

Economic ideas matter. They constitute economic discourses on all levels and layers of society, inform and frame policies, help define challenges, and shape the interests of economic players (Blyth 2002; Béland and Cox 2011). That is why the study of intellectual traditions in economic thought is an important foundation for the study of actual economies. Despite the fact that some scholars find it useful to distinguish ideologies (as more linked to politically engaged and purposive communities) and cultures (Berman 2013), for the purposes of this book, economic ideology, framed and communicated by economic theorizing, is considered a significant element of economic culture.

In this book, we investigate the link between economic theorizing and economic culture as part of national traditions. This chapter will provide a perspective on the French economic thought of the post-war years in order to link the normative ideas suggested by French economists, the sociology of the economics discipline in France, and the general role played by economic thought in the development of the French economy and society.

The storyline for this chapter is as follows. Already by the time of the Second World War, at the famous Lippman colloquium, which marked the birth of neoliberalism, the standard opposition between 'the market' and 'the state', between the policy of laissez-faire and interventionism in the spirit of German corporatism or Soviet planning, was considered obsolete, and there were calls to rethink the ideas of market liberalism. The post-war reconstruction only added new urgency to this problem.

Perhaps the most significant intellectual contribution that emerged in French economic thought in response to this event came from the future Nobel Prize winner Maurice Allais, who defended the idea of *competitive planning* (*planification concurentielle*). Allais was an active member of the Mont Pelerin Society but did not sign the final statement – because he refused to radically adhere to the idea of private property and was not sure this idea would be significant enough in future (Denord 2009). Nevertheless, Allais was also an adversary of traditional forms of centralized planning and, instead, sought to reconcile market thinking with the pressing problems that required state intervention and were

DOI: 10.4324/9781003208549-5

in line with the French tradition of regulation. In fact, the whole history of post-war French capitalism can be written from the perspective of finding the right balance between the 'state' and the 'market' (see one of the most recent attempts in Amable 2017). This balance was sought both by economists and by policymakers.

From the point of view of economic theory, another influential French tradition – that of economic engineering – became relevant here. Allais and his disciples, in particular Jacques Lesourne and Marcel Boiteux, started to implement the ideas of competitive market economics in practice and embarked upon the reform of tariffs at the huge natural monopolies, notably *Électricité de France* and *Charbonnages de France*. This was the way in which, first, free-market economics was explicitly invoked in the policy context of implementing 'competitive planning' (implementation having been for a long period in the hands of academic economists); and, second, it demonstrated how *'markets' could be constructed and maintained* in the post-war policy context of French planning (that was predominantly Keynesian, embodied/symbolized by experts like Claude Gruson). In the 1970–1980s, the theories and practices developed by this group of economists would give way to other ways of economic regulation that will be informed by different, more complex theories. One important stream of thought, French Neo-Keynesianism, would try to formalize and refine Keynesian ideas in the new framework of disequilibrium theory. Another, developed by Jean-Jacques Laffont and Jean Tirole, would bring to one of its originators (Tirole) a Nobel Prize. Importantly, there was a direct way, both conceptual and, arguably, institutional, that led from the policies of the kind developed by Boiteux to the more complex regulation frameworks involving agency theory and the new approach to industrial organization, of the kind suggested by the scholars from Toulouse School of Economics (TSE).

The chapter will trace the intellectual and policy contexts of this transformation, and, in particular, will concentrate on the interplay between *policy challenges* and *academic innovations*, as well as on *market values* implied in (and nurtured by) this interaction.

5.2 The starting point: What are the questions?

Economic thinking is often closely associated with market thinking, to the point that economics itself might be defined as the science of markets. Considering the connection of markets and values thus involves the crucial question of the *normativity of economic discourse*. The positions of economists on the normativity of economics are very diverse.

For example, Duncan Foley, in his *Adam's Fallacy*, argues that economics is built on the premise that one can indeed separate 'an economic sphere, with its presumed specific principles of organization, from the much messier, less determinate, and morally more problematic issues of politics, social conflict, and values' (Foley 2006: xiii). But in fact, Foley claims, 'the economic way of thinking is just as value-laden as any other way of thinking about society':

> at its most … interesting level, economics is a speculative philosophical discourse, not a deductive or inductive science. … The most important feature of Adam Smith's work is not what it tells us concretely about how the economy works … but its discussion of how we should feel about capitalist economic life and what attitude it might be reasonable for us to take toward the complicated and contradictory experience it affords us.
>
> (Foley 2006: xiv–xv)

Contrast this assertion with the recent overview of economics suggested by Dani Rodrik who limits the normative content of the market mechanism to the notion of Pareto efficiency:

> What are these market values? Deep down there is really only one: efficiency. All that an economist can claim about a market … is that it yields an efficient allocation of resources in a precise sense: there is no feasible way to make some people richer without making others poorer. Any economist who makes a broader argument about the fairness, justice, or moral worth of markets that is based on economics proper is simply engaged in malpractice.
>
> (Rodrik 2014: 105)

That opinions may diverge as much demonstrates that economic thinking, in its normative commitments, cannot be easily and unambiguously associated with any of the positions, be it a radical denial of any normativity whatsoever (Rodrik) or an explicit admission of the value-laden nature of economic knowledge (Foley).

By engaging with the specific views of economists, we can hope to shed more light on this controversy. The best entry point would be, on the one hand, the contextualization and implementation of the very idea of 'markets' and, on the other, the specific values that were associated with this 'messier' work. For in becoming applied, or in wishing to become applied, economics confronts itself with all kinds of normative challenges. It is this interface in which economics both shapes public opinion and broader layers of economic knowledge, and, at the same time, is further informed and influenced by these contexts. In what follows, I will thus focus on the ways economics understood itself as a policy science in the France of the second half of the twentieth century. In particular, I will try to demonstrate how the understanding of markets was connected to a certain set of normative ideas in post-war France.

The generally accepted notion in the history of post-war economic ideas is the rise of free market and liberal – or neoliberal – thought (see Backhouse 2005; Mirowski and Plehwe 2009; Burgin 2012 and many others) emphasizing the value of competition, deregulation, and decentralization, and private entrepreneurship. However, it is clear that these processes played out very differently in different European countries. This chapter is an attempt at a survey of the ideas and approaches to markets and market values in the discourses of French economic science in 1960–1990s.

In what way is France special in linking markets and morals? The French case is of interest here, because, in France, *the state* has traditionally played a powerful role in the economy, and the general trend for deregulation has not been much pronounced. In particular, the *planning* in France was essentially different in nature and less market-oriented, than, for example, in the Netherlands (Desrosières 1999). Planning is of particular interest here, because the debates on markets, implicit or explicit, were most often associated with forms of economic regulation, be it the arguments for 'more' or 'less' intervention.[2] According to the varieties of capitalism literature, 'what distinguishes France's market economy from the UK's financial market-driven model and Germany's managed market model is the hierarchical nature of both its state and its firm and labor relations' (Schmidt 2016: 624).

In France, the social and political contexts in which economists had to operate were defined by a deep *distrust towards markets*. This attitude was only reinforced by the institutional structure of the economy. At the same time, economics – as a science of markets – did develop in France (not with the same speed and intensity as in the United States) and had its own influential perspective on the idea of markets and its normative content. It is to this perspective, embedded in the specific institutional form taken by economic knowledge in France, that we now turn.

5.3 Economics and economists in France

In France, the autonomization and institutionalization of economics (especially from law) has been a lengthy process.[3] Perhaps ironically, the events of 1968 that shattered the liberal consensus in economics education (prevalent at the law departments) also contributed to the institutional support of a more autonomous and depoliticized, technical economic science.[4]

After the war, the idea of free markets in France was relegated to the background. Most economists and policymakers were convinced that more government intervention was needed to solve the immediate pressing problems of the post-war reconstruction. The state became a central reference point. 'In 1945, the state was celebrated in much the same way that the sovereignty of the nation had been celebrated in 1789' (Rosanvallon 1989: 187). Note that in practice, the state interventionism in that period did not mean the enlargement of the welfare system, but rather, the focus on industrial growth (Prasad 2005).

The French tradition of interventionism and, generally, the confidence in the power of the state to intervene have always played a major role both in the history of ideas and in the policy debate, beginning at least with Colbert. Even the Physiocrats, to whom we attribute the famous formula of laissez-faire, never doubted that the state (the monarch) should overlook the working of the economy and guarantee that the natural law is not violated. Rosanvallon (1989) argues that some sort of interventionism was so natural for France that

Keynesian ideas initially seemed to be an uninteresting commonplace, something unworthy of attention, because domestic policies had been Keynesian *avant la lettre*.

What role did economics play in this new consensus? After the war, French economic science was a fractured set of very different approaches and traditions. Most conspicuously, neoclassical ('marginalist') economists, as well as emerging adherents of Keynes, were *not* represented in the universities, but rather taught at engineering schools (*Grandes écoles*) and/or worked as administrators for the government or state corporations (Arena 2000; Benamouzig and Lebaron 2018). This, along with the long-standing French tradition of economic engineering (Etner 1987), defined their role in French economic thought and policy.

Interestingly, it was not that the economic engineers were always 'hands on' practitioners and far removed from 'abstract theory.'[5] However, their theoretical efforts were of course tightly connected to their engineering background. The engineers created a world parallel to the official academia, being clearly much closer to the economic policy institutions than the liberal economists at the universities were. Note that, as argued by Le Merrer (2011), an important ideational factor was the influence of social Catholicism in the French university law departments, a doctrine generally opposed to any ideology of utilitarianism that was so firmly associated with neoclassical economics.

Thus, economic engineering in France can be described as one element in the growing body of state bureaucracy. Marion Fourcade describes the rise of 'social engineers' after the war in the following way:

> A first change was the more assertive institutionalization of an economic orientation within the public administration, which created the conditions for the production of a critical mass of nonuniversity economists. A second important step was the progressive, somewhat serendipitous, establishment of research havens for these people within administrative agencies, where many ended up devoting themselves to academic work. The final step was their penetration of traditional academic institutions – that is, the universities and the CNRS[6] – after the 1970s.
>
> (Fourcade 2009: 202–203)

Fourcade (2009) argues that the new generation of economists was *created and supported by the state*. In fact, the jobs they were subsequently getting were also largely in the state institutions, and the expertise they were bringing in was, of course, also mostly connected to solving problems in state economic policy.

This type of socialization could thus easily involve certain elitist tendencies among the 'social engineers':

> The generation of high-ranking civil servants that emerged after the Liberation felt themselves in a certain sense above society, which they judged as obsolete and archaic; they assumed the roles of guides and

> pedagogues … Herein lies perhaps the most profound difference between France and the Anglo-Saxon countries: the anticapitalist ethic and the consecration of high-ranking civil servants as central elites were combined to relegitimate a state that had been strongly contested during the interwar period.
>
> (Rosanvallon 1989: 192)

Since the 1960s, a new regime of economic knowledge has started to emerge. The need to create technocratic elites who would solve the particular tasks of state policy was matched by the transformation of economic ideas, in semi-administrative institutions, in particular INSEE[7] and the *Direction de la Prévision*. Economics itself, in its significant part, moved towards becoming more 'technical', more standardized, and more closely resembling its American counterpart. In particular, INSEE economists played a significant role in setting the economic policy agenda, defining the policy options and forecasting their effects (see a fascinating case study by Angeletti [2021]).

5.4 Implementing markets and mediating between the market and the state in post-war French economic thought

Maurice Allais, the key figure in post-war French economic science, incorporated in his work many elements that are significant for our context. He was awarded the Nobel Memorial Prize in economics for 'pioneering contributions to the theory of markets and efficient utilization of resources.' In this formulation, and in its extension, the idea of 'maximum efficiency' ('how to promote the greatest feasible economic efficiency while ensuring a distribution of income that would be generally acceptable'[8]), we see the priorities for the economists working in this tradition.[9]

Allais himself formulated what is now known as theorems of welfare economics, linking the competitive market equilibrium with the notion of Pareto efficiency. By no means did this resolve the complex problems of how just the markets can be in their functioning and in their outcomes. However, it reflected the general intuition – very influential in standard economics – that 'perfect' markets create some kind of 'good' state: the society at large would prefer a Pareto-superior state over a Pareto-inferior one.

The students of Allais developed these ideas in different directions. In particular, Gerard Debreu, who went to work in the United States, made decisive contributions to the general equilibrium theory and became one of the founding fathers of rigorous economic analysis, while Marcel Boiteux, another bright mathematical economist, left 'pure' science and engaged in implementing the ideas of Allais in practice.[10]

The paths of these two scholars demonstrate the dual nature of the engineering approach to economic matters in France. On the one hand, French economists tried to be as rigorous as possible in formulating economic problems and in creating formal models to deal with them. On the other hand, they were very much driven by some kind of a *normative vision*, the one proposed by Allais. In fact, as Drèze (1964) admits in the first important overview of the work done at that time, most of the theory done by these economists was of normative nature.

Allais was connected with the famous Mont Pelerin Society. In fact, 'in predominantly socialist post-war France, Allais was considered a staunch liberal economist, bluntly advocating free markets' (Munier 1991: 185). The same could be said about one of the most influential French planners and economists, Pierre Massé, whose tensions with his more interventionist colleagues are now well documented (Spenlehauer 1999). Today, again, French economists (such as Kramarz and Tibi [2016]) still keep allegiance to market thinking (and still feel underrepresented).

Allais refused to sign the final statement of the Mont Pelerin Society in 1947, because he believed that there are limits to markets and that economic policy – and economic ideology – should recognize them. The idea of these limits came, again, with post-war reconstruction and with the creation of big monopolies. Allais claimed as early as 1943 that natural monopolies should be owned and managed by the government and (in 1947) that pricing of certain goods and services (such as transportation) should take into account peak-load periods (Munier 1991).

Yon (2014a, b) demonstrates how economic analysis has been prominent in constructing tariffs for *Électricité de France* (EdF), a new natural monopoly integrating the production and distribution of electricity in one single nationwide network. This new microeconomic policy can be seen as an embodiment of Allais' idea of 'competitive planning' and maximum social efficiency (*rendement social maximal*): the policy aimed at promoting competitive solutions even in the absence of a market as such.

Boiteux, who worked at the EdF, made a decisive contribution both to the theory and to the technology of this type of rational policy. In particular, he and his colleagues used the concept of long-term marginal costs – as a guidance for pricing that would be socially optimal and attach the natural monopoly to a particular pricing rule. As Yon (2014a, b) argues, the idea behind the EdF planning was to exactly mimic the perfectly competitive situation, in which prices would be equal to marginal costs, while allowing for certain adjustments that reflected the nature of the 'market' for electricity. This 'planning' implies that the guidance of consumers remains purely formal: the state never defines the precise content or structure of consumption. Instead, the rules are imposed on the state itself, and the rules imply that the state should follow the logic of the competitive pricing. The competitive prices (to be compatible with relative scarcities, cost minimization, and long-term optimality) were used to reveal consumers' (optimal) preferences. This creation of a market without a real market testifies to the general idea that, in order to maximize social welfare and fully utilize scarce resources (to satisfy the demand with the minimal cost), market pricing should be implemented in the form of precise (tariff-setting) rules. The *market* itself, in this vision, resembles more a tight *social agreement*, rather than the set of small independent entities competing with each other.

The role of the marginalist approach was no less important in the French fuel industry. The success of marginalist policies at the EdF praised for its efficiency and the mix of political and economic circumstances made it possible to extend the application of marginalist pricing to other nationalized industries, such as coal mining. However, this was a result of a political and economic serendipity (Chick 2006: 166),[11] with authoritative economic ideas (marginal cost pricing), which became the locus of policy discussions; energetic economists (Allais and Boiteux) willing to promote these ideas; and an institutional infrastructure (so-called 'Energy Section' of the Economic and Social Council [ESC]) that made this influence possible.[12]

However, as Fourcade (2009) claims, the influence of this pattern outside state monopolies was minimal and did not concern the rest of the French business world. Generally, Fourcade demonstrates that in France, establishing a good relationship with administrative powers turned out to be much more significant than relying on professional economic advice. As one of her interviewees said, characteristically, '[p]eople who live in an economy where administrative power is dominant do not believe in the pertinence of an analysis centered on the market. They simply do not see the usefulness of an economic discourse' (cited in Fourcade 2009: 229).[13]

Thus, markets were not just studied, explained, and predicted by economists in France. Rather, the economists developed tools and models of a normative kind: markets needed to be implemented. This was the response of economics to the challenge of moving beyond the simple opposition between laissez-faire and centralized planning.[14]

Later on, this tradition was revived and decisively rebuilt by the new generation of French economists, notably by Jean-Jacques Laffont and Jean Tirole. Both following the tradition of the French economic engineering, and being among the progenitors of contemporary theory of industrial organization, they were fully integrated into the economics mainstream and, at the same time, continued to develop the ideas of Allais. In fact, Laffont and Tirole built on Allais' idea of 'the economics of markets' (and not just 'economics of the market'), implying that there should not be a single and uniform logic of 'the market', but rather the continuum of different forms of imperfect competition that should be analyzed in a rigorous way. Thus, along with 'competition', the new keywords associated with the markets emerged as elements of the economic discourse (to be sure, not exclusively the French one): market failure and market power.

The pragmatic part of these models was associated with the new theory of regulation (Laffont and Tirole 1993).[15] It was based on the idea that a good governance is significantly hindered by major information asymmetries, in particular between the regulating state ('principal') and the regulated companies ('agent'). The models developed in this theory were conceived as solutions to these difficulties.

At the end of the 1970s, Jean-Jacques Laffont started to work on what is now known as the *Toulouse School of Economics*. This was done with the support of EdF and *Gas de France* (Fourcade 2009). The general climate of the 1980s was quite helpful: economists in France had been influential (as symbolized by the figure of Raymond Barre, a professor of economics who was prime minister in 1976–1981) and followed the general tendency towards deregulation and more market-oriented policies (Prasad 2005). Laffont and Tirole's approach (Tirole came to Toulouse at the beginning of the 1990s), however, has been pragmatic: as Tirole said in his Nobel lecture, in many cases 'neither laissez-faire nor a shotgun regulatory approach is warranted. Only sound economic analysis will do' (Tirole 2014: 519). This sound economic analysis implied the creation of simple models focusing on the informational structure of the markets, on the strategic interactions of market participants, on various market imperfections, and on the essential features of particular industries.

In terms of policy prescriptions, one of Tirole's (2016) major ideas has been to support independent agencies, that are situated – and mediate – between the market and the state, and weaken, for example, the incentives to 'capture' the regulator. These agencies already exist and play an important role in various industries within the French economy (Bacache-Beauvallet and Perrot 2017). Another important factor in the new regime of economic expertise has been associated, increasingly since the 1980s, with the European regulatory bodies and regulations that bring with them the universalization/internationalization of knowledge. Economic expertise had to lose its exclusively French character and to focus on France's role in the common European market.

It should also be said that until today, (public) economic discourse in France remains pluralist. Very different schools of thought are present, ranging from purely mainstream economists at the TSE or Paris School of Economics (PSE) to figures like Thomas Piketty (eager to develop his programme of rebuilding economics for the new century and to make it more empirical and more focused on the issues of inequality), to Marxists and institutionalists. What most of the schools share, however, is the importance of economic regulation, an interventionist ideological stance that has been and remains very prominent in France.

5.5 Ethical and ideological implications

Why was the normative paradigm so important for so many economists, including Allais, Laffont, and Tirole? Moreover, what does this case teach us? In particular, what does it bring in terms of the controversial claims of Foley and Rodrik I referred to at the beginning? We have seen that for many French economists, *markets themselves* were not a neutral object of study, but rather were *normative* concepts. They did not just address 'good' markets: they wanted (in line with the traditional neoclassical approach) to understand what it means for markets to be 'good', what would be the normative criteria of this 'goodness', and how one can best achieve this by engineering the optimal solutions.

Economists became the priests of this new optimal governance, paradoxically, even more so, in a society characterized by general mistrust towards markets and free market reasoning (emphasizing property rights, deregulation, and competition). Instead, French political economic discourse is still imbued with the idea of *solidarity* (Schmidt 2002). Markets thus could be introduced and sustained (along with other mechanisms, and never beyond them) to promote human flourishing.

To be implemented, market logic of optimality was instrumentalized, and there, various *values* were involved. In the case of Boiteux, it included, along with the standard efficiency considerations, an idea of some long-term stability. Tariffs, the products of economic reasoning, had to account for the possibility of planning investment and sustaining the working of the regulated industry. These long-term commitments became a part of the conceptual apparatus employed by economists in these sectors. The new perspective on economic regulation admitted that one had to take seriously the issue of incentives and asymmetric information. Economic agents might behave opportunistically, and we need a framework of rules that would mutually align their interests and nudge them to the social good. That would ultimately provide for overall human flourishing.

Tirole's (2016 and 2017) current position on markets and morals is very much in line with the standard response of economists to the challenges posed by ethicists. In response to the ethical critiques of markets and marketization, he urges us not to forget how much economists engage with various market imperfections and how important it is to understand the deeper social foundation of moral norms. In the regulative framework Tirole is thinking about, economists still engineer the best solutions (best in the sense of *social welfare*), and the lines dividing market activities from those exempt from market logic should not be strict and should be subject to critical scrutiny.

> Even when it neither strengthens nor weakens our social bonds, the market becomes a mirror to our souls that reflects realities of our societies, facets of our aspirations, and preferences that we would rather conceal – from ourselves as well as others. We can break the mirror by doing away with the market, but to do so only suspends judgment on our personal and collective values.
>
> (Tirole 2017: 50)

Where does it leave us in our analysis? Economists in France recognized the importance of markets for ensuring efficiency but feared the consequences of unregulated markets. Backed by the strong state and administrative bodies, in a country 'where a nationalized electricity company buys coal from nationalized coal mines in order to produce electricity to sell to nationalized railroads' (Drèze 1964: 33), economic engineers in France sought to implement their own – neoclassical – vision of markets. Subsequently, their academic heirs developed the intricate theoretical apparatus that was aimed at defining, theoretically and empirically, how much the markets should be regulated depending on specific circumstances, thus contributing, along with the growing internationalized body of economic discipline, to the new science of industrial organization.

Even as the French state becomes less interventionist, it still plays a crucial role in shaping the French economy. Here, the position of Tirole (2016) is also characteristic: for him, economics – scientific understanding of economic mechanisms – is a public good. Thus, the triangle of markets, values, and human flourishing in France was overlooked by economists as guardians of rationality, suggesting their normative vision as a common framework of reference and guide to action. The knowledge they produced was both a product and a factor of French economic ideologies throughout the last decades.

Notes

1 I am deeply grateful to my colleagues from the Templeton project. I also should thank Serge Benest, Yann Giraud, Matthieu Renault, Guillaume Yon, and the participants of the 2019 Annual History of Economics Society meeting in New York City, where the preliminary draft of this paper was presented. All remaining errors or omissions remain mine, of course.

2 Indeed, as shown by Sonia Amadae (2003), among others, the need to demonstrate that the rationality of markets that would be comparable with or superior to the rationality of socialist planning was one of the main factors that influenced the very emergence of mainstream economics.

3 The separate economics degree emerged only in 1959 and only at the end of the 1960s were economics and law separated administratively (Fourcade 2009).

4 However, the effect in applied economics might have been the reverse – see Mazoyer (2013) on the emergence of critical applied economists in the Ministry of Transport after 1968.

5 As Brunnermeier and co-authors seem to suggest at one place (Brunnermeier *et al.*, 2016: 68).

6 According to Le Merrer (2011), econometric analysis was present at the Centre National de la Recherche Scientifique (CNRS) almost immediately after its creation in 1939.

7 Institut National de la Statistique et des Études Économiques, headed, in various years, by technical economists (Claude Gruson, Edmond Malinvaud, Jean-Claude Milleron, and Paul Champsaur).

8 Cf. parallel discussion by Müller-Armack on social security and economic freedom in the chapter by Fritz and Goldschmidt in this volume.

9 Another significant post-war French economist explaining and defending the idea of market was Jacques Rueff. Rueff developed an account of markets as fundamental institutions implied by the system of secure property rights. Inspired by Walrasian vision of the competitive market, Rueff developed a statistical notion of equilibrium, without, however, developing the formal analysis in the Walrasian mode, something Allais and his students were up to. Importantly, Rueff was a fierce critic of Keynesianism, one of the participants of the famous *Colloque Walter Lippmann* in 1938, a member of Mont-Pèlerin Society, and a financial advisor to Charles de Gaulle.

10 Apart from Boiteux, other prominent scholars – such as René Roy, Jacques Lesourne, Thierry de Montbrial, Hubert Levy-Lambert, Edmond Malinvaud, Lionel Stoleru, Jean-Claude Milleron, Pierre Massé – were closely associated with bureaucracies (Fourcade 2009).

11 Thus, British economists arguing for the same cause were marginalized, overpowered by the strong coal-mining lobby (Chick 2006). Allais took part in the same discussion in France and defended the marginalist approach.

12 The implementation of marginalist policies was clearly made easier due to the influence of certain individuals, such as Jean-Marcel Jeanneney, an economist supporting marginalism and influenced by Allais, who was appointed Minister of Industry and Commerce in 1959 (Chick 2006).

13 The role of economists in formulating economic policies has long been a controversial subject. Thus, for example, today's French Council of Economic Analysis (*Conseil d'Analyse Economique*), a consulting body within the government, is staffed mostly with economists. In this chapter, I assume that, even if the immediate influence of economic ideas is limited and/or difficult to demonstrate with certainty, their influence on the intellectual climate and public discourse is beyond doubt.

14 This idea, like many others, has been rediscovered by today's economists: "The recognition that markets live on foundations laid by institutions – that free markets are not the same as unregulated markets – enriches both theory and its practice. We must now start building a theory of market transactions that is more in tune with their institutional and regulatory foundations." (Acemoglu 2009: 188)

15 It is interesting to note that this was, again, a normative theory. Parallel to that, an alternative economic theory of *régulation* was emerging in France, advanced primarily by Michel Aglietta (1979) and Robert Boyer (1979). This 'regulation school' was a qualitative macroeconomic structural theory of institutional systems focusing on long-term systemic patterns and their dynamics, and in that, a much more descriptive kind of analysis. For this school, the notion of *régulation* involved 'a conjunction of mechanisms and principles of adjustment associated with a configuration of wage relations, competition, state interventions and hierarchization of the international economy' (Boyer 2008: 11472f.) Jullien and Rochet (2005) still had to insert a caveat that regulation envisaged by Laffont and Tirole had nothing to do with the approach of 'regulationists', while Laffont (1995) himself used the term 'réglementation.'

References

Acemoglu, D. (2009) The crisis of 2008: Structural lessons for and from economics, *Critical Review* 21(2–3): 185–194.

Aglietta, M. (1979) *A Theory of Capitalist Regulation*, London: New Left Books.

Amable, B. (2017) *Structural Crisis and Institutional Change in Modern Capitalism: French Capitalism in Transition*, New York and Oxford: Oxford University Press.

Amadae, S. M. (2003) *Rationalizing Capitalist Democracy: The Cold War Origins of Rational Choice Liberalism*, Chicago, IL: University of Chicago Press.

Angeletti, T. (2021) How economics frames political debates: Macroeconomic forecasting in the French planning commissions, *Socio-Economic Review*, 19(2): 635–657.

Arena, R. (2000) Les économistes français en 1950, *Revue économique* 51(5): 969–1007.

Bacache-Beauvallet, M. and A. Perrot (2017) Régulation économique: quels secteurs réguler et comment?. *Notes du conseil d'analyse économique* 44(8): 1–12. https://www.cairn.info/revue-notes-du-conseil-d-analyse-economique-2017-8-page-1.htm.

Backhouse, R. (2005) The rise of free-market economics since 1945. In P. Boettke and S. G. Medema (eds.), *History of Political Economy 37 (supplement) Economists and the Role of Government*, Durham, NC: Duke University Press: 347–384.

Béland, D. and R. H. Cox (eds.) (2011) *Ideas and Politics in Social Science Research*, Oxford: Oxford University Press.

Benamouzig, D. and F. Lebaron (2018) Economics and policy analysis: From state to market?. In C. Halpern, P. Hassenteufel and P. Zittoun (eds.), *Policy Analysis in France*, Bristol: Policy Press.

Berman, S. (2013) Ideational theorizing in the social sciences since 'Policy Paradigms, Social Learning, and the State', *Governance* 26(2): 217–237.

Blyth, M. (2002) *Great Transformations: Economic Ideas and Institutional Change in the Twentieth Century*, Cambridge: Cambridge University Press.

Boyer, R. (1979) Wage formation in historical perspective: The French experience, *Cambridge Journal of Economics* 3(2): 99–118.

Boyer, R. (2008) Régulation. In S. Durlauf and L. Blume (eds.), *The New Palgrave Dictionary of Economics*, Basingstoke: Palgrave Macmillan.

Brunnermeier, R., H. James, and J.-P. Landau (2016) *The Euro and the Battle of Ideas*, Princeton, NJ and Oxford: Princeton University Press.

Burgin, A. (2012) *The Great Persuasion. Reinventing Free Markets since the Depression*, Cambridge, MA: Harvard University Press.

Chick, M. (2006) The marginalist approach and the making of fuel policy in France and Britain, 1945–72, *Economic History Review* 59(1): 143–167.

Denord, F. (2009) French neoliberalism and its divisions. From the Colloque Walter Lippmann to the 5th Republic. In P. Mirowski and D. Plehwe (eds.), *The Road from Mont Pèlerin. The Making of the Neoliberal Thought Collective*, Cambridge, MA: Harvard University Press.

Desrosières, A. (1999) La commission et l'équation: une comparaison des Plans français et néerlandais entre 1945 et 1980, *Genèses* 34: 28–52.

Drèze, J. (1964) Some postwar contributions of French economists to theory and public policy: With special emphasis on problems of resource allocation. *American Economic Review* 54(4 Part 2, Supplement): 2–64.

Etner, F. (1987) *Histoire du calcul économique en France*, Paris: Economica.

Foley, D. (2006) *Adam's Fallacy. A Guide to Economic Theology*, Cambridge, MA: Harvard University Press.

Fourcade, M. (2009) *Economists and Societies*, Princeton, NJ and Oxford: Princeton University Press.

Jullien, B. and J. Rochet (2005) La régulation en pratique, *Revue d'économie politique*, 115(3): 273–283.

Kramarz, F. and P. Tibi (2016) *Plus de marché pour plus d'Etat! Pref. de E. Macron*, Eyrolles, Revue Banque.

Laffont, J. J. (1995) Sur l'économie politique de la réglementation, *Réseaux, Communication - Technologie – Société* 72–73: 11–18.

Laffont, J. J. and J. Tirole (1993) *A Theory of Incentives in Procurement and Regulation*, Cambridge, MA: MIT Press.

Le Merrer, P. (2011) « L'affirmation de l'économie comme discipline scientifique : une histoire française particulière », *Tracés, Revue de Sciences humaines* [Online], n°11: 163–174.

Mazoyer, H. (2013) Réformer l'administration par le savoir économique: La Rationalisation des choix budgétaires aux ministères de l'Équipement et des Transports, *Genèses* 93(4), 29–52.

Mirowski, P. and D. Plehwe (2009) *The Road from Mont Pèlerin. The Making of the Neoliberal Thought Collective*, Cambridge, MA: Harvard University Press.

Munier B. R. (1991) The many other Allais paradoxes, *Journal of Economic Perspectives* 5(2): 179–199.

Prasad, M. (2005) Why is France so French? Culture, institutions, and neoliberalism, 1974–1981, *The American Journal of Sociology* 111(2): 357–407.

Rodrik, D. (2014) *Economics Rules: The Rights and Wrongs of the Dismal Science*, New York: W.W. Norton.

Rosanvallon, P. (1989) The development of Keynesianism in France. In P. Hall (ed.), *Political Power of Economic Ideas*, Princeton, NJ and Oxford: Princeton University Press.

Schmidt, V. A. (2002) *The Futures of European Capitalism*, Oxford: Oxford University Press.

Schmidt, V. A. (2016) Varieties of capitalism: A distinctly French model? In R. Elgie, E. Grossman and A. G. Mazur (eds.), *The Oxford Handbook of French Politics*, Oxford etc.: Oxford University Press.

Spenlehauer, V. (1999) Intelligence gouvernementale et sciences sociales, *Politix* 12(48): 95–128.

Tirole, J. (2014) *Market Failures and Public Policy*, Nobel Prize Lecture. https://www.nobelprize.org/uploads/2018/06/tirole-lecture.pdf.

Tirole, J. (2016) *Économie du bien commun*, Paris: PUF.

Tirole, J. (2017) *Economics for the Common Good*, Princeton, NJ: Princeton University Press.

Yon, G. (2014a) L'intérêt général et l'investissement. Coût marginal de long terme et tarification à Électricité de France (1948–1949), *Annales historiques de l'électricité* 1 (12): 43–63.

Yon, G. (2014b) L'économicité d'EDF. La politique tarifaire d'Électricité de France et la reconstruction de l'économie nationale, de la nationalisation au milieu des années 1960, *Politix* 1 (105): 91–115.

Part III

Policy

6 Three varieties of labour markets

Three varieties of human flourishing?

Lei Delsen

6.1 Introduction

In Chapter 1 of this book, three ideal-type market models were distinguished: the free or liberal market economy in the United States of America (US), the coordinated market economy in Germany, and the French hierarchical market economy. For these three countries, this chapter investigates when and why views, ideas, and economic thoughts were transformed into specific labour market policy. Can we observe a tendency to convergence? Although the pre-Second World War period will be addressed, the emphasis is on the post-Second World War period.

Labour markets concern an important institutional context in the study of the diversity of models of capitalism. The war of the economic models is about labour markets (Freeman 1998). Labour markets are not only of crucial importance for the performance of economies, but paid employment is also central to the functioning of societies. Meaningful work and work motivation affect productivity growth and the standard of living (Freeman, Dunlop and Schubert 1980; Goldin 2000). Work is a pivotal part of human life: work not only generates an income, but also social identity and individual self-esteem, and enables people to achieve their personal goals and expectations. Employment and working conditions are reflections and determinants of individuals' life chances. Work, employment, and education are pathways to human flourishing (Warr 1999; VanderWeele 2017; Nikolova and Cnossen 2020).

The structure of the chapter is as follows. Section 6.2 describes the changes in labour market institutions and regulations in the United States. Thereafter, Section 6.3 discusses the changes in Germany, and Section 6.4 those in France. These sections focus on the way industrial and employment relations are organized in the three countries. Section 6.5 focuses on the consequences for human flourishing. Section 6.6 concludes.

6.2 Changes in labour market policy and institutions in the United States

6.2.1 From classical to modern liberalism

Liberalism is deeply rooted and has a long-standing tradition in the American society. The eighteenth- and early-nineteenth-century liberalism was a highly

DOI: 10.4324/9781003208549-6

individualistic ideology. Laissez-faire economics were applied in law and policy. Adam Smith's ideas in The Wealth of Nations (1776) had their influence. As pointed out by Candela in Chapter 3, according to this view, catallactic competition tends to *liberate* the individual from *arbitrary* assignments of resources and income based on creed, gender, race, or legal status. The government should not play a large role because that easily leads to unjustifiable privileges. People should be allowed to have control over their own economic well-being. Equality of opportunity, i.e., life chances, is advocated, not equality of results (Zafirovski 2007; Starr 2007).

In the late nineteenth and early twentieth century, the United States was confronted with the 'social question' (Vercherand 2014). Industrialization and urbanization were accompanied by bad working conditions and extreme poverty of many workers. The Industrial Revolution created a group of alienated employees whose skills were diminished by the division of labour and machinery (Goldin 2000). The response during the Progressive Era (1890–1920) included labour reform and increased government regulation. For instance, in the early 1910s, the Workers' Compensation legislation for workers injured on the job was the first social insurance act passed in the United States (Goldin 2000), equivalent to the 1884 German legislation. Disability insurance was preferred to costly and unpredictable legal proceedings.

At the beginning of the twentieth century, employment-at-will became a well-established ideal throughout the United States. Employers could fire employees for any reason, good or bad (Thurow 1992). It reinforced laissez-faire economics and freedom to contract. Labour contracts were supposed to be entered upon freely, and employer and worker to bargain as equals. Courts generally did not intervene to protect the employee from unfair treatment. In the 1910s and 1920s, almost all states introduced rules restricting the hours of work of women. For instance, in the state of Oregon, the Supreme Court decided that the right of the individual to contract freely was outweighed by the right of the unborn. Women required protection because they give birth to children. In 1916, the federal government passed legislation restricting the employment of children under 14, but this law was found unconstitutional in 1918. In the 1920s, immigration from Europe was restricted to protect the standard of living of American workers. The final 1929 quota act, the National Origins Act, was applied until the Immigration Act of 1965 that freed restrictions on country of origin (Goldin 2000).

During the 1930s, both changes in the dominant economic view and the Great Depression led to a move towards more protection for workers. In the pre-Second World War period, economic institutionalists dominated labour economics. John Commons, the founding father of American labour economics and industrial relations, rejected the idea that workers do not need state protection. In his view, labour markets are imperfect by nature, and the inferior bargaining position of the individual worker harms both worker and society. Moreover, labour markets are imperfect because of externalities and public goods in the workplace (Commons and Andrews 1936; Kaufman 1994).

Institutionalists advocated floors for wages and working conditions, arrived at through legislation or collective bargaining, to be set at the level that would prevail if the labour markets were truly competitive – maximizing economic efficiency and social welfare. It provided much of the intellectual rationale for the New Deal legislation in the 1930s.

The Great Depression also led to a change in the common view on an individual's responsibility. No longer was each individual responsible for one's own fate. The state had to intervene in order to protect the people against hardship. Laissez-faire economic policy was replaced by the view that the government has to take on broader functions without sacrificing individual freedom as long as the law provides strong safeguards against arbitrary power. This modern liberalism, inspired by John Maynard Keynes' The General Theory of Employment, Interest and Money (1936), remains fundamentally based on key classical liberal principles (Zafirovski 2007; Starr 2007).

6.2.2 Expansion of protection by laws and regulations

At the beginning of the Great Depression, President Herbert C. Hoover (1929–1932) was still in favour of self-reliance, i.e., individuals have the responsibility to take care of themselves and not rely on assistance from the government. As part of President Franklin D. Roosevelt's first New Deal (1933–1934), the 1933 National Industrial Recovery Act (NIRA) restricted labour contracts by the federal minimum wage and the maximum working week of 44 hours, and introduced the right of workers to organize trade unions, to bargain collectively, and to strike. This led to a dramatic increase in collective-bargaining coverage, but only to a modest increase in union density. The NIRA was declared unconstitutional in 1935. Measures continued under the 1935 National Labor Relations Act (NLRA) in the second New Deal (1935–1938). This so-called Wagner Act gave more bargaining power to workers than had the NIRA and encouraged faster growth in unionism.

The Social Security Act of 1935 introduced a federal unemployment insurance scheme,[1] the Old Age and Survivors Insurance (OASI) for the elderly, and the means-tested Aid to Dependent Children (ADC) for needy children without fathers that became the Aid to Families with Dependent Children (AFDC), the core New Deal welfare programme for poor families. Disability insurance was added in 1956: OASI became the federal Old-Age, Survivors, and Disability Insurance (OASDI), the official name for Social Security in the United States. President John F. Kennedy started the War on Poverty. In 1965, new federal programmes – Medicaid for the aged and Medicare for the needed and disabled – were introduced. The programmes became the most powerful anti-poverty programmes. Based on payroll contributions, employee status provides access to Social Security (Goldin 2000; Plotnick *et al.* 2000; Polaski 2018).

In 1938, the Fair Labor Standards Act (FLSA) established the maximum 44-hour working week, a minimum working age of 16, a minimum wage of \$0.25 per hour, and overtime pay of at least 150%. In 1940, the legal maximum weekly working hours were reduced to 40. In the 1950s, in the United States, the 40-hour working week was widely accepted and set the example for Germany and France. The FLSA only protects employees. Working persons who are not classified as employees, for example independent contractors, temporary, and on-call workers, do not enjoy these rights. Practice and court applications have eroded the FLSA (Polaski 2018).

In the period between the two World Wars, the United States also introduced highly progressive income taxes. Since the 1930s until the end of the 1970s, the United States had the most progressive tax system in the world, including marginal income tax rates of 90% (Alesina, Glaeser and Sacerdote 2001; Brady 2019).

The Civil Rights Act of 1964 prohibited employment discrimination against both minorities and women. The 1967 Age Discrimination and Employment Act banned employment discrimination against workers aged 40 to 70. These laws partly offset the high external labour market flexibility. The 1970 Occupational Safety and Health Administration (OSHA) ensured safe and healthful working conditions, and the 1974 Employee Retirement Income Security Act (ERISA) set minimum standards for retirement and health plans.

In response to increasing unemployment rates, the 1973 Comprehensive Employment and Training Act (CETA, 1973–1982) offered training to economically disadvantaged persons and provided them with subsidized jobs in the public service (Freeman, Dunlop and Schubert 1980; Goldin 2000; Krueger 2000). The 1975 Earned Income Tax Credit (EITC) provides refundable tax credits to low-income working families with children. It was considered a pro-work, low-cost alternative to public assistance programmes. Congress repeatedly liberalized the EITC. It became the largest anti-poverty programme (Plotnick *et al.* 2000).

6.2.3 Revival of classical liberalism

Already by the late 1940s, trade unions were increasingly regarded as obstacles to economic growth. In response to a wave of strikes, the 1947 Taft-Hartley Act revised the NLRA. It redressed the imbalance favouring unions that many saw in labour law. It became more difficult to strike (Freeman, Dunlop and Schubert 1980; Krueger 2000; Goldin 2000). Managerial opposition against unions in enterprises increased. It became possible for states to outlaw closed shops. The introduction of so-called 'right-to-work' laws made it no longer compulsory for workers covered under a company collective-bargaining agreement to pay their union dues. It weakened unions by allowing free riding by workers covered under a union contract (open shop). Union density in the United States peaked in 1954 at almost 35%, and dropped, continuously, to 20% in 1983 and 11% in 2016 (Addison 2020).

Because of the focus on the individual, industrial relations between management and labour are hostile; management mistrusts its workforce and trade unions, and workers are not loyal to their firm (Thurow 1992). Works councils operate in the form of company unions. Plant-level bargaining dominates, but multi-employer bargaining had, since the 1930s, advanced in many parts of manufacturing. In the 1980s, these agreements were abandoned, or firms withdrew (Wallerstein 1999; Visser 2013). The majority of employees are not covered by collective agreements. The coverage rate decreased from 26% of employees in 1980 to 14% in 2000, and 11.5% in 2016 (Kügler, Schönberg and Schreiner 2018).

President Jimmy E. Carter changed the perception of the government. In his 1978 State of the Union address, he said: 'Government cannot solve our problems, it can't set our goals, it cannot define our vision.' President Ronald W. Reagan was even more sceptical in his inaugural address in 1981: 'Government is not the solution, but is the problem', signalling the re-emergence of classical liberalism and laissez-faire economics. The Reagan administration replaced CETA by the Job Training Partnership Act (JTPA, 1982–1998). The public service job programme was abolished. The JTPA budget and Department of Labor job training budget dropped sharply. In part, this was related to the general increase in formal education. In 1998, JTPA was replaced by the Workforce Investment Act (WIA, 1998–present), introducing training vouchers. Funding cuts followed (Freeman, Dunlop and Schubert 1980; Goldin 2000; Krueger 2000).

By the 1980s, tax change had started. Gradually the tax rates were reduced to 28% and 23% for the super-rich; in other words, the tax system became regressive. The tax brackets are higher for low levels of income (up to about 50% of the average worker's wage) and lower for higher levels of income (Alesina, Glaeser and Sacerdote 2001; Brady 2019). President Donald J. Trump's 2017 Tax Cuts and Jobs Act was a massive regressive tax cut to boost the economy.

In 1996, the Clinton administration replaced the AFDC by the more restrictive Temporary Assistance for Needy Families (TANF) programme, i.e., welfare with strong work requirements. The same welfare reform law also introduced work requirement for Supplemental Nutrition Assistance Program (SNAP), i.e., food stamps. In 2019, President Trump introduced work requirement for all public housing residents. In 2015, the Department of Labor addressed the erosion of the labour and social protection system. In 2017, the Trump administration withdrew the Department of Labor's broad interpretation of employee (Polaski 2018). In 2019, President Trump presented a plan for a dramatic reshaping of the 1965 Immigration Act in order to protect American workers. This included a merit-based entry system.

6.3 Changes in labour market policy and institutions in Germany

6.3.1 The origin and birth of the social market economy

Ordoliberalism, the Freiburg School, provided the theoretical foundation of the German social market economy after the Second World War (see Chapter 4). Ordoliberalism shares with the free market theorists an appreciation of individual freedom and self-realization. Ludwig Erhard and Alfred Müller-Armack were the two main campaigners and 'godfathers' of the social market economy. According to Müller-Armack, who coined the term 'social market economy' in 1946, individual freedom should be safeguarded against both the power of the government and the power in the hand of companies or pressure groups. The market, and thus competition, is regarded as an instrument to restrict the power of the government and to control the impact of interest groups. The welfare state is a helpful component that would manage to undo some of the hardships that some people had to endure in a market economy. The German ordoliberals tried to find a 'third way', a middle way between collectivist socialism (and fascist *dirigisme* concentration under the Nazi regime) and laissez-faire capitalism. German economic liberalism was mixed with a *Sozialstaat*, already created by Otto von Bismarck[2] in the 1880s (Schmidt 2002; Stolper and Roskamp 1979; Hagemann 2017; Warlouzet 2019).

Social insurance schemes financed by earning-related contribution are the core of the Bismarckian welfare state. It included obligatory sickness, health, accident, and old-age insurances for wage labourers. In 1927, compulsory unemployment insurance was added. After the Second World War, a generous benefit system, financed by contributions and taxes, emerged. Supplementary benefits were added in 1961. The dependent worker was supposed to be a male breadwinner on a permanent full-time contract. There was little attention to atypical or marginal employment and temporary income. The earnings-related benefits were also meant to reduce dependence on regularly lower, subsidiary means-tested assistance benefits (Hinrichs 2010).

The core of the German wage setting system is the right of codetermination and works councils (*Mitbestimmung*) and *Tarifautonomie* that had their roots in the Works Council Act of 1920,[3] and were emphasized by the Codetermination Act in 1951 and the consensual pension policy based on the 1957 Pension Insurance Law. The principle of autonomy of wage bargaining is laid down in the German Constitution and implies that negotiations take place without the government directly exerting influence. Negotiation with unions and the participation of works councils in the decision-making process are an important cornerstone in furthering common interests. The recognition of union agreements is left to the discretion of the firms. It fosters consensus-based negotiations. Union wages typically act as sector-wide minimum wages. These union wages may also be considered as 'fair payment' or a 'social norm' and it may be costly for firms to deviate from this norm (Kügler, Schönberg and Schreiner 2018).

In 1938, the legal working week was 48 hours. In 1956, collective agreements reduced the working week to 45 hours and in 1959 to 44 hours. The 1950 tax reform reduced the marginal income tax rate from 85% to 18% for an annual income of about 2,400 Deutschmark. At the same time, trade unions postponed wage increases, minimized strikes, and supported technological modernization. Unlike in France, the powerful West German unions were able to colonize works councils and use them as a source of strength in a period of economic restructuring (Howell 1992; Thelen 2001).

6.3.2 Erosion and strengthening of the market principle

After 1967, the emphasis on 'social' suggested by Müller-Armack allowed for the erosion of the market principle in the name of social market economy. With the entry of the Social Democratic Party (SPD) into government, between 1966 and 1974, neo-Keynesianism took hold and a countercyclical policy was implemented. In the mid-1970s, the German unemployment rate rose to around 4%, and active labour market measures were introduced. The unemployed only had to take up work that matched their qualifications and experience (Spohr 2019).

Stagflation characterized the 1970s, due to which Keynesianism lost ground against Milton Friedman's monetarism (Hagemann 2017). This change in the dominant policy paradigm reinforced market-type solutions. In the early 1980s, the retreat of the state and the emergence of more free markets under Christian Democratic Union (CDU) Chancellor Helmut Kohl echoed Reagan's classical liberal themes. However, the major policy objective was a 'renewal of the social market economy', not its dismantling (Cox 2001). In 1985, the social partners negotiated a mandatory reduction in the working week from 40 to 36, in return for an increase in working hours' flexibility. The 1985 Employment Promotion Act abolished the requirement to specify a reason for employers using fixed-term contracts and lessened other restrictions. At the same time, expenditure on welfare programmes was reduced in order to balance the budget, not for ideological reasons (Schmidt 2002). Moreover, reductions were offset by an increase in expenditure on redistributive programmes that were focused on the family. From the 1970s onwards, the German social policy paradigm changed. The level of social insurance contributions was reduced by retrenching wage earner-centred benefits, in order to expand the provision of public support and services for families with a view to reconciling paid work and family obligations. In addition, from 1997 onwards, those who were unemployed had to accept work offers outside their occupation or level of qualification (Seeleib-Kaiser 2002). The Kohl government used external factors such as globalization, and internal factors like unification and demographic conditions, to legitimize welfare reforms, e.g., stronger work requirements in social assistance in 1996 (Schmidt 2002).

Until the 1990s, the post-Second World War policy paradigm of the social market economy, as well as the discourse that legitimized it, were largely unquestioned and remained intact (Schmidt 2002). However, by the mid-1990s, the German social model was under attack. German unification in 1990 appeared to be costly and further aggravated the unemployment problem. A dual labour market developed, with a growing share of long-term unemployed (Paqué 1990; Jacobi and Kluve 2007). Employers blamed rising social security costs for rising unemployment rates and non-wage labour costs. The public was hostile to reform; see, e.g., the 1996 conflict over the reduction in sick pay from 100% to 80%. Politicians implemented new costly welfare state programmes to please voters, e.g., the compulsory long-term care insurance in

1995 (Kinderman 2017). Reforms came even later, as successive governments did not want to jeopardize non-market coordinating institutions. Governments also lacked the political institutional capacity to negotiate reforms in the labour market and the pension system (Thelen 2001; Schmidt 2002).

6.3.3 The 'work first' paradigm shift and dramatic decentralization

In the late 1990s and into the early 2000s, Germany was referred to as 'the sick man of Europe.' At the beginning of the twenty-first century, the unemployment rate went up to 9.6% in the West and 18.6% in the East. In both the political and academic debates, the benefit system was criticized for creating adverse work incentives and increasing long-term unemployment. Public employment services were criticized as ineffective (Jacobi and Kluve 2007; Rinne and Zimmermann 2013). It prepared the population for accepting agreements for the sake of economic growth, which saw inequality rise dramatically for the first time after the Second World War (Dustmann *et al.* 2014; Stockhammer 2013; Kügler, Schönberg and Schreiner 2018).

German employers favoured modelling Germany on the flexible labour market and low level of regulation in the United States. In 2000, the New Social Market Economy Initiative (*Initiative Neue Soziale Marktwirtschaft*, INSM) was founded, funded by the employers' federation *Gesamtmetall* to lobby for far-reaching institutional change and to shape public opinion. INSM aims to revive Ludwig Erhard's policy principles and to bring the discourse closer to the origins of the social market. The aim of social policy should be to create jobs. 'Badly paid jobs are better than none at all.'

The guiding principle of the ISNM was 'just is whatever creates employment.' It became the motive in the Agenda 2010 labour market reform by SPD Chancellor Gerhard Schröder (begun in 2003) to attract voters through economic growth and lower unemployment (Kinderman 2017). Agenda 2010, of which the Hartz reforms were part, included measures to make social insurance systems, especially pensions, fiscally sustainable, labour market deregulation, and a radical restructuring of the welfare state. The aim was to improve incentives for the jobless to take up work and to reduce labour costs (Odendahl 2017). The reforms were also driven by political concern: a 'second Godesberg.'[4] In 2002, the Schröder government took advantage of a political scandal related to massive fraud by the Federal Employment Office to overcome the *Reform Stau*, resulting in the contested – a blessing or a misery? – Hartz reforms during the period 2003–2005 (Spohr 2019).

The Hartz reforms concern a comprehensive modification of active and passive labour market policies, a paradigm shift from a passive towards an active welfare state, and the introduction of the American 'work first' principle. The employment offices were transformed into temporary work agencies to create additional jobs. Deregulation of non-standard employment, including fixed-term contracts and temporary agency work, and of marginal part-time jobs (mini-jobs and midi-jobs), extended the exit options available to employers.

In addition, dismissal protection was deregulated. The unemployment benefits for the long-term unemployed were significantly cut to basic social assistance, and the generosity and duration of unemployment insurance was reduced. The unemployed were subjected to increased pressure to accept almost any job offer. Support for vocational training was increased, and unemployed people were encouraged to start their own businesses (Jacobi and Kluve 2007; Bosch and Weinkopf 2017; Spohr 2019; Eichhorst and Marx 2020). At that time there was widespread political agreement: liberalization and welfare reform are necessary. Global competition, increasing unemployment, demographic ageing, and the deficit limits imposed by the Stability and Growth Pact made the German welfare state unsustainable. Trade unions were challenged by the motto 'Less welfare state means more jobs.' The positions of trade unions and employers were too far apart. The government had the responsibility for acting and creating jobs (Camerra-Rowe 2004).

German union density showed a slow decline in the 1960s from 34% to 33%, and an increase in the 1970s from 33% to 37%; in the 1980s, it stagnated and showed a small decline in 1990 to 34% (van Ruysseveldt and Visser 1996). It decreased to 23% in 2003 and further to 15% in 2017. German unification was an important reason for the decrease in the coverage rate of collective agreements, which dropped from 85% in 1990 to 54% in 2018; 56% in West Germany and 45% in East Germany. The unification opened low-cost labour markets and thus altered the balance of power between employer and employee associations in favour of the former. It became increasingly costly to pay union wages (Dustmann *et al.* 2014; Kügler, Schönberg and Schreiner 2018). Trade unions agreed to so-called opening clauses that allowed firms recognizing a union to nevertheless pay wages below the industry-wide standards. German trade unions were willing to make these concessions to avoid further marginalization. It strengthened the role of works councils in wage determination relative to trade unions. A works council elected by the employees does not have to represent the union, and works councils may act in greater independence from a union if the survival of their firm is at stake.

Germany's particular system of industrial relations allowed for an unprecedented decentralization of the wage-setting process, leading to a decrease in real wages, in particular at the lower end of wage distribution (Dustmann *et al.* 2014; Kügler, Schönberg and Schreiner 2018). In 2015, for the first time in German history, a statutory nationwide minimum wage was introduced to increase gross hourly wages for low-wage workers.

6.4 Changes in labour market policy and institutions in France

6.4.1 The origin of post-Second World War dirigisme

France has a long tradition of state interventionism. This goes back to Minister Jean-Baptiste Colbert who, under Louis XIV in the seventeenth century, tried to build a strong French economy by using the tax system to sell goods abroad and buy domestically. *Dirigisme* was the dominant political-economic paradigm in the post-Second World War period until 1983.[5] French *dirigisme* denotes directive state intervention in economic activity. *Dirigiste* policies include centralized economic planning, directing investment, controlling wages and prices, and supervising labour markets (see also Chapter 5). The state tends to intervene where it sees fit, where it considers the interest of the national economy to lie (Schmidt 2002, 2003).

After 1945, French state officials were entrusted with the task of reconstructing and modernizing the economy, resulting in a comprehensive state-led social security scheme, nationalizations, and indicative planning. The main components of the French welfare system reflect the Bismarckian tradition of social insurance, financed only through contributions, and independent of the state. The French social security system is a fragmented corporatist system. Numerous complementary collective insurances have developed (Lynch 2006; Palier 2010; Jabbari 2012). Full-timers enjoy adequate social protection; less so the long-term unemployed, and the poor and socially marginalized. Income should be obtained from the labour market by salary or unemployment benefit (Barbier and Théret 2001).

Indicative – non-binding but influential – planning was introduced in 1946 to coordinate the process of reconstructing the economy. *Dirigisme* was given full legitimacy in 1958 in de Gaulle's discourse appealing to French grandeur and independence. From 1962 onwards, the five-year plan also included social aims, such as social investments like schools. In 1963, it contained an attempt to incorporate income policy to ensure fairness and economic soundness (Warlouzet 2019).

In 1950, the national minimum wage, the *Salaire Minimum National Interprofessionnel Garanti* (SMIG), was introduced to allow the lowest-paid employees to meet their basic family needs. SMIG was pegged to consumer prices. In 1970, SMIG was replaced by the *Salaire Minimum Interprofessionnel de Croissance* (SMIC) because the bargaining system was unable to protect workers from low wages. SMIC was automatically adjusted to economic growth so that employees could participate more in the benefits of growth and so that wage inequality could be reduced.

The French government not only determines conditions of employment and the structure of wages, but also the very conditions of union functioning in the plant. Rival unions most often do not coordinate their demands and tactics, resulting in competitive and often irresponsible bargaining (Lorwin 1957). The 1950 Law on Collective Bargaining protected unorganized workers and strengthened trade unions. A strict hierarchy applied. Legislation had priority over collective agreements and higher-level collective agreements over lower ones. Collective agreements at least provide workers with the minimum wage and working conditions set down in legislation. French trade unions, although weak, remain remarkably influential within the public discourse (Howell 2009). Coverage by union wage contracts is one of the highest among the OECD countries, but union density has traditionally been low. However, state intervention and industrial conflicts are far more important for regulating employment relationships (van Ruysseveldt and Visser 1996). The state organized collective bargaining, and unions relied on strikes or the government to settle conflicts. Union density steadily declined after the Second World War from around 48% in 1946 (Lorwin 1957) to 8.5% in the 1980s.

6.4.2 Changes in the role of the state: Paradigm shifts

Unlike in Germany, the economic crises in the mid- and late-1970s changed the discourse and policy paradigm in France. In the 1980s, Europeanization was used to incite change or excuse it (Schmidt 2002, 2003). At the beginning of the 1980s, a rival discourse by the parties on the left called for more state interventionism, neo-Keynesianism, and generous social policies. However, at the same time, the radical neoliberal ideology of the right pleaded for the retreat of the state. Even among socialists, liberal ideas were gaining ground between 1981 and 1983. In 1982, to restore full employment, François Mitterrand, who was president from 1981 to 1995, imposed a mandatory reduction of the working week from 40[6] to 39 hours – without loss in workers' pay. In 1983, the retirement age was reduced from 67 to 65.

In 1983, the Mitterrand government made a U-turn (see also Chapter 7). Mitterrand had started his period in office with an expansionary Keynesian-type economic policy. However, this policy proved to be unsustainable. Unemployment rates remained high and the French franc had to be devalued repeatedly. In March 1983, the government decided that such a policy was no longer trustworthy and changed course to monetarist budgetary austerity, and the retreat of the state. Retrenchment consisted mainly of stricter eligibility criteria in social insurance. Benefits were insufficient to sustain the standard of living of the insured. It implied a paradigm shift from guaranteeing a substitute income to modifying behaviour with regards to employment, and was a tool for spurring the economy. It attempted this not by supporting household consumption but by encouraging citizens to work as much as possible. Social security became an instrument of competitiveness, and thus was adapted to the supply side (Palier 2010).

To dismantle the dysfunctional *dirigiste* industrial policy system, in the 1980s and 1990s the social and labour market programmes were massively expanded to buy off the industrial workers who had lost their jobs in the process and those other groups made vulnerable by pro-market reform. These state programmes and policies have allowed employers to reorganize their companies, closing unprofitable factories and downsizing plants. Social solidarity played only a small role in the expansion of unemployment and early-retirement programmes. Between 1984 and 1999, public labour market programmes expanded 250%. The role of the state changed from that of leader to that of enhancer (Schmidt 2003; Levy 2008; see Chapter 7 for a similar attitude towards the financial system). In 1988, a national social safety net was established, the *Revenu Minimum d'Insertion* (RMI). The RMI replaced a patchwork of local and targeted social assistance programmes that had left large segments of the population uncovered, notably the long-term unemployed (Levy 2008). In the 1983–1997 period, there was a marked shift in the tax burden: increasing taxation on labour and reducing taxation on capital (Marchand and Minni 2019).

The French system of industrial relations prevented a decentralization of the wage-setting process similar to Germany. The government intervenes extensively in labour relations (Lorwin 1957) and plays an active role in the wage-setting process. The government sets a wage floor through a statutory minimum wage that is binding for all workers and firms in the economy. The minimum wage is set at a high level, resulting in a low share of low-paid employment. The collective bargaining coverage rate increased considerably, in spite of union decline and the growing importance of enterprise rather than industry bargaining resulting from public policy, including the imposition of a duty to bargain on employers (Visser 2013). The French government extended virtually all collective agreements negotiated between trade unions and employer federations to all firms and workers in the economy. Due to the legal extension, the coverage by union wage contracts has remained remarkably stable at very high levels – around 90% during the 1990s and the 2000s. It prevented a downward adjustment of wages.

6.4.3 German style reforms of industrial relations

During the long post-Second World War boom, unions were useful agents in institutionalizing class conflict and permitting steady, predictable wage growth that increased mass consumption. By the end of the 1970s, flexibility and adaptability were preferred over rigidity and predictability. Trade unions were less able or less willing to deliver what employers wanted (Howell 2009).

Until 1982, company agreements were not allowed to provide less favourable provisions than those set by law or higher-level agreements. The so-called Auroux Laws of 1982–1983, on working time flexibility and on collective bargaining, breached this hierarchy (Glendon 1984; Howell 1992). These laws aimed at reforming the industrial relations system by strengthening trade unions, encouraging collective bargaining, giving new power to works councils, allowing workers to express themselves in their workplace, and establishing more direct management–worker dialogue inside the firm, in line with German practice (Schmidt 2003; Howell 1992). The Auroux Laws brought about fundamental changes in French collective bargaining. A duty to bargain annually at industry and company levels was imposed on employers. These reforms ended the trade union monopoly in expressing workers' views within the workplace (Glendon 1984; Visser 2013).

However, results were different from intention, due to the economic crisis, employers' hostility to unions, and labour union weakness. The reforms resulted in a decline in union density to 7–10% in the 1980s; trade unions became marginalized outside the public sector. In 2015, union density was 8%. A reversal of the usual bargaining pattern and hierarchy occurred. It was an incentive for employers to bargain at firm level, where unions were weak and interests more firm-centred. From 1982, a decline in branch-level bargaining and an explosion of firm-level agreements were recorded. In 1985, 20% of all firm-level agreements were derogatory. It also resulted in an increase in coverage by branch- and firm-level agreements, mainly achieved through the government's extension procedure. French works councils possess little formal bargaining power or rights of codetermination. However, in many firms the head of the enterprise and the works council concluded agreements that were accepted by the labour courts (Schmidt 2003; Howell 1992).

After 1997, there was a marked reversal in the tax burden from labour to capital. In the 1990s, lowering employers' social contributions for low-wage jobs became a key policy instrument in France. Expenditure on these policies increased more than three times between 2000 and 2016 to 85% of all support measures. The cost of specific employment support was 15% (Marchand and Minni 2019).

The incentives to work longer were bolstered by pension reforms, for private-sector employees in 1993 and for civil servants in 2003 that increased the number of years necessary to qualify for a full pension (Levy 2008). In March 2020, the National Assembly approved President Emmanuel Macron's radical overhaul of the post-Second World War pension system into a unified points-based system to replace the existing 42 mandatory public pension schemes and to increase retirement age.

The reduction of the working week from 39 to 35 hours in 2000 for large firms, and in 2002 for small firms, involved a general framework set by the French state, within which labour and business were to negotiate in order to boost job growth. It resulted in rules about work shifting massively and largely in favour of business (Estevão and Sá 2008).

In 2014, the Hollande government took a first step in introducing German-style reforms to promote economic growth and reduce unemployment. From 2016 onwards, extension requests could be rejected when collective agreements undermined competition, vulnerable workers, or firms. Until December 2018, no rejections were recorded. In 2018, President Macron went a step further with his reforms aimed at liberalizing the labour market in the spirit of the Hartz reforms (Kügler, Schönberg and Schreiner 2018; Carcillo *et al.* 2019).

To make work pay, in 2019 social security contributions at the minimum wage level were reduced. To reduce unemployment, subsidized jobs were encouraged. The French effective tax rate at minimum wage level is now one of the lowest in the OECD. Due to implicit costs imposed by laws, business is reluctant to use permanent contracts and governments do not dare to alter fixed-term employment contracts (Tirole 2017: 237–238; Carcillo *et al.* 2019). French employment protection of permanent contracts against individual and collective dismissals has become less rigid. Since 2018, employment protection of permanent contracts has been more flexible than in Germany. French regulation of temporary contracts is still one of the highest in the OECD (Carcillo *et al.* 2019).

6.5 Consequences for human flourishing

6.5.1 Wages and inequality

The distribution of income is crucial for human flourishing. People care about relative rather than absolute treatment and wages. Feelings of well-being depend on a reference or comparison of levels of income. Workers are concerned about their relative place in the wage distribution (Varian 1980; Agell 1999). Until the 1980s, the share of the income of the top 1% in the United States was similar to Germany and France. It increased from 8% in 1975 to 18% in 2014. In Germany it increased from just above 10% to about 14% and in France from 7–8% to over 9% (Furman 2016). Post-Second World War regulations in the United States reduced child labour, and considerably improved the economic position of black workers and women. The increase in the level of education also played a role. In the 1950s and 1960s, black, older workers, less-skilled and less-educated workers experienced more rapid increases in wages. In the 1970s, this was reversed (Freeman, Dunlop and Schubert 1980; Goldin 2000). From the 1950s, the income distribution was fairly equal. From the 1980s, the highly progressive income taxes were gradually abolished, and turned into strongly regressive taxes. In the 1950s and 1960s, hourly compensation in the United States grew at roughly the same rate as productivity. However, from 1973 to 2016 productivity grew six times as fast as compensation for typical workers.

The increase in wage inequality in the United States experienced between 1995 and 2016 is to a significant extent driven by changes in the remuneration of top managers (Stockhammer 2013; Kügler, Schönberg and Schreiner 2018). The benefits of economic growth are largely being captured by those at the top of the income distribution, leaving most workers behind. The Kaitz index, the ratio of minimum wage to median wage, was 48% in 1960. It reached its maximum in 1968 at 55%, and steadily decreased to 33% in 2018. The fall in federal minimum wages and the drop in unionization rates have been drivers of stagnation and declining wages for low-paid workers and of the increase in wage inequality in the 1979–2017 period (DiNardo, Fortin and Lemieux 1996; Fortin, Lemieux and Lloyd 2018; Polaski 2018). Increasing unemployment rates have played a role too. Income and wage inequality in the United States is now among the highest in the OECD (Furman 2016; OECD 2014).

In Germany, the transfer of codetermination to works councils partly accounts for the low growth in mean wages relative to productivity growth and for the increase in inequality at the bottom end of the wage distribution between 1995 and 2008. The decline in unionization has also played a role. As in the United States, the dramatic rise in overall wage inequality was caused by the increase in inequality at the top of the wage distribution in the sector that was not covered. The low aggregate wage growth and the increase in inequality were, at least to some extent, supported by trade unions and works councils (Dustmann *et al.* 2014; Kügler, Schönberg and Schreiner 2018). Wage inequality forced or at least supported the introduction of a statutory nationwide minimum wage in 2015. The Kaitz index was 48% in 2015 and 49% in 2018.

In France too, codetermination moved to the works councils. However, due to the increasing statutory minimum wage and the legal extension, wages grew much faster in France than in Germany, in particular at the lower end of wage distribution between 1995 and 2016, although labour productivity rose at a similar rate of 1.5% in the two countries. In 1960, the Kaitz index was 42%. It decreased to 35% in 1967 and increased gradually to 52% in 1995, 60% in 2005, and 62% in 2018. It also explains the low share of low-paid employment as well as structural unemployment that was higher than in Germany and the United States (Stockhammer 2013; Kügler, Schönberg and Schreiner 2018; Carcillo *et al.* 2019). In Germany, the proportion of low-wage earners increased from 20.3% in 2006 to 22.5% in 2014, in France from 7.1% to 8.8% (Piasna 2017). Kügler, Schönberg, and Schreiner (2018) argue that in France, one of the most egalitarian distributions of wages to be observed since the 1960s can be attributed to the high and rising legal minimum wage and the legal extension.

A high level of income inequality is associated with lower equality of opportunity, hampers social mobility, and is bad for health, education, innovation, and economic well-being (Furman 2016; OECD 2014; Rowlingson 2011; Wilkinson and Pickett, 2009). It impedes human flourishing. Income inequality also harms the standard of living of a country. Cingano (2014) estimates that the increase in income inequality from 1985 to 2005 (Gini coefficient) has resulted in a loss in GDP per capita of 6.0%-points for the United States and 5.7%-points for Germany, while in France greater equality helped increase GDP per capita prior to the 2009 crisis (3.6%-points). Moreover, societies with higher levels of income inequality display less happy and less fulfilling personal lives. Income inequality causes social problems such as drug addiction, obesity, imprisonment, and health problems (Wilkinson and Pickett 2009; Rowlingson 2011).

During the past century, the US labour market and its institutions have come full circle in various ways. Unionization in the private sector has returned to the level achieved immediately before the Wagner Act of 1935. Wage growth for low-wage workers during recent decades looks similar to that between 1900 and 1920. The public social safety net developed between the 1930s and 1960s was rolled back from the 1980s. From the early 1970s, inequality steadily increased, by the 1990s reaching levels comparable to those in the early twentieth century (Plotnick *et al.* 2000; Piketty and Saez 2003). The rise in earnings inequality is the biggest difficulty in the American labour market (Goldin 2000; Furman 2016; Hamermesh 2019).

6.5.2 Unemployment

Being unemployed is associated with low levels of life satisfaction and happiness and with health problems; in other words, it is detrimental to human flourishing (Layard, Nickell and Jackman 1991; Warr 1999; Burgard and Lin 2013; Nikolova and Cnossen 2020). Between 1960 and 1973, the unemployment rate as a percentage of the total labour force was 4.8% in the United States, 2.0% in France, and 0.8% in West Germany. After 1990, it changed. From 1990 to 1995, the unemployment rate in the United States was 6.4%, compared to France at 8.6% and 7.1% in Germany (Brady 2019). These figures may suggest that when it comes to reducing unemployment, the United States performs better than the two other countries. This perception, however, is misleading, as in the United States the high number of people in prison reduces the official unemployment rate. In the United States, incarceration increased from 500,000 in 1980 to almost 2.3 million people in 2019. Besides artificially reducing the unemployment rate, this practice of putting people in jail also increases inequality and damages human flourishing, as it reduces the prisoners' skills and chances of obtaining a job on release. In 1992/1993, the incarceration rate per 100,000 adults in the United States was 519,[7] in France 84, and in Germany 80. Consequently, the unemployment rate in the 1990s in the unregulated American labour market was worse, not better, than in the regulated labour markets of, e.g., France or Germany (Western and Beckett 1999).

German unemployment peaked at 11% in 2005. In contrast to France and the United States, Germany experienced almost no increase in unemployment during the Great Recession. After the crisis, the German labour market also performed well. The crucial labour market policy in mitigating the recession's impact was part-time work (Spohr 2019; Cléaud *et al.* 2019). In 2016, unemployment was 4% and 3.4% in 2018, levels not seen since the early 1980s.

The low aggregate wage growth and the smaller increase in inequality have consistently improved Germany's competitive position. Between 1994 and 2012, unit labour costs decreased relative to France and the United States (Dustmann *et al.* 2014; Kügler, Schönberg and Schreiner 2018). This may also have contributed to its 'employment miracle' that brought down unemployment to record low levels. The share of fixed-term contracts and temporary jobs increased. The Hartz reforms are another factor (Odendahl 2017; Kügler, Schönberg and Schreiner 2018; Spohr 2019). Dustmann *et al.* (2014) argue that while the Hartz reforms have contributed to the recent decline in long-term unemployment and to the continued increase in wage inequality at the lower end of the wage distribution, they were not essential in the process of improving the competitiveness of German industry. The specific governance structure of the German system of industrial relations played a decisive role (see also Spohr 2019; Rinne and Zimmermann 2013).

Even though unemployment in France was not much affected by the Great Recession, it has been consistently high at about 9–10% throughout the last two decades. The high level of long-term unemployment is a concern in France. It is harmful to the individual, leads to stigma, and stifles human flourishing. To address structural unemployment, Tirole (2017) recommends a transformation from protecting jobs to protecting employees, by making companies accountable for the costs of dismissal by experience rating (see note 1) and by giving them more flexibility, as in the United States in 1935, while reducing the role of the courts. This, however, does not sit comfortably with the French tradition.

6.5.3 Quality of the jobs

Over past decades, growing income inequality has been caused partly by the quality of jobs, i.e., the increasing number of non-standard jobs (OECD 2015; Brady 2019). In the United States, Germany, and France, part-time and temporary jobs, and self-employed workers in particular, are excluded from labour law and social security coverage. Employers prefer these cheaper non-standard workers to permanent employees. Active labour market policy, stronger work requirement, and lower unemployment and social assistance benefits have forced workers to accept insecure low-paid and flexible work. Precarious employment is detrimental to workers' health and well-being, i.e., human flourishing (Burgard and Lin 2013; Piasna 2017; Hohendanner and Krug 2018; Pförtner, Pfaff and Hower 2019). Having a bad job can be worse for one's health than being unemployed (Grün, Hauser and Rhein 2010; Chandola and Zhang 2018). Meaningless work constrains human flourishing. Survey data show that in 2015 the percentage of socially useless jobs was 9% in Germany and France, and 7% in the United States. Socially useless jobs are not productive, i.e., they are inefficient. People having socially useless jobs are not compensated by higher wages for this disadvantage and this is associated with a drop in job satisfaction (Dur and van Lent 2019). The lower rate in the United States may be related to work itself being much vaunted.

In the United States, the share of freelancers, on-call workers, temporary help agency workers, and contract workers increased from 10.7% to 15.8% between February 2005 and late 2015 (Polaski 2018; Katz and Krueger 2019). In Germany, fixed-term employment increased from 6.5% in 2003 to 8.5% in 2015. After the Hartz reforms, the number of subcontracted workers in temporary jobs tripled between 2003 and 2016, to almost 3% of all employees (Odendahl 2017). In France, temporary employment increased from 15% in 2007 to 17% in 2017, one of the highest in the OECD, and is associated with low wages and one of the lowest transition rates to regular employment in the OECD (Tirole 2017: 237–238; Carcillo *et al.* 2019). In Germany, the Hartz mini- and midi-jobs hardly built a bridge into regular employment and resulted in an increasing number of working poor (Spohr 2019). Low transition rates imply traps that hinder human flourishing. In-work poverty in the United States is among the highest in the OECD: over 12% in both 2005 and 2017. In Germany, the in-work poverty rate increased from close to 5% to 9%; in France from around 5% to 7.4% (Furman 2016; OECD 2014; Piasna 2017).

The Hartz reforms turned out to be a dualizing reform package. Due to these negative effects, from the mid-2010s public policy has shifted from job creation to reducing labour market inequality and segmentation. The focus has moved to limiting temporary agency work, to equal treatment, and to narrowing the gap between permanent and temporary employment contracts (Eichhorst and Marx 2020). The rise in inequality has led to an intense debate about its social consequences and its effect on poverty and social justice (Dustmann *et al.* 2014; Odendahl 2017).

6.5.4 Working time

Working time per person employed may serve as an indicator for individual control of time. The latter is an important job characteristic linked to job as well as life satisfaction, i.e., human flourishing. In 1950, the average annual hours worked per employed person in the United States (1,867) was lower than in West Germany (2,316) and France (1,989) (*Monthly Labor Review*, August 1963: 925–934). In 2018, it was 1,786 hours in the United States, higher than the 1,520 hours in France and 1,363 hours in Germany.

Legislation and collective working time reduction played a role. Individual working time reduction, i.e., the growth in the voluntary part-time employment rate also played a considerable role in Germany and France, less so in the United States (Cléaud *et al.* 2019). The proportion of part-time employment in total employment gradually increased between 1973 and 2018 from 7.7% to 22.0% in Germany, and from 5.1% to 14.0% in France. In the United States, the part-time rate dropped from 13.9% to 12.7%.

German survey data show that fewer hours worked is associated with greater life satisfaction (Alesina, Glaeser and Sacerdote 2005). Reduction in working time and part-time employment redistribute employment, reduce unemployment rates, and give people quality of life, well-being, work-life balance, and productivity growth (Knight, Rosa and Schor 2013).

6.6 Conclusions

The developments in the labour market policies in the United States, Germany, and France that are researched in this chapter lead to the following conclusions. The political colour of the government, the actual economic climate and in particular the situation in the labour market, and the then dominant school of economic thought determine the combination of objectives and instruments chosen at any point in time. Although the dominant view on markets changes over time, the national differences in priorities, as set out in previous chapters, are still found.

No convergence towards a particular model is observed. Before the First World War and after the Second World War, labour market performance, institutions, and policies in the three countries converged upwards: employment and working conditions improved; performance developed economically and socially. From the 1980s, downward convergence can be recorded, although the timing differs. Employment and working conditions have been eroded. Labour market performance is accompanied by distribution issues. In both periods, the United States set an example for France and Germany. The developments show, contrary to Schmidt (2002, 2003), that the German labour market institutions and outcomes do not always occupy middle ground between the United States and France.

Trifurcated convergence applies in selective areas of the labour market. From the 1980s onwards, the three countries experienced a shift from Keynesian full-employment macro-economic policy to monetarist and supply micro-economic policy, from passive to active labour market policy, from insurance to provision, influenced by economic and budgetary consideration and trends in the labour market. The conditions for human flourishing deteriorated in the three countries; in the United States more than in Germany and France. Although endangered by increasing wage inequality, Germany outperforms the United States and France.

A liberal, laissez-faire type of view dominates labour market regulations in the United States. Employees can easily be fired. From the 1930s, the American labour market became increasingly regulated to protect workers, and the United States became an egalitarian society. The legal minimum wage was higher and the weekly and annual working hours lesser than in Germany and France. Between the 1930s and the 1970s, Roosevelt's New Deal and Kennedy's War on Poverty marked the development of the social safety net but its expansion came to a halt after the 1960s. From the 1980s onwards, a trend towards liberalization can be observed. Practice eroded protection by labour law and social security. The social assistance programmes were rolled back, and work requirements introduced, notably in the 1990s. In the 1980s, multi-employer bargaining disappeared; labour contract negotiations between the individual employee and employer dominate even more. The New Deal legislation and regulations to protect workers can be regarded a detour from the classical liberal economic thinking and practice. The current US labour market shows similarities with that of the 1920s and 1930s. Will the COVID-19 crisis trigger a New Deal 2.0 after the 2020 elections?

The German labour market policy is highly influenced by the ordoliberals' idea of a social market economy. The idea is to strike a balance between market forces and state intervention. Markets are a way of structuring the economy. The system assigns an important role to trade unions and codetermination within firms. After 1967, the market principle was eroded. The costly German reunification in the early 1990s altered the balance of power in favour of employers. Moreover, the 2004 enlargement of the European Union by the formerly centrally planned economies increased foreign competition. As a result, at the turn of the century Germany was Europe's sick man. The market part of the social market economy was emphasized. Extensive labour market (Hartz) reforms (deregulations, flexibilization, and work first) were introduced during the first decade of the twenty-first century. Wage negotiations gradually moved from industry level to firm level, between the employer and the works council. Wage inequality and poverty increased and will be issues in campaigns for the 2021 elections. The 2015 statutory minimum wage, designed to increase wages at the bottom, signifies a limited departure from *Tarifautonomie*. A rebalance of the market and the social part of the social market economy may follow.

France had, and still has, a more influential state. This is reflected in continual detailed labour market regulation. For example, in recent years the statutory minimum wage has increased. In 2016, the state regulation of the conditions of union functioning in plants has been intensified by the conditional legal extension of collective agreements. In March 1983, France made a U-turn and shifted its policies towards a more liberal system. High unemployment rates proved expansionary economic policy unsustainable. In 1988, the national social safety net was established to dismantle *dirigiste* policy. In the 1980s and 1990s, social and labour market programmes were expanded, and incentives to work and the retreat of the state were used to reform and boost the French economy. The wage bargaining system was decentralized from sector level towards firm level, and codetermination towards works councils. High long-term unemployment rates still need to be addressed, either by the market or by the government.

Notes

1 Experience rating determines tax liabilities of firms on the basis of their previous unemployment, to internalize the costs of unemployment. Commons used this classic Pigouvian argument.
2 This first welfare state was created to prevent social unrest, to undercut the appeal of the new Social Democratic Party (SPD), to secure the support of the working classes for the German Empire, and to reduce emigration to the United States, where wages were higher but welfare did not exist (Prevezer 2017).
3 Abolished in 1934.
4 The Bad Godesberg Program in 1959 was designed to broaden SPD support among middle-class voters by gaining acceptance for the social market economy, the Western alliance, and private property.
5 Howell (2009) argues, the French state continues to intervene strategically, mainly to protect workers and firms from the worst effects of the markets.
6 The legal 40 hours workweek was introduced in 1936.
7 This meant that 1,947 per 100,000 blacks and 306 per 100,000 whites were imprisoned.

References

Addison, J. T. (2020) The consequences of trade union power erosion, *IZA World of Labor*, 68. doi: 10.15185/izawol.68.v2.

Agell, J. (1999) On the benefits from rigid labour markets: Norms, market failures and social insurance, *Economic Journal* 109: F143–F164. doi:10.1111/1468-0297.00406.

Alesina, A., E. Glaeser and B. Sacerdote (2001) *Why doesn't the US have a European-style welfare system?*, NBER Working Paper 8524, Cambridge, MA: National Bureau of Economic Research. doi: 10.3386/w8524.

Alesina, A., E. Glaeser and B. Sacerdote (2005) *Work and Leisure in the United States and Europe: Why So Different?*, NBER Working Paper 11278, Cambridge, MA: National Bureau of Economic Research. doi: 10.3386/w11278.

Barbier, J.-C. and B. Théret (2001) Welfare-to-work or work-to-welfare: The French case?. In N. Gilbert and R. A. Van Voorhis (eds.), *Activating the Unemployed: A Comparative Appraisal of Work-Oriented Policies*, New Brunswyck: Transaction Publishers: 135–183.

Bosch, G. and C. Weinkopf (2017) Reducing wage inequality: The role of the state in improving job quality, *Work and Occupations* 44(1): 68–88. doi:10.1177/0730888416683756.

Brady, A. M. E. (2019) The decline of employment protection and the rise of precarious work. In R. Tausendfreund (ed.), *Reassessing 1989: Lessons for the Future of Democracy*, Washington, DC: The German Marshall Fund of the United States: 53–62. http://www.gmfus.org/sites/default/files/1989_FINAL.pdf.

Burgard, S. A. and K. Y. Lin (2013) Bad jobs, bad health? How work and working conditions contribute to health disparities, *The American Behavioral Scientist* 57(8): 1105–1127. doi: 10.1177/0002764213487347.

Camerra-Rowe, P. (2004) Agenda 2010: Redefining German social democracy, *German Politics and Society* 22(1): 1–30. doi:10.3167/104503004782353311.

Carcillo, S., A. Goujard, A. Hijzen and S. Thewissen (2019) *Assessing recent reforms and policy directions in France: Implementing the OECD jobs strategy*, OECD social, Employment and Migration Working Papers No. 227, Paris: OECD Publishing. doi:10.1787/657a0b54-en.

Chandola, T. and N. Zhang (2018) Re-employment, job quality, health and allostatic load biomarkers: Prospective evidence from the UK Household Longitudinal Study, *International Journal of Epidemiology* 47(1): 47–57. doi:10.1093/ije/dyx150.

Cingano, F. (2014) *Trends in income inequality and its impact on economic growth*, OECD Social, Employment and Migration Working Papers, No. 163, Paris: OECD Publishing. doi:10.1787/5jxrjncwxv6j-en.

Cléaud, G. *et al.* (2019) *Cruising at Different Speeds: Similarities and Divergences between the German and the French Economies*, Luxembourg: Publications Office of the European Union.

Commons, J. R. and J. Andrews (1936) *Principles of Labor Legislation*, New York: Harper & Brothers.

Cox, R. H. (2001) The social construction of an imperative: Why welfare reform happened in Denmark and the Netherlands but not in Germany, *World Politics* 53(3): 463–498. doi:10.1353/wp.2001.0008.

DiNardo, J., N. Fortin and T. Lemieux (1996) Labor market institutions and the distribution of wages, 1973–1992: A semiparametric approach, *Econometrica* 64(5): 1001–1044. doi:10.2307 / 2171954.

Dur, R. and M. van Lent (2019) Socially useless jobs, *Industrial Relations. A Journal of Economy and Society* 58(1): 3–16. doi:10.1111/irel.12227.

Dustmann, C., B. Fitzenberger, U. Schönberg and A. Spitz-Oener (2014) From sick man of Europe to economic superstar: Germany's resurgent economy, *Journal of Economic Perspectives* 28(1): 167–188. doi:10.1257 / jep.28.1.167.

Eichhorst, W. and P. Marx (2020) How stable is labour market dualism? Reforms of employment protection in nine European countries, *European Journal of Industrial Relations* 27(1): 93–110. doi:10.1177/0959680119899199.

Estevão, M. and F. Sá (2008) The 35-hour workweek in France: Straightjacket or welfare improvement? *Economic Policy* 23(55): 417–463. https://www.jstor.org/stable/40071859.

Fortin, N. M., T. Lemieux and N. Lloyd (2018) *Labor Market Institutions and the Distribution of Wages: The Role of Spillover Effects*, Vancouver: Vancouver School of Economics, University of British Columbia.

Freeman, R. B. (1998) The war of the models: Which labour market institutions for the 21st century? *Labour Economics* 5: 1–24. doi:10.1016/S0927-5371(98)00002-5.

Freeman, R. B., J. T. Dunlop, and R. F. Schubert (1980) The evolution of the American Labor Market 1948–1980. In M. Feldstein (ed.), *The American Economy in Transition*, Chicago, IL: University of Chicago Press: 349–414. http://www.nber.org/chapters/c11299.

Furman, J. (2016) Forms and sources of inequality in the United States, *Vox CEPR's Policy Portal*, 17 March. https://voxeu.org/article/forms-and-sources-inequality-united-states.

Glendon, M. A. (1984) French labor law reform 1982–1983: The struggle for collective bargaining, *The American Journal of Comparative Law* 32(3): 449–491. doi:10.2307/840424.

Goldin, C. (2000) Labor markets in the twentieth century. In S. L. Engerman and R. Gallman (eds.), *The Cambridge Economic History of the United States* (Vol. 3), Cambridge: Cambridge University Press: 549–623.

Grün, C., W. Hauser and T. Rhein (2010) Is any job better than no job? Life satisfaction and re-employment, *Journal of Labor Research* 31: 285–306. doi:10.1007/s12122-010-9093-2.

Hagemann, H. (2017) Ordoliberalism, the social market economy, and Keynesianism: Germany after 1945. In R. E. Backhouse, B. W. Bateman, T. Nishazawa and D. Plehwe (eds.), *Liberalism and the Welfare State: Economists and Arguments for the Welfare State*, Oxford: Oxford University Press.

Hamermesh, D. (2019) The labor market in the US, 2000–2018, *IZA World of Labor*: 361. doi:10.15185/izawol.361.v2.

Hinrichs, K. (2010) A social insurance state withers away. Welfare state reforms in Germany - or: Attempts to turn around in a cul-de-sac. In B. Palier (ed.), *A Long Goodbye to Bismarck? The Politics of Welfare Reform in Continental Europe*, Amsterdam: Amsterdam University Press: 45–72.

Hohendanner, C. and G. Krug (2018) *Does the impact of fixed-term contracts on health in Germany depend on "objective" job (in)security?* https://www.aiel.it/cms/cms-files/submission/all20170603161057.pdf

Howell, C. (1992) The contradictions of French industrial relations reform, *Comparative Politics* 24(2): 181–197. doi:10.2307/422277.

Howell, C. (2009) The transformation of French industrial relations: Labor representation and the state in a post-dirigiste era, *Politics and Society* 37(2): 229–256. doi:10.1177/0032329209333993.

Jabbari, E. (2012) *Pierre Laroque and the Welfare State in Postwar France*, Oxford: Oxford University Press.

Jacobi, L. and J. Kluve (2007) Before and after the Hartz reforms: The performance of active labour market policy in Germany, *Journal for Labour Market Research* 40(1): 45–64.

Katz, L. F. and A. Krueger (2019) The rise and nature of alternative work arrangements in the United States, 1995–2015, *ILR Review* 72(2): 382–416. doi:10.1177/0019793918820008.

Kaufman, B. E. (1994) The evolution of thoughts on the competitive nature of labor markets. In C. Kerr and P. D. Staudohar (eds.), *Labor Economics and Industrial Relations. Markets and Institutions*, Cambridge, MA: Harvard University Press: 145–188.

Kinderman, D. (2017) The Initiative for a New Social Market Economy and the transformation of the German welfare regime after unification. In R. E. Backhouse, B. W. Bateman, T. Nishazawa and D. Plehwe (eds.), *Liberalism and the Welfare State: Economists and Arguments for the Welfare State*, Oxford: Oxford University Press.

Knight, K. W., E. A. Rosa and J. B. Schor (2013) Could working less reduce pressures on the environment? A cross-national panel analysis of OECD countries, 1970–2007, *Global Environmental Change* 23(4): 691–700. doi:10.1016/j.gloenvcha.2013.02.017.

Krueger, A. B. (2000) Labor policy and labor research since the 1960s: Two ships sailing in orthogonal directions?. In J. L. Perry and J. Tobin (eds.), *Economic Events, Ideas, and Policies: The 1960s and After*, Washington, DC: Brookings Institution Press: 299–332.

Kügler, A., U. Schönberg and R. Schreiner (2018) Productivity growth, wage growth and unions. In *Proceedings of ECB Forum on Central Banking*, June 20th 2018, Frankfurt am Main: European Central Bank: 215–247.

Layard, R., S. Nickell and R. Jackman (1991) *Unemployment: Macroeconomic Performance and the Labour Market*, Oxford: Oxford University Press.

Levy, J. D. (2008) From the dirigiste state to the social anaesthesia state: French economic policy in the longue durée, *Modern and Contemporary France* 16(4): 417–435. doi:10.1080/09639480802413371.

Lorwin, V. R. (1957) Collective bargaining in postwar France, *The ANNALS of the American Academy of Political and Social Science* 310(1): 66–74. doi:10.1177/000271625731000108.

Lynch, F. M. B. (2006) Finance and welfare: The impact of two world wars on domestic policy in France, *The Historical Journal* 49(2): 625–633. doi:10.1017/S0018246X06005371.

Marchand, O. and C. Minni (2019) The major transformations of the French labour market since the early 1960s, *Economie et Statistique /Economics and Statistics* 510–512: 89–107. doi:10.24187/ecostat.2019.510t.1989.

Nikolova, M. and F. Cnossen (2020) What makes work meaningful and why economists should care about it, *Labour Economics* 65. doi:10.1016/j.labeco.2020.101847.

Odendahl, C. (2017) *The Hartz Myth: A Closer Look at Germany's Labour Market Reform*, London: Centre for European Reform.

OECD (2014) *United States: Tackling High Inequalities Creating Opportunities for All*, Paris: OECD Publishing.

OECD (2015) *In It Together: Why Less Inequality Benefits All*, Paris: OECD Publishing.

Palier, B. (2010) The dualizations of the French welfare system. In B. Palier (ed.), A Long Goodbye to Bismarck? The Politics of Welfare Reform in Continental Europe, Amsterdam: Amsterdam University Press: 73–99.

Paqué, K.-H. (1990) *Unemployment in West Germany: A survey of explanations and policy options*, Kiel Working Paper, No. 407, Kiel: Institut für Weltwirtschaft (IfW). https://www.econstor.eu/bitstream/10419/47240/1/25609974X.pdf.

Pförtner, T.-K., H. Pfaff, and K. Hower (2019) Trends in the association of different forms of precarious employment and self-rated health in Germany. An analysis with the German Socio-Economic Panel between 1995 and 2015, *Journal of Epidemiology and Community Health* 73: 1002–1011. doi:10.1136/jech-2018-211933.

Piasna, A. (2017) *'Bad jobs' recovery? European Job Quality Index 2005–2015*, Working Paper 2017.6, Brussels: European Trade Union Institute. https://www.etui.org/publications/working-papers/bad-jobs-recovery-european-job-quality-index-2005-2015.

Piketty, T. and E. Saez (2003) Income inequality in the United States, 1913–1998, *Quarterly Journal of Economics* 118: 1–39. doi:10.3386/w8467.

Plotnick, R., E. Smolensky, E. Evenhouse and S. Reilly (2000) The twentieth-century record of inequality and poverty in the United States, Volume 3. In S. L. Engerman and R. Gallman (eds.), *The Cambridge Economic History of the United States*, Cambridge: Cambridge University Press: 249–300.

Polaski, S. (2018) *Building an adequate U.S. labor and social protection system for the 21st century*, ESS — Working Paper No. 60, Geneva: International Labour Office.

Prevezer, M. (2017) *Varieties of Capitalism in History, Transition and Emergence: New Perspectives on Institutional Development*, New York: Routledge.
Rinne, U. and K. F. Zimmermann (2013) Is Germany the North Star of labor market policy?, *IMF Economic Review* 61(4): 702–729. doi:10.1057/imfer.2013.21.
Rowlingson, K. (2011) *Does Income Inequality Cause Health and Social Problems?* York: Joseph Rowntree Foundation. https://www.jrf.org.uk/report/does-income-inequality-cause-health-and-social-problems.
Schmidt, V. A. (2002) *The Futures of European Capitalism*, Oxford: Oxford University Press.
Schmidt, V. A. (2003) French capitalism transformed, yet still a third variety of capitalism, *Economy and Society* 32(4): 526–554. doi:10.1080/0308514032000141693.
Seeleib-Kaiser, M. (2002) A dual transformation of the German welfare state?, *West European Politics* 25(4): 25–48. doi:10.1080/713601641.
Spohr, F. (2019) German's labour market policies. How the sick man of Europe performed a second economic miracle. In P. 't Hart and M. Crompton (eds.), *Great Policy Successes*, Oxford: Oxford University Press: 283–303.
Starr, P. (2007) *Freedom's Power: The True Force of Liberalism*, New York: Basic Books.
Stockhammer, E. (2013) *Why Have Wage Shares Fallen? A Panel Analysis of the Determinants of Functional Income Distribution*, Conditions of Work and Employment Series No. 35, Geneva: International Labour Office. https://www.ilo.org/wcmsp5/groups/public/---ed_protect/---protrav/---travail/documents/publication/wcms_202352.pdf.
Stolper, W. F. and K. W. Roskamp (1979) Planning a free economy: Germany 1945–1960, *Journal of Institutional and Theoretical Economics* 135(3), Currency and Economic Reform: West Germany After World War II: A Symposium: 374–404. https://www.jstor.org/stable/40750150.
Thelen, K. (2001) Varieties of labor politics in the developed democracies. In P. A. Hall and D. Soskice (eds.), *Varieties of Capitalism: The Institutional Foundations of Comparative Advantage*, Oxford: Oxford University Press: 71–103.
Thurow, L. (1992) *Head to Head: The Coming Economic Battle Among Japan, Europe, and America*, New York: William Morrow.
Tirole, J. (2017) *Economics for the Common Good*, Princeton, NJ: Princeton University Press.
VanderWeele, T. J. (2017) On the promotion of human flourishing, *Proceedings of the National Academy of Sciences of the United States of America* 114(31): 8148–8156. doi:10.1073/pnas.1702996114.
Van Ruysseveldt, J. and J. Visser (eds.) (1996) *Industrial Relations in Europe. Traditions and Transitions*, London: Sage.
Varian, H. R. (1980) Redistributive taxation as social insurance, *Journal of Public Economics* 14(1): 49–68. doi:10.1016/0047-2727(80)90004-3.
Vercherand, J. (2014) *Labour: A Heterodox Approach*, London: Palgrave Macmillan.
Visser, J. (2013) *Wage Bargaining Institutions - from crisis to crisis*, Economic Papers 488, Brussels: European Commission Directorate-General for Economic and Financial Affairs. https://ec.europa.eu/economy_finance/publications/economic_paper/2013/pdf/ecp488_en.pdf.
Wallerstein, M. (1999) Wage-setting institutions and pay inequality in advanced industrial societies, *American Journal of Political Science* 43(3): 649–680. doi:10.2307 / 2991830
Warlouzet (2019) The EEC/EU as an evolving compromise between French dirigism and German ordoliberalism (1957–1995), *Journal of Common Market Studies* 57(1): 77–93. doi:10.1111/jcms.12817.

Warr, P. (1999) Well-being at the workplace. In D. Kahneman, E. Diener and N. Schwarz (eds.) *Well-Being: Foundations of Hedonic Psychology*, New York: Russell Sage Foundation: 392–412.

Western, B. and K. Beckett (1999) How unregulated is the U.S. labor market? The penal system as a labor market institution, *American Journal of Sociology* 104(4): 1030–1060. doi:10.1086/210135.

Wikinson, R. and K. Pickett (2009) *The Spirit Level: Why More Equal Societies Almost Always Do Better*, London: Allen Lane.

Zafirovski, M. (2007) *Liberal Modernity and its Adversaries: Freedom, Liberalism, and Anti-Liberalism in the 21st Century*, Leiden: Brill.

7 Do national financial systems still reflect national values?

The case of the United States, Germany, and France[1]

Eelke de Jong

7.1 Introduction

In the previous chapters, we have presented economic theories representing the free market economy, the coordinated market economy, and the hierarchical market economy. In Chapter 2, we have recast this as different ways of dealing with uncertainty. According to Chapter 3, the free market economy is in favour of competition as it liberates individuals from arbitrary assignments and thus enables them to flourish. As a consequence, the inhabitants of these countries accept uncertainty to a great extent and favour flexible arrangements. In coordinated market economies, competition is also thought to be good but should be restricted from the outset. Market participants have to acquire the capacity to act and competition can be restricted in order to protect the common interest. Uncertainty is not readily accepted and one copes with it by relying on rules. The hierarchical market economies don't favour competition per se. It is just one possibility along with state intervention. In Chapter 2, we have argued that uncertainty is restricted by concentrating power in the hands of a higher level, an elite. In France, this elite is the government.

This chapter will investigate to what extent these characteristics of the three different types of market economy have played a role in the development of the financial systems in the United States of America, Germany, and France. Many have argued that since the 1980s these systems have converged towards a market-based system, which is characteristic of the United States. Therefore, this chapter investigates in particular whether this convergence has taken place, and if so, whether this convergence holds for all aspects of the financial system. For each country, three aspects of its financial system are considered: the way the system finances firms, the way pensions are financed, and the manner in which it provides finances for housing (the mortgage markets).

The rest of the chapter is organized as follows. The subsequent sections describe the evolution of the financial system of, respectively, the United States (free market economy), Germany (coordinated market economy), and France (hierarchical market economy). For each country we focus on the arguments and implicit values underlying each original structure. The focus will be on developments since the Second World War, although we will also discuss some

DOI: 10.4324/9781003208549-7

elements of earlier periods. Per country, we consecutively describe the system in general which is directed at financing firms' activities, the way pensions are financed, and the manner by which housing is financed.[2] The final section presents the conclusions.

7.2 The free market economy: The United States

7.2.1 The period before the Second World War

The history of the United States' financial system is characterized by a distrust of concentration of power, often expressed in the form of populism, and a favouring of competition between small units. Distrust and populism were already apparent at the end of the eighteenth and the beginning of the nineteenth century. For example, in 1830, President Jackson announced that, in his view, the Second National Bank of the United States was a dangerous monopoly which only served the interests of its wealthy owners. This populist position helped him get re-elected in 1832. In 1833, he decided to redistribute the federal deposits over different state banks and thus undermined the position of the Second National Bank, which in the end was not chartered.

Of course the different state banks supported the president's position against the Second National Bank as the latter was a competitor and could control them. This illustrates another reason for the fragmented position of US banking, namely the infighting among different groups and the power of local and state banks. Within the federal structure, each state has the power to charter banks. In practice, each state protected the banks in its territory by excluding branches from other states' banks. Moreover, frequently states prevented single-location banks from branching, so that a bank was restricted to a single office. This unit banking system hampered banks in diversifying their risks and limited their growth. Often these regulations were established in order to protect rural interests, in the sense that locally collected deposits would not be invested in other communities (Berger *et al.* 1995: 185 and 186). As a result, banks were small and by the beginning of the twentieth century, insurers were the largest financial institutions in the United States. Banks were confined to a single state and in many instances to a single location (Roe 1994: 59). The McFadden Act of 1927 consolidated this situation by imposing restrictions on interstate banking.

The 1929 Wall Street Crash and the resulting Great Depression of the 1930s led to the Banking Act of 1933, better known as the Glass-Steagall Act. This act prohibited the banks from engaging in both commercial activities (providing loans to firms and private persons) and investment banking. Investment banking refers to the activities of banks on stock exchanges, such as trading in stocks and organizing the initial public offerings (IPOs). At that time, a dominant view was that the 1929 panic was caused by 'excessive use of bank credit for the purpose of stock speculation, or, more generally stated, for the excessive carrying of securities with borrowed money' (Senate Banking Act

Report 1933: 9). From 1922 to June 1929, the commercial loans of all incorporated commercial banks on securities increased by 126% whereas commercial loans increased by only 12% (Sissoko 2017: 91). In accordance with this view, Section 11 of the Banking Act prohibited commercial banks from investment banking activities such as 'making loans on the securities of stocks, bonds and other investment securities to brokers or dealers in such securities' (Sissoko 2017: 91). The public mood also played a role as the Pecora Investigation[3] revealed that some rich bankers had not paid any taxes since 1930. This was legal because they had incurred large losses on their portfolios of stocks.[4]

Another important view in the 1920s and 1930s was that the financial crisis and Great Depression were a result of excessive competition, or 'ruinous competition' (see, e.g., Wheelock 1992b: 326). Prices had declined too much, so that many companies (including banks) went bankrupt. In order to stem this 'excessive' competition, the Banking Act of 1933 prohibited banks from paying interest on demand deposits and gave the Federal Reserve System (FED) the authority to introduce ceilings on interest rates of time deposits and savings deposits. The FED exercised its authority through a regulation known as Regulation Q.

In summary, after the crisis of the 1920s and 1930s, the United States' financial system was characterized by restrictions on interstate banking, a separation of commercial and investment banking, and restrictions on interest rates. The first two were introduced as a reaction to populistic mood and a distrust of large financial institutions. The last measure (Regulation Q) aimed at mitigating the consequences of too severe competition. However, from an outsider's perspective it appears strange, as it seemed to restrict competition by restricting prices in order to enable competition, which is a contradiction in terms.

7.2.2 Reforms after the Second World War

After the Second World War, these regulations were still in place. During the first decades after 1945, these restrictions did not cause serious problems, because the international financial system itself was tightly regulated.

From the beginning of the 1960s, pressure started building up against the ceilings imposed by Regulation Q. The Eurodollar market, which trades US dollar loans outside the jurisdiction of the American authorities, began to flourish and offered an alternative for investing in US dollars at higher rates than were possible in the United States, where the deposit rates were still limited by Regulation Q. As a reaction, money flew out of America (see Johnston 1983; Wheelock 1992b: 327). In the 1970s, the situation worsened as inflation increased and nominal interest rates rose above the ceilings set by Regulation Q, generating an outflow of funds from banks and thrifts. Meanwhile, money market funds were created by other financial institutions. These funds pooled small investors' money to purchase commercial paper and were not restricted with respect to the interest that could be offered. As a consequence, small investors invested via money market funds in more attractive assets outside of banks and thrifts. These developments undermined the profitability of commercial banks. In the period 1980–1982, acts were passed in order to phase out interest ceilings (Sherman 2009: 6) and to allow banks to offer money market deposit accounts that could compete with money market funds (Berger *et al.* 1995: 179). In the end, Regulation Q was abolished because the economic situation made it counterproductive. Instead of protecting banks and thrifts against ruinous competition, it placed these institutions in an unfair position against newcomers such as money market funds and participants in the Eurodollar market.

The restrictions on interstate banking were largely the result of the McFadden Act of 1927 and other laws (Medley 1994). These restrictions were motivated by concerns about the power of concentrated financial institutions and about the possibility of adequately supervising banks operating in multiple states. Starting in the early 1980s, some states made changes to their own laws that permitted out-of-state banks to enter their states under specific conditions (see Berger *et al.* 1995: 185–190, for an overview). By 1990, 46 states had laws which permitted out-of-state banks to acquire in-state banks under certain circumstances. The result was a patchwork of regulations. The Clinton administration made clear that it would like to move away from this patchwork and formulated a law that would suggest uniform rules for all states. Large banks were in favour, and the opposition by small banks was not as vocal as it had been before. This could be because the proposal allowed states to limit interstate entry and also set a minimum age requirement for the banks that could be acquired. Moreover, the law contained conditions aimed at restricting the power of individual institutions, such as ceilings on the percentage of the nation's total deposits (10%) and an individual state's deposits (30%). On September 29, 1994, President Bill Clinton signed the Riegle-Neal Interstate Banking and Branching Efficiency Act that allowed for different types of interstate banking. As the title suggests, at least according to the proponents of this law, it would enhance the banks' efficiency and 'help American banks better meet the needs of our people, our communities, and our economy' (Clinton 1994). The law contained criteria for out-of-state banks with respect to their investments in favour of poor persons and poor neighbourhoods. These criteria came from the Community Reinvestment Act (CRA) of 1977. The CRA is a federal law which aims at encouraging commercial banks and savings associations to provide loans to all segments of the society, including low- and moderate-income neighbourhoods (see Bernanke 2007, for a brief overview). It is one of many laws aiming to reduce discriminatory credit practices such as redlining.

During the 1970s, commercial banks and investment banks each began activities that traditionally belonged to the other type (Wheelock 1992a: 244). Commercial banks began to offer various kinds of securities services (e.g., assistance in buying stocks) and corporate finance services (e.g., advice on merger and acquisitions). Investment banks, in their turn, encouraged companies to borrow money through bond issuance rather than through loans with commercial banks. They supported actions by the Government National Mortgage Association to securitize residential mortgages, so that these mortgages were financed through securities markets instead of deposits. The Money Market Mutual Funds (MMMF) also increased the relevance of investment banking over commercial banking. By the end of the 1990s, most financial institutions offered both saving and investment accounts, and in some cases even insurance. In addition, those in favour of allowing banks to execute both activities argued that in good times people invest, so that the money flows to investment banks, whereas in bad times there is a tendency to put money into savings accounts that are part of commercial banks. Allowing investment banks and commercial banks to merge would reduce the institutions' sensitivity to business cycles and hence make the financial system more stable.[5]

Opposition to a repeal of the Glass-Steagall Act argued that abolishing this act would undermine competition in two ways.[6] First, holdings of commercial and investment banks would become too big to fail. Since bankruptcy is a crucial element of competition, such too-big-to-fail institutions would undermine competition because these institutions know they cannot go bankrupt. Second, these large institutions can acquire a monopoly in some fields and thus undermine competition. Over time the arguments against universal banks became less relevant, amongst other reasons due to developments in the financial world where the importance of financial institutions covering both commercial and investment banking increased. These events led to the Gramm–Leach–Bliley Act (GLBA), also known as the Financial Services Modernization Act of 1999. The act allows financial institutions to offer commercial banking, investment banking, and insurance. Some restrictions remained in place, among which was that in case of a merger, each of the parties and affiliates should meet the criteria set by the regulatory bodies responsible for the Community Reinvestment Act. In practice this meant that each institution should lend enough money to minorities and the poor.

7.2.3 Pensions and the market for mortgages

A large part of the American pensions are funded (see Table 7.1), which is in accordance with the importance of financial markets.

The value of outstanding residential loans is slightly more than 40% of GDP (Table 7.1). Mortgage contracts are very flexible. No fee is required for early repayment. A typical mortgage contract has a term to maturity of 30 years. Homeowners can borrow against the current value of the asset and thus their ability to borrow is influenced by the development of the house prices. The proceeds of the loan may be used for financing other expenses than buying a house (equity withdrawal in Table 7.1). The average loan to value ratio is about 80%. These characteristics of mortgage contracts imply that within a group of industrialized countries, US inhabitants can most easily acquire a mortgage for financing their home (CESifo 2008).

The US government stimulates homeownership by enhancing the availability of cheap financial instruments via financial markets. Since 1916, the federal government has created so-called Government Sponsored Enterprises (GSE) (see Pollin and Heintz 2013, Chapter 12). These are privately owned

Table 7.1 Characteristics of the financial systems in the three countries

	USA	*Germany*	*France*
Stock market capitalization as a % of GDP in 2015	143	47	79
Pension funds as % GDP: private	134.9	6.8	9.8
Pension funds as % of GDP: public	15.4	1.1	2.5
Loan to value as a % in 2017	90	78	86
Typical maturity of a residential loan in 2017	15-30	25	18
Mortgage equity withdrawal	yes	no	no
Refinancing (fee-free prepayment)	yes	no	no
Outstanding residential loans as a % of GDP in 2017	45.5	42.3	41.6
Covered bonds % of total residential loans in 2017	–	15.6	19.5
Residential mortgage-backed securities as % of total residential loans in 2017	–	2.0	8.3

Source: Stock market capitalization to GDP source; World Bank (undated).
Pensions funds as a % of GDP (both private and public): OECD (2017), Table 8.4
Mortgage equity withdrawal and refinancing (fee-free prepayment) refer to the early 2000s: IMF (2008), Table 3.
The other data are from European Mortgage Federation (2018).

enterprises with a public mission that have been established by the federal government. The purpose has been to create favourable conditions for credit in areas regarded of public importance such as agriculture, education, and housing finance.[7] The most important GSEs are in the area of housing finance and are Fannie Mae established in 1938, and Freddie Mac established in 1970. Both were created 'to provide a stable source of funding for residential mortgages across the country, including loans on housing for low- and moderate-income families. Fannie Mae and Freddie Mac carry out that mission through their operations in the secondary mortgage markets' (Congressional Budget Office 2010: viii). Although the debt securities of these institutions were not officially backed by the federal government, the common opinion was that the government would not allow a default of their obligations. In September 2008, they were nationalized and are still (as of June 2021) owned by the federal government.[8] Between 1980 and 2006, these two institutions bought between 40% and 50% of all original mortgages (Fieldhouse *et al.* 2018: 1509). In the United States, the secondary market of mortgages is larger than that in other countries (CESifo 2008).

7.2.4 Conclusions

This brief survey of the history of the American financial system reveals that competition between small units (unit banking), populism, and an aversion to the concentration of power have been important ingredients for the development of the American financial system. Of course the country's federal structure also stimulated the fragmented system for a long time. The federal government takes measures at the moment the consequences of the prevailing system are considered to be bad. In the 1930s, this meant that competition was restricted because it became 'too ruinous.' After the Second World War, the restrictions on interest rates (Regulation Q) served to harm the American financial sector and stimulated offshore markets. This resulted in a process of deregulation in which subsequently Regulation Q, the ban on interstate banking, and the ban on universal banking were lifted. The last two deregulations benefited large banks more than small banks and thus, in that respect, went against the American population's favouring of competition between small units.

7.3 Coordinated market economies: Germany

7.3.1 Structure of the financial system

Germany's financial system has always been dominated by banks, whereas markets have played a minor role (see Welker 1992, for a brief description of the history). After the Second World War, the country was divided into four occupational zones. During the years immediately after the war, the three big private banks were each split into ten regional institutions. From 1956 onwards, the three banks were allowed to re-establish. The Deutsche Bank and the Dresdner Bank were re-established in 1957 and the Commerz Bank in 1958. No restrictions apply to the activities banks are allowed to conduct, so that, in principle, all banks can be universal banks. Traditionally, investment banking activities have been of minor importance. Four groups of banks can be distinguished, namely publicly owned savings banks, cooperative banks, commercial banks, and specialized banks.

The savings bank sector consists of the primary savings banks, the regional *Landesbanken*, and the DekaBank. The majority of these banks are owned by governmental bodies: municipalities, counties (*Kreis*), and *Länder* (federal state). The primary savings banks, *Sparkassen*, are required to serve the public interest in their community and are expected to avoid losses but they are not required to maximize their profits. Operations outside of their own territory are forbidden. Their clients are households and small and medium-sized enterprises. The regional *Landesbanken* are often jointly owned by regional associations of the *Sparkassen* and the regional state governments (*Landesregierung*). At the time of writing, 2020, there are six *Landesbanken*. Originally, these *Landesbanken* acted as the banker of the federal states (*Länder*) and the central bank of the *Sparkassen*. Over time, however, they developed activities in commercial and investment banking and in this way became state-guaranteed competitors of commercial banks. Since 2005, these activities have operated from a separate unit and receive no government guarantee. The last type of savings banks consists of one bank, the DekaBank. It is owned jointly by the *Landesbanken* and the German Savings Banks Association (DSGV) and serves as the central asset manager of the savings bank sector.

The cooperative banking sector consists of two levels: the primary cooperative banks and two regional institutions. The primary cooperative banks (*Volksbanken*) are owned by their members and fulfil banking functions similar to the *Sparkassen*, while the DZ bank and the WGZ bank act as the central banks for the primary cooperative banks.

The private banks are the big banks, regional banks, and branches of foreign institutions. By 2010, there were four big banks, of which Deutsche Bank is by far the largest and the only major international player. The big private banks have traditionally acted as house banks for the big industrial concerns, providing long-term loans and having representation on the supervisory boards of these firms. The second group of private banks consists of small stock-owned banks, which operate regionally. The third group consists of branches of foreign banks. There are many of these, but the total sum of their assets is relatively small.

The three previously described groups are universal banks. In addition to these banks, Germany also has specialized banks which perform a specific function. These are mortgage banks, building and loan associations, and banks providing funds for investments in particular sectors. The largest are the *Kreditanstalt für Wiederafbau* (KfW), which provides loans for infrastructure and other government supported projects, and IKB (German Industrial Bank) which provides loans for small and medium-sized enterprises.

Traditionally, security markets play a minor role in the German financial system. The largest stock exchange is in Frankfurt and there are five minor ones in different cities, such as Hamburg and Hannover, Berlin and Bremen, Düsseldorf, Munich, and Stuttgart (Detzer *et al.* 2013: 83). In the 1990s, the stock exchanges grew due to the privatization of large state-owned enterprises such as Lufthansa and Deutsche Telekom, and of firms in the former German Democratic Republic. Nevertheless, the size of the equity market is still small compared to the Anglo-Saxon world (see Table 7.1).

7.3.2 Degree of competition and the government's role

The local *Sparkassen* and the *Volksbanken* are all independent legal entities. This implies that a national concentration index will reveal a very low level of banking concentration (Detzer *et al.* 2103: Ch. 7). At the local level, however, concentration is much higher, as only one savings bank (the area a savings bank operates in is preset and restricted) and a few cooperative banks are active in one region. These banks have close ties with the small and medium-sized enterprises, which makes it difficult for other banks (the foreign ones and the big German banks) to enter the market. There are indications that the local banks are more willing to extent credit in bad times and thus provide stable finance to their customers (Detzer *et al.* 2013: 80).

The lack of competition at the local level can lead to a relatively high interest rate spread for German banks. A comparison of interest rate spreads over the period 1979 to 2009 in different countries confirms this impression (Detzer *et al.* 2013: Figure 7.2). The introduction in 1995 of money market funds almost immediately decreased the spread, indicating that the competition from these funds has had an effect (Detzer *et al.* 2013: 144).

Different layers of the government, municipalities, counties (*Kreis*), and the governments of the *Länder* own a share of the *Landesbanken* and the *Sparkassen*. One could argue that the resulting government guarantee gives these banks a competitive advantage, but as far as we know, this has never been regarded as a problem at the local level, where potential competitors are German. It became a problem at the moment that the *Landesbanken* entered into business and foreign banks became their competitors. The latter regarded the implicit government guarantee as unfair and illustrated that at international capital markets the spread for *Landesbanken* was lower than for commercial banks. After an appeal to the European Commission, the *Landesbanken* had to separate their commercial business from their other activities as of 2005. As a consequence, the *Landesbanken* began investing in foreign assets, in particular mortgage-backed securities, and were severely hit by the subprime crisis. In sum, within Germany, banks compete but that is at the regional level and often the close ties between local banks and their costumers restrict this competition.

The government ownership of the *Sparkassen* does raise issues with respect to the banks' governance. Now and then, the close ties between local politicians and the local *Sparkasse* lead to scandals in the sense that money is used for politically motivated projects.[9]

7.3.3 Reforms towards a market-based system

Since Germany already had a universal banking system, no initiatives were taken to enlarge the scope of bank activities, except that nowadays insurance is also part of the all-service banks. Restrictions on deposit interest rates were also lifted much earlier than in other countries. In the 1970s, German bank regulation still suited the dominant position of banks. It allowed cross-shareholdings between firms and between banks and firms and, often, banks had a dominant position on the supervisory boards of large firms. Regulation did not require high standards of transparency or the prohibition of insider trading, which are crucial for the well-functioning of financial markets. From the 1980s onwards, pressure for reforms came from three sources: the large commercial banks, the German government, and foreign actors. The foreign forces came with the wish to integrate the German financial sector with that of other industrialized, in particular European, countries. The European integration required a harmonization of national laws. All drivers resulted in legal changes that improved the position of financial markets.

In the mid-1980s, the big banks saw their profits declining due to a decrease in the services they provided to the big industrial firms. The latter moved abroad and listed their shares on foreign equity markets, such as the New York Stock Exchange and Tokyo Stock Exchange. Moreover, the international bond market grew, and new technology enabled long-distance trading. In order to increase their competitiveness, the big banks formed a consortium to promote the so-called *Finanzplatz Deutschland*; Germany as a financial centre. A key element of this initiative was to expand the securities markets. The banks hoped that an increase in the activities of securities markets would increase their income from fees and investment banking activities. The Kohl government also wanted to strengthen Germany's role in international financial markets to support German financial institutions and to reduce the financing costs of the government's deficits (Mügge 2015: 184 and 185).

As a consequence of the desire to make the German financial system more market friendly, four financial market promotion acts have been legislated over the period 1990–2002. These acts broadened the products that could be traded and increased transparency. The act of 1990 was the first unified capital market law in German history, and was the first law to have investor protection as one of its objectives (Bradley and Sundaram 2003). Over the course of a decade, the laws allowed new activities such as money market funds, introduced a prohibition of insider trading (1994),[10] increased transparency, enhanced investor protection, and improved supervision. In 2002 the Federal Financial Supervisory Authority was established as the single integrated financial markets supervisor, to supervise 'same businesses' with the 'same risks' and the 'same rules.' This was needed because of an increase in the variety of activities that different institutions involved in, partly due to the establishment of large financial groups.

Besides a sound legal framework, enhancing investment bank activities also requires that banks and firms have no tight relationships. If they do, then some banks could have prior information which sets them at a competitive advantage. However, until 2002, German banks still held large shares of equity in different industrial firms because selling it was unattractive due to a 50% capital gains tax they would have to pay if they sold their holding. In 2002, the Social Democratic–Green government abolished this capital gains tax, which encouraged the large banks to divest.

In the 1990s, stock markets were given an important impetus by the privatization of a number of large state-owned enterprises, such as Lufthansa and Deutsche Telekom. In addition, in 1997, the *Neue Markt* was opened, which targeted growth stocks, much like the New York Nasdaq. In 1999, the SMAX for smaller firms was opened. Both markets were closed in 2003.

These reforms towards a more market-oriented financial system have had only limited effect. First, despite the attempts to promote an 'equity culture' so that private individuals would invest a larger share of their possessions in equity, private persons' investment in equity did not increase in a systematic way. The amount invested by private individuals increased during the 1990s but decreased again after the dot com bubble of 2000 (Detzer *et al.* 2013: 85, 86, 89, and 245).

7.3.4 Pensions and housing finance

In Germany, pensions are based to a large extent on a Pay-As-You-Go system. The assets of private pension plans and public pension reserve funds are low (see Table 7.1). In order to increase their income, relatively many Germans act as landlords. In addition to these individuals, the group of private landlords consists of housing companies, institutional investors, and companies controlled by financial institutions. This group of private landlords owns 47% of all dwellings, which is a very high percentage by international standards (Kofner 2014: 264). Of the privately rented dwellings in Germany, 84% are owned by private households, i.e., individuals, couples, estates, or civil partnerships. The figure for all rental apartments is more than 60%.

The *Bauspar* system is very popular for financing privately owned houses. In 2012, there were about 26 million *Bauspar* savers with a total contract sum of about 763 billion euros (around 30% of German GDP) (Kofner 2014: 272). A *Bauspar* contract consists of three phases: a savings phase (*Sparphase*), an eligible phase (*Zuteilungsphase*), and a loan phase (*Darlehensphase*). The idea is that all participants contribute to a fund that enables contributors to borrow in order to finance a house. During the savings phase, participants save and receive an interest. When the total amount saved is high enough, the saver can use this amount as a down payment for buying a house and financing the additional amount needed by means of a mortgage. Before the credit crisis, the savings had to be at least 50% of the amount the participants want to borrow. After the crisis, conditions became less strict. The *Bauspar* mortgage offers a fixed interest rate over the entire time to maturity. The typical term to maturity is 25 years. The proceeds of the loan may not be used for other expenses than buying the house and prepayment is often restricted. The average age of first-time buyers is high, about 40 years (Kofner 2014: 272), and the average loan-to-value (LTV) is relatively low (see Table 7.1). Moreover, innovative products such as adjustable rate mortgages and interest-only mortgages are scarce. Subsidies for home-ownership are low and much lower than in other countries (Kofner 2014: 263).

The mortgages are provided by banks whose funding is also conservative. The majority of mortgages are financed by deposits and *Pfandbriefe* which are covered bonds that remain on the balance sheet of the issuing banks. The amount of residential mortgage-backed securities is small (Table 7.1).

In sum, in Germany the financing of residential buildings is bank-dominated and conservative. Germans initially save a large proportion of the money needed to buy a house and then obtain a mortgage which has a fixed rate for a long period of time. Both the mortgages and their funding focus on a distant horizon.

7.3.5 Conclusion

In summary, the German financial system was, and still is, a bank-based system, with a large share of not-for-profit banks (*Sparkassen* and *Volksbanken*). These banks are independent legal entities. Except for a few specialized banks, all banks are universal banks. Different layers of the government, most importantly municipalities and the governments of the *Länder*, own a share of the banks – the *Landesbanken* and the *Sparkassen*. Due to the close ties between the banks and their customers, competition on the local level is subdued and it is difficult for outsiders to enter the market.[11] Contracts have a long term to maturity and are not flexible, with no equity withdrawal and a fee for prepayment. The minor role of financial markets and the conservative attitude towards new products illustrate the German aversion to uncertainty (see Chapter 2). Moreover, the stability-oriented macro-economic and monetary policy (see Chapter 9), along with restrictions on the use of particular financial instruments, have minimized the incentives to innovate new financial products (Houben 1999: 161). In short, Germans appreciate a *Stabilitätskultur* (stability culture).

7.4 Hierarchical market economy: France

7.4.1 Structure and reform after the Second World War

In France, the government has always played a dominant role in many sectors of society. This also holds for the financial sector.[12] At the end of the nineteenth century, the Paris Bourse was as important as the London Stock Exchange (Cerny 1989: 170). In 1913, stock market capitalization to Gross Domestic Product (GDP) in France was twice that of the United States (Rajan and Zingales 2003, Table 3). The importance of financial markets declined due to the First World War, the depression of the 1930s, and the move towards regulation in and after the Second World War. After the Second World War, the French financial system was dominated by banks under strict regulation by the government. It was an 'overdraft economy' instead of an 'auto economy' (a distinction made in Hicks 1974). 'In an overdraft economy, deficit units do not borrow from the markets (which are non-existent or only residual), but they rely on bank credit' (de Boissieu 1992: 186). Over the years, many reforms were suggested and, in some cases, partly implemented. The final and largest move towards a deregulated system came after Mitterrand's U-turn in March 1983. In this section, we first describe the system as it was before the deregulation of the 1980s and then how it rapidly changed from the mid-1980s onwards.

In 1945, three categories of banks were established: deposit banks, investment banks, and medium- and long-term lending banks. The competition between the different types of banks was low and each bank had its own preassigned field, objectives, and instruments. The Treasury Circuit provided a good illustration of the high degree of regulation imposed by the French government. This circuit worked as follows (see Butzbach 2015: 1171–1172, for a schematic representation). The local savings banks (575 in 1945, Butzbach 2015: 1161) collected private savings. Until 2007, these banks were the only providers of the Livret A,[13] a savings deposit of which the interest rate and conditions were set by the Caisse des Dépôts et Consignations (CDC), a specialized state-affiliated and -controlled financial institution. These conditions reflected the Treasury's priorities. The funds collected by savings banks were not invested by these banks themselves but transferred to the CDC. The latter, in turn, converted these funds into medium- and long-term financing, granting loans directly to local authorities and financing social housing construction through the Crédit Foncier de France, a state-owned mortgage credit institution. The CDC also made productive investments through the Crédit National, a state-owned credit bank. The so-called Minjoz Law, passed in June 1951, authorized the savings banks to propose to the CDC that loans be made to local authorities representing up to 50% of the annual increase in deposits (Butzbach 2015: 1163). It remained the case that savings banks were not permitted to invest these funds themselves. This nicely illustrates that, at that time, banks were very specialized and often held a state-endowed (partial) monopoly in a specific niche.

The first deregulation came in 1966–1967. The lending rates of banks were deregulated, although ceilings remained, and branch banking was liberated, creating intense competition for market share (de Boissieu 1992: 186). During these years the government intended to end exchange controls and to move towards a more flexible monetary policy. However, these intentions were thwarted by the events of May 1986 (Cerny 1989: 171).

French firms relied heavily on debt provided by banks. The French government controlled the allocation of loans from banks to firms through its control of Banque de France. In the early 1970s, about 80% of all loans were directly controlled by the Banque de France (Loriaux 1991).

During the same period, about 60% of the medium- to long-term loans allocated to French companies were provided by government and semi-government agencies. These agencies' aim was to facilitate and subsidize lending to specific sectors. In 1973, the *encadrement du credit* system was implemented. This was a system of credit ceilings so that individual banks could control the quantity of money and the direction of financial flows (Cerny 1989: 172). Foreign influences were restricted by means of capital controls, and financial markets were of minor importance. In 1977, IBM's market capitalization was about twice that of the Paris Bourse. Moreover, through different government institutions, such as CDC, the government owned about 55% of French company shares (Cerny 1989: 174).

This system had various drawbacks. First, efficiency was low due to an almost complete absence of competition. Second, since interest rates did not reflect market forces, they could be set too low so that too much credit was provided and inflation was created. Third, over the years it appeared that the money market was too small so that it could not provide enough finance for French firms. From the beginning of the 1980s, the financial system also had to be reformed in order to finance the government's deficits. Finally, the system of *encadrement du credit* was very costly and complex because it sets limits to the credits to be provided by individual banks. Hence, the authorities had to conduct detailed oversight of the behaviour of individual banks.

At the end of the 1970s and the beginning of the 1980s, the disadvantages of this overregulated system emerged. The first disadvantage was triggered by international developments, such as floating exchange rates and the rise in foreign interest rates due to the restrictive monetary policy in the United States and the UK. In the first instance, the French government tried to shield the French economy from these developments by means of capital controls. However, these controls appeared to be unsustainable in the longer run and forced the authorities to implement structural changes so that the economy became more open to the outside world. These international developments put stress on the French banks. This sector appeared to be overregulated. The different segments introduced after the Second World War could not handle foreign pressure. In 1979, the Mayoux Report recommended the introduction of universal banking, so that an individual bank could diversify its portfolio.

Second, the system of *encadrement du credit* had always been subject to exemptions for credits to low-cost housing, exports, agriculture, and other investment projects favoured by the government. In 1976 Raymond Barre, who at that time became prime minister and minister of finance and economic affairs, announced a target for the growth rate of M2 money. With the founding of the European Monetary System (EMS) in March 1979, these monetary targets became of greater importance as they signalled French willingness to stick to the agreed fixed exchange rates within the EMS. The *encadrement du credit* was the main instrument for controlling M2. However, since the subsidized credits often exceeded M2 targets, the growth of the non-subsidized credits had to be set at an extremely low level, so that adhering to the system would undermine the business of banks without access to subsidized credit. These banks were therefore allowed to provide bank credit with money acquired by issuing bonds at financial markets (Melitz 1990: 396). These bonds had a long term to maturity, whereas the loans provided were short term. This maturity transformation is the reverse of the normal one and in many cases is not a profitable arrangement, as long-term interest rates are generally higher than short-term rates. In addition, the habit of providing exemptions to the rules for preferred credits gave a boost to institutions with privileged access to the socially expensive credits (Melitz 1990: 396). In conclusion, during the 1970s it became clear that the French government's great influence on the financial system had been detrimental and that this system was in need of a total overhaul.

In the first half of the 1980s, the initiative for reform rested with the *Trésor*, and thus with the government (see, e.g., Métais 1996: 367). Two phases can be distinguished. First, the nationalization phase during the first years of President Mitterrand's government. In 1982, the socialist government nationalized the banks in order to direct the banks' policies towards financing small and medium-sized firms (de Boissieu 1992: 189). During these years, the government followed a Keynesian policy in order to stimulate economic activity. Capital controls were used to limit the flight of capital.

The second phase started in March 1983 when the franc was devalued again, and the Mitterrand government changed course and aimed at a fixed peg between the French franc and the German mark and thus at a stability-oriented policy. In 1982, the socialist government had nationalized banks in order to radically overhaul the French banking system so that it could withstand international pressures. It nationalized 36 deposit banks including large banks such as Paribas. As a result, it controlled almost the entire banking sector. The government's aims were to finance priority investments, to improve control of credit, and to reduce the costs of bank loans. Nationalized firms made huge losses in 1981–1982. In addition, the former shareholders had to be compensated according to a ruling by the Constitutional Council (Cerny 1989: 173). Both events required new funds. Moreover, since the second oil shock of 1979 the French government's budget had shown a deficit, whereas during previous years its budget had always been in balance (Melitz 1990: 395). In 1984, the minister of finance started a process of deregulation which strove for a unified financial market where prices would be set freely. The Banking Act of 1984 aimed at tearing down the barriers between the different segments and introducing competition between the different financial institutions. This competition was still state-controlled (Mügge 2015: 180). From 1986 onwards, banks were gradually privatized again. At that time, the conservative government 'justified the privatization by the pressures of competition and the need for French credit institutions to increase their capital' (de Boissieu 1992: 189). In 1988, the French state still had control over 69% of the commercial banks and 42% of the banking sector. During the 1980s and 1990s, the local savings banks merged into larger units, as a result of which the number of savings banks decreased from 470 in 1982 to 17 in 2000 (Butzbach 2015: 1171).

The French stock market was very small in the 1960s and 1970s. The trade was monopolized by the *agents de change*. From 1985 onwards these agents lost their monopoly (Cerny 1989: 175). The nationalization in 1982 had an unintended stimulating effect on the Paris Bourse; the funds acquired through the compensation the government had to pay to the former shareholders of the nationalized companies were invested in companies listed on the Bourse (Cerny 1989: 178). In 1988, the French stock market was reformed; the *petit* Big Bang. The aim of the Stock Exchange Reform Act was to create a French investment banking industry that could compete with the banks in London. Ultimately, the overregulated financial system of the 1980s had to be replaced by a dynamic financial system which would rely, much more than before, on financial markets.

The establishment and further development of the French market for derivatives illustrate the declining influence of the state in favour of private participants (Mügge 2015: 182). The MATIF, the French market for derivatives, was introduced in 1986. The *Tresor* had played an important role in establishing this market and it immediately became a success, leading to high profits for those who were allowed to trade at MATIFF. These profits caused jealousy among the banks that did not have a permit to trade, a conflict that had to be settled by the Treasury. The conflict remained, however, since a consortium of three French banks and a Swedish specialist set up a rival exchange, named OMF.

Two of the three French banks, BNP and Paribas, had already established capital market operations in London.

In the meantime, from the end of 1983 onwards, the government also lifted restrictions on international capital flows. It started with a restriction that hurt the constituency of the Socialist Party, the middle classes, most: travel allowances and the *carnet de change* (liberalized in 1984). In 1985, other transactions were liberalized, such as Eurobond[14] issues in French francs. In January 1990, France's capital account was fully liberalized (Abdelal 2006: 8).[15]

Despite this trend towards a market-based financial system, the ties between the French government and the financial and nonfinancial institutions remain closer than in many other countries. The state still holds shares in large companies, among which are financial institutes. Top managers are recruited from the students and alumni of the *Grandes écoles* (Métais (1996: 369). In finance, the graduates of the specialization *Inspecteurs des Finances* of the École National d'Administration (ENA) play a large role.[16] They typically start their career at the ministry of finance and then move to top management roles in banking (among which is the central bank) and to the top positions in industrial groups.

7.4.2 Pensions and housing finance

The French Pay-As-You-Go pensions system is relatively sober, and funded pension schemes are small (see Table 7.1). The lack of funded schemes is a reflection of the French aversion to the Anglo-Saxon type of institutions (Chavannes 2000: 189). Consequently, owning a house is a good way of increasing income (reducing costs) when old, and also of smoothing consumption over time.

Since the Second World War, the French government has had many schemes in place to subsidize housing loans and stimulate private savings with a view to house purchase. In the 1960s, over half of the housing loans were subsidized. This gave the French government the ability to control many of the terms on which housing loans were made, including maturity terms and interest rates. From 1966, the Debré reforms were introduced, reducing the government-sponsored circuit and introducing savings schemes to stimulate household savings to finance housing. As of January 1, 2018, these savings schemes still exist but no longer offer the right to a subsidized loan.

Until the mid-1980s, subsidized loans played an important role in financing housing. In 1985, about 67% of new housing credit was in the form of a subsidized loan (van der Valk 2018, Table 4). A popular loan type was the *Prêts en accession a la propriété* (PAP), introduced in 1977 as part of the Barre Reforms. In 1995, the PAP loan was replaced by the *Prêts a taux zéro* (PTZ). The PTZ is targeted at lower- to middle-income households that want to buy a house for the first time. It is still available and offers a loan without paying interest for a targeted group of first-time owners.

In the second half of the 1980s, a growing share of the population was confronted with an increase in debt. This led to a debate about over-indebtedness that resulted in the Neiertz Law in 1989. According to this law, the creditor should prevent the over-indebtedness of consumers. In the case of arrears, and after the failure of mediation, a judge can impose a reduction in the debt or reduce the interest rate (van der Valk 2018: 23). From 1985 onwards, the percentage of non-regulated credits for housing increased.

Nowadays housing finance is dominated by large universal banks of French origin. These banks are very cautious when providing housing credit. Loan to value is around 90% for first-time buyers. This is relatively high, whereas the percentage of the outstanding amount of guaranteed loans for house purchases is also high at 14% (see ECB 2009, Table 2). Interest bands prescribe that interest rates cannot deviate by more than one-third from the average over the previous period. This is a measure to prevent large increases in interest payments and thus reduce the chance that a private individual will fall into arrears while servicing their debt. The Neiertz Law (on over-indebtedness) has a similar aim. Since profits on mortgage loans are low, banks require an extensive set of insurance products. A consequence of this behaviour is that low-income households, the elderly, and those without a steady employment are largely excluded from the market. This system of housing finance was hardly affected by the subprime crisis, probably due to the fact the French banks did not enter into securitization products and there was a limited possibility of credit providers experimenting.

In the 1960s, the funding of mortgages was arranged via Crédit Foncier de France and the rediscounting facility of Banque de France (van der Valk 2018: 14). In the mid-1960s, monetary financing was restricted and by 1973 most refinancing had been halted. To compensate for the reduction in rediscounting, in 1966, the Banque de France allowed the banks to issue medium-term covered bonds. The Crédit Foncier de France became the regulator of the mortgage bond market and set the interest rates. The French government strictly regulated the type of bonds that could be employed as collateral on this market. Maturity was set at 10 and 20 years and mortgages, or a *privilège immobilier,* served as the guarantee. A *privilège immobilier* is an alternative to a mortgage. It gives the creditor a priority right in case the debtor fails to pay. No notary is required, but the holder risks other creditors being faster at making a claim. The latter is not possible with a mortgage (van der Valk 2018, note 21). In 2017, covered bonds and mortgage-backed securities accounted for slightly more than 25% of the funding of mortgages (Table 7.1).

7.4.3 Conclusion

After the Second World War, the French government assigned niches to different types of banks and the entire system came under the control of the ministry of finance. Over the years, this highly regulated system was able to meet the financial needs of neither the private sector nor the government and had to be overhauled. Initially this restructuring was led by the Treasury. At a later stage, private agents took the lead. This is a very good example of an economy in which an elite takes care of uncertainty (see Chapter 2).

7.5 Concluding remarks

In this chapter, we have discussed the development of the financial systems in the United States, Germany, and France. Besides the actual developments, we have focused on the underlying principles of these financial systems. It appeared that in the United States the ideal person acts independently, and competition between individual (small) actors is assumed to be good. Public debate can be very populistic and the general public has a distrust in large financial institutions as these are often owned by 'foreigners', that is, people who do not belong to the persons' own state. Banks, and the financial system at large, must serve the people. In the 1930s, these national traits led to three measures: a prohibition of interstate banking, a distinction between commercial banking and investment banking, and a restriction on competition by capping interest rates (Regulation Q). From the beginning of the 1960s, changes in circumstances forced American authorities to abolish these restrictions: first those of Regulation Q, then the ban on interstate banking, and finally, at the end of the century, the prohibition on combining investment banking and commercial banking in one institution.

The stability culture of Germans fits with the dominant role of banks that were already universal banks. The close ties between local banks and their clients, and the conservative nature of both, limit the effect of competition. Moreover, the *Sparkassen* operate in a pre-assigned area. Until the 1990s, the French financial system was, to a great extent, under control of the Treasury. The necessary reforms of the 1980s were also led by the government. This represents the view that an elite takes charge of the uncertainties a country faces. Changes in legislation were also important drivers for the savings banks being centralized.

During the 1990s, the financial systems of Germany and France moved towards a more market-based system, with fewer close ties between large firms (France) or large firms and large banks (Germany). Nevertheless, the financial markets are still not as important as in the United States (see Table 7.1). Moreover, German investors are very reluctant to invest in equity (see OECD 2019). National differences are certainly still present when it comes to the financing of pensions and of housing. Pensions are funded (relying on markets) in the United States and are Pay-As-You-Go systems in the other two countries, where pension funds are small. Mortgage contracts are very flexible in the United States. In Germany these contracts are spread over a long period and are very restrictive. One has to adhere to the original scheme and changes are not permitted. In France the term to maturity is shorter than in Germany, and the French restrictions aim at protecting the borrower against over-indebtedness.

In sum, the financial systems of the three countries nicely illustrate the different ways of coping with uncertainty: acceptance by the United States, controlling by means of rules and restrained (conservative) behaviour in Germany, and protection by an elite in France. Although the national differences are less than they were 40 years ago, they can still be found in markets targeted at local consumers.

Notes

1 I thank Merijn Jacobs and Annelie Kroese for research assistance and the following persons for comments on previous versions: Johan Graafland, Andrée Kartchevsky, Carolyn Sissoko, Tim van der Valk, Michel Vigezzi, participants at the EPCS annual meeting, April 2019, in Jerusalem, and those of the WINIR conference in Lund, September 2019.

2 A description of the mortgage markets in several countries which have these three types of economies can be found in de Jong and van Dijk (2019).

3 This was the popular name of the United States Senate Committee on Banking and Currency, which was installed on March 4, 1932, to investigate the causes of the crisis.

4 The opposition by the large banks to the introduction of a deposit insurance system also played a role, see, among others, Tabarrok (1998: 7 and 8).

5 In addition, academic articles published in the 1980s and 1990s did not find empirical support for the hypothesis that a universal bank could lead to conflicts of interest (Rheinholdson and Olson 2012, Table Selected papers), and that many of the allegations in the 1930s of misconduct and increased financial risk of the securities trading activities were unfounded (White 1986). A comparison of different financial systems revealed that only Japan and the United States still maintained a separation between commercial and investment banking (Barth *et al.* 1997).

6 See Chapter 3 for the importance of competition according to free market economists.

7 Besides these institutions initiated by the federal government, the state of North Dakota owns the Bank of North Dakota (BND), the only state-owned bank in the United States. The bank was founded in 1919. At that time, most of the credit to companies (farmers) in the state was provided by financial institutions from other states. The farmers thought these institutions charged excessive rates and provided insufficient credit. The BND was founded as a bankers' bank to help increase private banks' lending power and it could purchase part or all of a loan after it had been issued. The BND has done very well during the subprime crisis (Pollin and Heintz, 2013: 173, 174).

8 Many argue for privatizing these firms again. The subprime credit crisis originated in the mortgage market and a large part of this market was held by Fannie Mae and Freddie Mac (27% in 2006 and 69% of new mortgages in 2012). This gave rise to a debate about these institutions' role in originating the crisis. Opinions differ widely (Pollin and Heintz, 2013: 168–170), but at least one can conclude that these institutions had not adhered to their standards strictly enough to prevent the crisis. Nor had they signalled problems.

9 After some failures had occurred in the 1930s, the savings banks (*Sparkassen*) had been separated from municipal administrations and were organized as autonomous bodies under public law (Welker 1992: 231). But local politicians could still have a seat on the supervisory board. A recent study (Markgraf and Véron 2018) for eight German federal states found that between 16% and 18% of these board members and more than 80% of their chairs are elected local politicians – a phenomenon unknown in other countries. Allegations of misuse of power by local politicians still occasionally pop up (see, e.g., Kahl *et al.* 2018). In addition, Gropp and Saadi (2015) found evidence of political business cycles in commercial lending by the *Sparkassen* over the years 1995–2006. The provision of loans is higher in the years of local elections and the creditworthiness of these loans is lower than those provided in non-election years.

10 Germany was the last country in the European Community to prohibit insider trading.

11 In a private conversation with the author, a German representative of a foreign bank complained that it was difficult to attract rich people for asset and wealth management, because they already conducted business with the local banks (*Sparkassen* and *Volksbanken*). They remained loyal to these banks when they became rich.
12 A brief description of the French financial system's history can be found in Blot *et al.* (2013) and Metais (1996: 364 and 365).
13 The Livret A was established in 1818 by Louis XVIII to pay back the debts incurred during the Napoleonic wars. It has since been a popular savings instrument because of government guarantees and reasonable interest rates.
14 Note Eurobonds refer here to the Eurocurrency market and not to the currency euro, which was created by the establishment of the Economic and Monetary Union.
15 It is noticeable that it was French leaders who, as chairs of international organizations, Camdessus (IMF), Delors (EC), and Chavranski (OECD), led the movement towards codifying liberal capital flows worldwide. An argument for the latter was, according to Lamy, 'if you liberalize you must organize' (Lamy, cited in Abdelal 2006: 7).
16 In April 2021, President Macron announced to close the ENA and replace it with a public management school that will draw from a more diverse pool of candidates and teach a broader curriculum (Abboud 2021).

References

Abboud, L. (2021) Macron to close training school of French elite, *Financial Times*, April 8.

Abdelal, R. (2006) Writing the rules of global finance: France, Europe and capital liberalization, *Review of International Political Economy* 13(1): 1–27.

Barth, J. R., D. E. Nolle and T. N. Rice (1997) *Commercial banking structure, regulation, and performance: An international comparison*, Economics Working Paper, Washington, DC: Office of the Comptroller of the Currency.

Berger, A. N., A. K. Kashyap, J. M. Scalise, M. Gertler and B. M. Friedman (1995) The transformation of the U.S. banking industry: What a long, strange trip it's been, *Brookings Papers on Economic Activity* 2: 55–218.

Bernanke, B. S. (2007) *The Community Reinvestment Act: Its Evolution and New Challenges*, speech at the Community Affairs Research Conference, Washington, DC, March 30, retrieved at April 18, 2018 from https://www.federalreserve.gov/newsevents/speech/Bernanke20070330a.htm.

Blot, C., J. Creel, A.-L. Delatte, K. Durand, A. Gallois, P. Hubert ... and M. Viennot (2013) *The French Financial System, From Past to Present.* Financialisation, Economy, Society & Sustainable Development (FESSUD) Project.

Bradley, M. and A. K. Sundaram (2003) *The Emergence of Shareholder Value in the German Corporation*, SSRN, doi:10.2139/ssrn.463840.

Butzbach, O. (2015) From thrifts to universal banks: The sources of organisational change in French savings banks, 1945–2000, *Business History* 57(8): 1155–1191.

Cerny, P. G. (1989) The 'Little Big Bang' in Paris: Financial deregulation in a *dirigiste* system, *European Journal of Political Research* 17: 169–192.

CESifo (2008) Institutional features of mortgage markets across countries, *CESifo DICE Report, 2008 / 3*: 70 and 71.

Chavannes, M. (2000) *Frankrijk achter schermen: De stille revolutie van een trotse nation (France Behind the Scene: The Silent Revolution of a Proud Nation)*, Amsterdam: Prometheus.

Clinton, W. J. (1994) Statement on Senate Action on Banking Legislation, September 13, 1994. In *Public Papers of the Presidents of the United States: William J. Clinton (1994, Book II)*. Washington, DC: Government Printing Office.

Congressional Budget Office (2010) *Fanny Mae, Freddy Mac, and the Federal Role in the Secondary Mortgage Market*, Washington, DC: The Congress of the United States, Congressional Budget Office, December 2010.

De Boissieu, C. (1992) France monetary and financial system. In J. Eatwell, M. Milgate and P. Newman (eds.), *The New Palgrave Dictionary on Money and Finance* (Part 3, Vol. 2), London: Macmillan: 185–190.

De Jong, E. and J. van Dijk (2019) *Financing Residential Housing in Three Types of Market Economies*, mimeo, Nijmegen: Radboud University.

Detzer D., N. Dodig, T. Evans, E. Hein and H. Herr (2013) *The German Financial System*, FESSUD, Studies in Financial Systems no. 3.

European Central Bank (2009) *Housing finance in the euro area, ECB*, Occasional Paper 101, Frankfurt am Main: European Central Bank.

European Mortgage Federation (2018) *Hypostat 2018*, Brussels: European Mortgage Federation.

Fieldhouse, A. J., K. Mertens and M. O. Ravin (2018) The macroeconomic effects of government asset purchases: Evidence from postwar US housing credit policy, *The Quarterly Journal of Economics* 133(3): 1503–1560.

Gropp, R. E. and V. Saadi (2015) *Electoral Credit Supply Cycles among German Savings Banks*, Halle: IWH Online 11/2015.

Hicks, J. R. (1974) *The Crisis in Keynesian Economics*, Oxford: Basil Blackwell.

Houben, A. C. F. J. (1999) *The Evolution of Monetary Policy Strategies in Europe*, PhD dissertation, Groningen: University of Groningen.

Johnston, R. B. (1983) *The Economics of the Euro-Market: History, Theory and Policy*, London: MacMillan.

Kahl, S., P. Skolimowski and B. Groendahl (2018) How Germany's little savings banks threaten big financial woes, *Bloomberg Businessweek*, October 5.

Kofner, S. (2014) The German housing system: Fundamentally resilient? *Journal of Housing and the Built Environment* 29: 255–275.

Loriaux, M. M. (1991) *France after Hegemony: International Change and Financial Reform*, Ithaca, NY: Cornell University Press.

Markgraf, J. and N. Vérnon (2018) *Germany's Savings Banks: Uniquely Intertwined with Local Politicians*, Brussels: Breugel Institute. http://bruegel.org/2018/07/germanys-savings-banks-uniquely-intertwined-with-local-politics/.

Medley, B. (1994) Riegle-Neal Interstate Banking and Branching Efficiency Act of 1994, *Federal Reserve History*, https://www.federalreservehistory.org/essays/riegle_neal_act_of_1994.

Melitz, J. (1990) Financial deregulation in France, *European Economic Review* 34: 394–402.

Métais, J. (1996) French banks: The challenge of competition and globalization. In L. Schuster (ed.), *Banking Cultures Around the World*, Frankfurt am Main: Fritz Knapp Verlag: 363–384.

Mügge, D. (2015) Competitive concern and imaginaries in the liberalization of European finance. In B. Jessop, B. Young and C. Scherrer (eds.), *Financial Cultures and Crisis Dynamics*, New York: Routledge: 176–188.

OECD (2017) *Pensions at a Glance 2017*, Paris: OECD.

OECD (2019) *Household Financial Assets (indicator)*, Paris: OECD. doi: 10.1787/7519b9dc-en (Accessed on 30 July, 2019).

Pollin, R. and J. Heintz (2013) *Study of U.S. Financial System*, FESSUD Studies in Financial Systems no. 10. European Union: Project on Financialization, Economy, Society and

Sustainable Development (FESSUD), file:///C:/Users/rpollin.PROVOST/Downloads/USA-FinancialSystems-Studies10%20(6).pdf

Rajan, R. G. and L. Zingales (2003) The great reversals: The politics of financial development in the twentieth century, *Journal of Financial Economics* 69: 5–50.

Rheinholdson, F. C. J. and H. S. Olson (2012) *The Separation of Commercial and Investment Banking: A Literature Review*, Master Thesis, Gothenburg: University of Gothenburg.

Roe, M. (1994) *Strong Managers, Weak Owners: The Political Roots of American Corporate Finance*, Princeton, NJ: Princeton University Press.

Senate Banking Act Report (1933) *Operation of the National and Federal Reserve Banking Systems*, Senate Report no. 73-77.

Sherman, M. (2009) *A Short History of Financial Deregulation in the United States*, Washington, DC: Center for Economic and Policy Research.

Sissoko, C. (2017) The plight of modern markets: How universal banking undermines markets, *Economic Notes by Banca Monte dei Paschi di Siena* 46(1): 53–104.

Tabarrok, A. (1998) The separation of commercial and investment banking: The Morgans vs. The Rockefellers, *Quarterly Journal of Austrian Economics* 1(1): 1–18.

Van der Valk, T. (2018) *Housing Finance, Policy Traditions and the Pension System: The Case of France and The Netherlands (1960–2018)*, mimeo, Utrecht: University of Utrecht.

Welker, J. (1992) Germany: Monetary and financial system. In J. Eatwell, M. Milgate and P. Newman (eds.), *The New Palgrave Dictionary on Money and Finance* (Vol. 2), London: Macmillan: 226–239.

Wheelock, D.C. (1992a) Glass-Steagall Act. In J. Eatwell, M. Milgate and P. Newman (eds.), *The New Palgrave Dictionary on Money and Finance* (Vol. 2), London: Macmillan: 243, 244.

Wheelock, D. C. (1992b) Regulation Q. In J. Eatwell, M. Milgate and P. Newman (eds.), *The New Palgrave Dictionary on Money and Finance* (Vol. 3), London: Macmillan: 326, 327.

White, E. N. (1986) Before the Glass-Steagal Act: An analysis of the investment banking activities of national banks, *Explorations in Economic History* 23: 33–55.

World Bank (undated) *Financial Development and Structure Dataset*, Washington, DC: World Bank, https://www.worldbank.org/en/publication/gfdr/data/financial-structure-database.

8 Competition policy within the free, hierarchical, and coordinated market tradition[1]

Iwan Bos

Introduction

This chapter considers competition policy within the context of the different varieties of capitalism as described in other parts of this book: the free, hierarchical, and coordinated market models.[2] Specifically, we discuss US, German, and French competition policy in relation to these three traditions.[3] We first focus on American competition policy and the free market tradition. Since competition policy by its very nature limits the freedom of market participants and leads to a larger government, it seems *a priori* at odds with the free market philosophy. We argue, however, that competition policy is consistent with the free market model when the free market would effectively disappear without these rules of the competition and show that politicians involved in the development of the US competition law framework considered this possibility real.

We then proceed with German and French competition policy, both of which are discussed in connection to the hierarchical and coordinated market traditions. It is argued that these policies initially fitted well within the hierarchical framework, but became more consistent with the coordinated market model during the last decades. We further argue that this transformation is not (yet) complete in the sense that both competition policies still provide scope for direct government intervention. Indeed, both the French and German minister of economic affairs can overrule a competition authority's merger decision when public interest demands it. This may be the case when the merger is viewed as essential to the merging firms' competitiveness in international markets. We show that such calls for 'national champions' are echoing throughout European competition policy history and are still present today.

8.1 US competition policy and the free market philosophy: a moral justification

8.1.1 Introduction

The year 1776 AD witnessed two landmark events in the history of the Free World. In the United Kingdom of Great Britain, a book by Scottish scholar Adam Smith (1723–1790) was published, titled *An Inquiry into the Nature and*

DOI: 10.4324/9781003208549-8

Causes of the Wealth of Nations. A main takeaway of this manuscript is that a decentralized free market system in which individuals solely pursue their self-interest may be more beneficial than a centralized system in which a few decide for the many. On the other side of the Atlantic, enemies of this Kingdom announced the Declaration of Independence, which marked the birth of the United States of America. Ever since the start, the free market philosophy such as set out in the *Wealth of Nations* has been part of this country's DNA.

In spite of the widespread belief in the merits of the free market, it did not take long before US legislators limited market participants' freedom through the adoption of antitrust laws. First at the state level and since the late 1800s at the federal level, these rules of competition intended to combat particular business practices such as price-fixing and monopolizing conduct. After a somewhat hesitant start, competition policy quickly became a key factor in all kinds of business transactions. The first national US antitrust law (i.e., the Sherman Act) was even perceived as having near-constitutional status at some point. Chief Justice Hughes, for instance, wrote that:[4]

> As a charter of freedom, the [Sherman] Act has a generality and adaptability comparable to that found to be desirable in constitutional provisions.

And in the early 1970s, the US Supreme Court stated:[5]

> Antitrust laws in general and the Sherman Act in particular, are the Magna Carta of free enterprise. They are as important to the preservation of economic freedom and our free enterprise system as the Bill of Rights is to the protection of our fundamental personal freedoms.

Without debating the impact and importance of competition policy, there is something inherently paradoxical about its presence in a free market-based society like the United States. After all, the free market tradition as it evolved through Scottish Enlightenment and British nineteenth-century liberalism essentially identifies a trade-off between government and market. Simply put, more market means less government and vice versa. Proponents of this philosophy generally favour the market and advocate a laissez-faire policy. Yet the development of US competition policy unquestionably led to more government intervention and, although celebrated by many as an expression of freedom, therefore seems at odds with the free market philosophy.[6]

The thesis in this first part of the chapter focusing on the United States is that competition policy is compatible with the free market philosophy but only to the extent that it is essential for free market existence. More rather than less government intervention may be warranted when the free market would effectively disappear absent competition law enforcement. In that case, government and market are no longer communicating vessels; less government might no longer imply more market but rather no market (in the sense proper) at all.

In the next section, we briefly describe the historical context within which US competition policy emerged. Section 8.1.3 offers a rough overview of this policy and shows how it slowly but surely expanded. The main argument of how competition law enforcement fits within the free market tradition is developed in detail in Sections 8.1.4 and 8.1.5. Section 8.1.6 concludes.

8.1.2 Historical context

Let us begin by briefly sketching the historical context within which American competition policy emerged. The body of antitrust laws did not just fall from the sky. Rather, there were significant economic, social, and political developments in the second half of the nineteenth century that formed a fertile soil for its creation. At the heart of it was the rise of big business, which was increasingly frowned upon, debated, and even feared by economists, legislators, and the American people.

Around 1800, the United States was already clearly developing as a nation. Market competition was, however, still mainly local and among small suppliers. Manufacturers typically controlled no more than 10% of their industry's production, for example (see Heilbroner and Milberg 2002: 87). Markets tend to work reasonably efficiently in such an environment, because neither buyers nor suppliers possess the power to upset the price mechanism. The absence of two vital ingredients prevented producers from growing into bigger enterprises. The first was monetary means to invest in large quantities of input to produce large quantities of output. The second was a significant level of demand for the product to make such an investment worthwhile. Both became increasingly available throughout the nineteenth century, which in turn enabled the rise of some of the most iconic American corporations (e.g., American Telephone & Telegraph, General Motors).

Regarding the first ingredient, substantial expansion investments came within reach primarily through the separation of ownership and control. At the time, it was common for owners to run their own business. And although this ensures extensive control on daily operations, it also limits investment opportunities. By giving up (part of) the ownership through the issuing of stocks, monetary means could be generated in a relatively short period. In turn, this made it possible to set up large production facilities. But what good is large-scale production when there are not enough customers to purchase the output?

This brings us to the second ingredient, which became available primarily through the development of infrastructure. Both communication devices and means of transportation improved with an unprecedented speed. In 1844, for instance, Samuel Morse succeeded in connecting Baltimore and Washington by telegraph. Just a few years later, cables linked New York to New Orleans and Chicago. Postal services developed in a similar fashion. Whereas US Postal Service mainly used horses and coach to transport mail around 1830, railways were developing westward and quickly became a superior substitute. A network of waterways further facilitated flows of products. Already in 1825, the famous Erie Canal became functional and many more canals were built in the ensuing decades. Together, these developments led to a rapid and substantial growth of markets as well as of some of the suppliers who now started to operate on a national scale.

Next to this expansion of markets, there was growing social and political unrest. Not long after the ending of the Civil War (1861–1865), Americans witnessed the advent of what became known as the *Long Depression*. This period of downturn is considered to have started with the Great Panic of 1873, a financial crisis that led to strikes and economic instability. The resulting downward drop in demand provided the new-born corporations with a strong and natural incentive to reduce their prices. A more profitable alternative to such a cutthroat strategy, however, was to restrict or even eliminate market competition. This is precisely what happened. Indeed, the United States saw a rise in horizontal price-fixing agreements and large-scale mergers unequalled in its young history.[7] Railroad companies, for instance, coordinated their actions to drive up prices.[8]

One consequence of these anticompetitive business practices was that a substantial amount of wealth ended up in the hand of a few. This, in turn, fuelled public opinion against the fast emergence of big business and trusts. These anti-bigness sentiments, combined with the fear for concentrations of market power, were at the heart of the development of the first antitrust laws. Towards the end of the nineteenth century, many considered the significant consolidation of industry and the emergence of powerful business combinations a severe threat.[9] In fact, some politicians vividly argued that this perceived danger could not be ignored. Indeed, Senator John Sherman from Ohio stated that[10] 'You must heed their [the voters] appeal or be ready for the socialist, communist, and the nihilist', therewith paving the way for US competition policy.

8.1.3 US competition policy

Though certainly not the first collection of competition rules in history, competition law enforcement is widely acknowledged to have been born with the passage of Bill S. I in the United States on July 2, 1890.[11] Today, this bill is known as the Sherman Act, named after Senator Sherman who proposed it at the 51st Congress and who at the time appeared one of the most articulate spokespersons on the subject. Together with the Clayton Act and the Federal Trade Commission (FTC) Act of 1914, this law still forms the foundation of today's US federal competition policy.

The Sherman Act has two substantive sections, namely Sections 1 and 2. As noted by many, however, the wording in both provisions is fairly vague and flexible so that the actual meaning of concepts like 'conspiracy', 'restraint of trade', and '(attempt to) monopolize' had to be determined in concrete court cases. In their search for sound judicial interpretations, some judges turned to common law from the pre-Sherman Act period.[12] Although no directly comparable common law principles existed, useful elements could be found in ancient private and criminal doctrines. Cases concerning restraints of trade were, for instance, commonly dealt with under contract law. Interestingly, several of these cases already revealed clear anti-monopoly sentiments as the next quote illustrates:[13]

> The clear tendency of such an agreement is to establish a monopoly and to destroy competition in trade, and for that reason, on grounds of public policy, courts will not aid in its enforcement.

In fact, this statement reflects the overall common law stance on anticompetitive combinations such as cartels; they were typically tolerated, but not legally enforceable.

During the decades after the passage of the Sherman Act, legal discussions mainly revolved around the question of whether challenged business practices should be subject to a reasonableness test or be declared illegal per se. Under a rule-of-reason standard, the court balances adverse and beneficial effects of a particular business act in order to judge its legality. This approach was explicitly embraced as the standard in two cases in 1911.[14] However, it did not take long before the Supreme Court established a per se prohibition for fixing prices.[15] Over time, the scope of the per se rule has widened and an increasing number of business practices (e.g., market division, customer allocation) are held illegal independent of their actual effect on the market.

Pleas by defendants and prominent economists on the potential beneficial effects of combinations increasingly fell on deaf ears, therefore. Cartels, for example, were recurrently referred to as 'children of distress' that ensured order and stability, particularly during economic downturns.[16] The central argument was that in the presence of high fixed and low variable costs, excess production capacity would trigger ruinous competition resulting in bankruptcies and unemployment. Cartels were considered a natural way out of such slumps. Not long after the Great Depression of the 1930s, however, the Supreme Court reconfirmed the per se approach towards price-fixing by reasoning that:[17]

> Ruinous competition, financial disaster, evils of price-cutting, and the like appear throughout our history as ostensible justifications for price-fixing. If the so-called competitive abuses were to be appraised here, the reasonableness of prices would necessarily become an issue in every price-fixing case. In that event, the Sherman Act would soon be emasculated; its philosophy would be supplanted by one which is wholly alien to a system of free competition; it would not be the charter of freedom which its framers intended.

Apart from these developments in the courtroom, two companion laws were enacted in 1914: the Clayton Act and the FTC Act. The Clayton Act outlaws a number of specific business practices such as price discrimination, tying, and exclusive dealing contracts. Its Section 7 prohibits mergers to the extent that they would substantially lessen competition. Moreover, it contains an incipiency standard that is intended to 'arrest the creation of trusts, conspiracies and monopolies in their incipiency and before consummation.'[18] The key provision of the FTC Act, Section 5, declares unlawful unfair methods of competition.

Similar to the Sherman Act, however, these laws were not very effective at first. Congress attempted to address this problem through the adoption of various amendments in the ensuing decades. It, for example, passed the Robinson-Patman Act in 1936. This law substantially amended the Clayton Act by making it applicable to a wider class of business situations and by enhancing enforcement possibilities. In particular, this act aimed to protect small businesses by countering the advantageous market position of big enterprises somewhat. With the passage of the Clayton Act and the FTC Act, US competition law enforcement changed from a primarily reactive to a more proactive policy, a trend fuelled by several amendments like the Robinson-Patman Act and the Hart-Scott-Rodino Antitrust Improvements Act throughout the twentieth century.[19]

During the past few decades, the most prominent changes took place in enforcement policy and the courtroom. An amnesty programme has been installed, for instance, which induces firms involved in competition law violations to self-report in exchange for a reduction of the antitrust penalty. The role of economic analysis in competition cases has grown substantially and facilitated the development of this programme as well as in the estimation of antitrust damages. However, it is debatable whether this has indeed led to an increase in antitrust enforcement.[20]

8.1.4 Preservation of the free market institution

The above description of US competition policy development sketches a picture of (directly and indirectly) increasing government intervention. Anticompetitive agreements between firms were often tolerated under nineteenth-century common law, but generally not legally enforceable. This ended with the passage of the Sherman Act, which made illegal particular monopolizing business practices. A few decades later, its companion laws introduced an incipiency standard and declared unfair methods of competition unlawful. Further restrictions on market transactions were imposed throughout the twentieth century and merger policy became tighter overall.[21]

This expanding set of restraints seems fundamentally at odds with the free market philosophy. Not only did it limit the liberty of market participants, but it also led to a larger rather than a smaller government. As we will argue in the following, however, competition policy is compatible with the free market tradition if one considers it a prerequisite for the preservation of the free market institution.

To begin, let us clarify what we mean when we qualify the market as *free* by means of a simple diagram. Imagine a remote village with a single *representative* marketplace where merchants offer their products to potential buyers. When

Supply Barriers \ Demand Barriers	High	Low
High	Non-Free	Demand Free
Low	Supply Free	Free

Figure 8.1 Stylized model of a (non-)free market definition.

would we consider such a market to be (non-)free? Figure 8.1 sheds light on this question.

A market is a (potentially abstract) place where buyers and sellers interact. Figure 8.1 combines this in one particular fashion. The rows represent the supply side and the columns capture the demand side. Starting with the supply side, a distinction is made between high and low entry barriers. These barriers are considered *high* when it is prohibitively costly for newcomers with a competitive value proposition to enter the market. They are considered *low* when these potential entrants find it profitable to access this market through setting up their own stands. The demand side in some sense mirrors the supply side perspective by distinguishing between high and low exit barriers. Exit barriers are considered *high* when actual buyers lack a reasonable alternative, which may be reflected by a low demand elasticity and a high willingness to pay. Instead, these barriers are *low* when buyers face attractive outside options.

This approach identifies four possible scenarios. One case is when both entry and exit barriers are low. This is characteristic of a *free* market. In this situation, entrepreneurs do not encounter unnatural barriers when pursuing new business opportunities in this market. Likewise, customers face no difficulties in leaving this market when confronted with suboptimal value propositions. A market can also be *semi-free*. It is *supply free* when entry barriers are low and buyers lack attractive outside options. If the opposite holds, then the market is *demand free*. The market is *non-free* when both barriers are high. Firms willing to enter such a market face severe obstacles, whereas consumers have no reasonable alternative.

It is clear that actual markets may vary in their degree of entry and exit barriers and therefore in the extent to which they are supply or demand free. Moreover, one should bear in mind that both entry and exit barriers may be in part endogenous. Markets that are initially free might through time transform into semi-free or non-free ones. If a few free market firms become dominant, for instance, they may successfully adopt lobbying tactics or entry deterring strategies.[22] Similarly, exit barriers may be raised over time. Buyers might, for example, experience switching costs after getting used to existing products. In addition, they may sign long-term contracts that strongly attach them to incumbent suppliers.

In terms of concentrations of economic power and market performance, however, there is no reason to consider free and semi-free markets problematic. After all, under such market conditions supra-competitive profits cannot be sustained for long. In supply-free markets, for example, above normal industry performance would attract newcomers, which in turn would create a downward pressure on prices and profits. In demand-free markets, incumbents are naturally constrained by the attractive outside options of their customers. This too precludes excessive profits and abuse. This is not to say that market performance will be poor in non-free concentrated markets. In fact, it is well-known that perfectly competitive outcomes may emerge even in isolated price-setting duopolies.[23] High entry and exit barriers are, therefore, a necessary, but not a sufficient, condition for high market power and poor market performance.

If even non-free markets may de facto function as free ones, then how can we reconcile the presence of competition policy with the free market philosophy? One answer lies in the fear that absent rules of competition the free market would effectively disappear. This fear is understandable when two conditions hold. First, it must be considered likely that non-free markets emerge on a large scale. It is noteworthy that this fear was reflected recurrently in US antitrust history. In 1889, for example, Senator Jones and Senator Turpie respectively stated that:[24]

> These commercial monsters called trusts ... [are] preying *upon every industry*, and by their unholy combinations robbing their victims, the general public.

And

> The conspirators of the trust ... are hunting the prey, dividing the spoil *in every market*.

Second, non-free markets must be viewed as breeding grounds for enduring concentrations of power, which in turn would severely limit the freedom of (a substantial part of) businesses and consumers. This belief was also widespread. In the famous *Alcoa* antitrust case, for example, Judge Hand referred to an observation by Sherman:[25]

> combinations already defy or control powerful transportation corporations and reach State authorities. They reach out their Briarean arms to every part of our country ... Congress alone can deal with them, and if we are

> unwilling or unable there will soon be a trust for every production and a master to fix the price for every necessity of life.

Of course, this is not to say that these expressed fears were justified. Although market concentration was increasing rapidly in many industries, one might argue that even after the rise of the corporation, most markets were still (semi-) free in the sense defined above.[26] Rather, the point is that the presence of competition law enforcement is compatible with a free market system if one considers it essential to its existence.

8.1.5 Promotion of the free market spirit

The approach of US competition policy to preserve the free market institution has been to prohibit particular anticompetitive business practices and to shape industry structures (e.g., through merger policy). This, one might argue, is its direct effect: the creation of a context within which individuals and firms are free to pursue their own best interests. Yet these competition rules arguably not only affect the stage on which the game is played, but also the players themselves. In particular, they not just face protection from anticompetitive measures by rivals, but are simultaneously incentivized to behave more competitively. We now turn to this indirect effect of US competition policy.

There are at least two ways through which US competition policy may stimulate the free market spirit. The first is due to the idea that freedom requires balance of power. More specifically, one of the main merits of a decentralized market system is that none has the power to dominate others. This, in turn, is considered to safeguard freedom for all. The free market philosophy is thus in some sense more about equality than about freedom; it is the equality of condition and opportunity that is thought to ensure freedom for American citizens and undertakings.[27] It is precisely this equality that was threatened by the emergence of the giant corporations and trusts.

It is then not surprising that the rise of oligarchs as well as a dominant managerial class was met with great suspicion.[28] There was (and, in fact, still is) strong sympathy for the small business owner who attempts to make a living through hard work and dedication. This widespread sympathy is also reflected in US competition policy. For instance, Judge Hand once reasoned that:[29]

> It is possible, because of its indirect social or moral effect, to prefer a system of small producers, each dependent for his success upon his own skill and character, to one in which the great mass of those engaged must accept the direction of a few. These considerations, which we have suggested only as possible purposes of the [Sherman] Act, we think the decisions prove to have been in fact its purposes.

One major risk of a severely unbalanced allocation of economic power is that those who find themselves with a lack of it may be discouraged to compete and challenge the establishment. The significant increase of market concentration in many industries was indeed thought to deprive ambitious Americans of the opportunity for prosperity.[30] One of Congress' goals was, therefore, to restore the balance of power somewhat and to encourage small businesses by establishing a playground on which they have a fair chance of success.[31]

This is not to say that anything goes within the boundaries of US competition policy, however. In fact, one of the prime benefits of maintaining a free competitive order is considered to be its presumed disciplinary value. Within such a setting, rewards come to those who seek and grasp the opportunities given to them. To be effective in such an environment, then, requires a certain character. Richard Hofstadter once formulated this as follows:[32]

> America was thought to have been made possible by the particular type of character that was forged by competitive individualism, a type that had flourished in the United States because competitive opportunities had been so widespread that alert men could hardly fail to see them, to grasp and use them, and, hence, to be shaped by them.

The merits of a decentralized free market system were frequently argued to surpass mere economic considerations. A competitive order in which each is offered a fair chance of prosperity imposes discipline and incentivizes all to embrace those values consistent with a free market economy. Small entrepreneurs who constantly seek to improve their situation are thought to stimulate 'expression of the fundamental virtues of thrift, industry, intelligence, schooling, home ties, and family pride.'[33]

In turn, these values enable free market-based societies to flourish as a whole. For example, to reap the gains from trade requires men to control their emotions and passions sufficiently. A working free market system can therefore be argued to contribute to a safe society. Moreover, since one is considered primarily responsible for one's self and relatives, there is a strong sense of community building. Indeed, absent a paternalistic government, individuals quite naturally rely on those around them and who find themselves in a similar position.[34] This creates mutual sympathy and social stability provided that everyone is given a fair chance to get ahead. The latter imposes a limit on inequality. In particular, losers in the free market should not lose too much as that is likely to create social costs as reflected by limited education and increasing crime rates.[35]

US competition policy may thus enhance the free market spirit in two ways. On the one hand, it offers small business owners a carrot by striving for a sufficiently balanced and fair playground. That is, a self-reliant, hard-working, and efficient businessperson should have a fair chance of reaping the fruits of his efforts. On the other hand, by protecting and stimulating the competitive process, it provides a stick to discipline all industry members. To be effective within a free market environment, hard work and efficiency are arguably less of a choice and more of a necessity.

8.1.6 Concluding remarks

Few today doubt the need for competition rules in a free marked-based society like the United States of America. From a free market philosophy perspective, however, there is something inherently paradoxical about the presence of competition policy. After all, the competition laws that are intended to combat restraints of trade are, in fact, themselves restraints of trade. We have argued that competition policy is compatible with the free market philosophy if the free market system would effectively disappear without it and have shown that this possibility was considered real in the history of US competition law enforcement.

At the heart is the idea that freedom is best preserved when no one is in the position to dominate others. Taking this perspective, the emergence of trusts and large corporations implied a reduction of freedom for both American citizens and firms. This freedom is, in the words of John Stuart Mill: 'that of pursuing our own good in our own way, so long as we do not attempt to deprive others of theirs or impede their efforts to obtain it.'[36] A free market rationale for US competition policy is that those with market power cannot be trusted to abide by this principle.

8.2 Competition policy within the hierarchical and coordinated market tradition: The case of Germany and France

8.2.1 Introduction

In the spring of 1950, the French foreign minister Robert Schuman stated:[37]

> Europe will not be made all at once, or according to a single plan. It will be built through concrete achievements, which first create a de facto solidarity. The coming together of the nations of Europe requires the elimination of the age-old opposition of France and Germany. Any action taken must in the first place concern these two countries.

In the same speech, now known as the Schuman Declaration, Schuman proposed setting up a supranational organization to pool European coal and steel production. About a year later, the establishment of the European Coal and Steel Community (ECSC) was among the first concrete achievements towards building a united Europe.[38]

The ECSC Treaty contained two explicit competition provisions, both of which foreshadowed the European competition policy of today.[39] These competition rules were poorly enforced, however, which was not least due to the lack of independence of the ECSC High Authority, an executive commission in charge of the implementation of the Treaty's goals. Although the member states clearly agreed on the High Authority's sovereignty, the political reality at the time was one of continuous interference by primarily France and Germany.[40] This naturally called for a different competition policy design for the European Economic Community (EEC). Some years later, under the heavy influence of the German-driven ordoliberalism doctrine, a strong European competition policy framework was established with an independent supranational competition authority.[41]

The ECSC and EEC competition policy experience can be embedded in the discussions on different types of capitalist systems that are central to this book, particularly the hierarchical and coordinated market models.[42] The ECSC case fits well within the hierarchical market tradition, for example. In the hierarchical archetype, competition policy is characterized by weak enforcement as well as close ties between big business and the political system (see, in particular, Schneider and Soskice 2009). Additional, complementary traits include the dominance of family and multinational corporations as well as the relatively weak position of workers (see Schneider 2009). By contrast, the EEC case reflects the ordoliberal philosophy and is therefore primarily compatible with the coordinated market tradition. In the coordinated archetype, competition policy is characterized by strong enforcement and a clear dividing line between the private and the public sphere. More specifically, the aim is to safeguard the competitive process, while reducing concentrations of market and political power.

In the following, we argue that German and French competition policy can also be placed within the hierarchical and coordinated market tradition. Akin to the European story, both originate from a mainly hierarchical-based framework and evolved towards a system compatible with the coordinated market model. At the same time, however, we argue that this transformation to date has been incomplete in the sense that both competition policies still contain some hierarchical elements. Specifically, both the German and the French economic ministries can legally interfere with merger cases and, in the name of public interest, overrule a blocking decision by the national competition authority. Therefore, and despite the dominance of the ordoliberal doctrine, both the German and the French states are not (yet) out of sight when it comes to shaping industry structures.

The case of Germany and France thus stands in stark contrast to the American case as discussed above. American competition policy has always been embedded within the free market tradition. In both Germany and France, competition policy has changed position over time. There was a period where the hierarchical model was dominant, but there has been a clear shift towards the coordinated model in both countries since the Second World War. That said, there currently is an increasing perceived threat from Chinese competitors in several key industries, which may well trigger a shift back to the hierarchical approach.

The next section provides a brief history of German competition policy and discusses the transformation from a hierarchical-based system to the coordinated-based framework of today. Section 8.2.3 takes a similar approach to discuss the French case. Section 8.2.4 concludes.

8.2.2 The German case

8.2.2.1 A brief history of German competition policy

The first German competition law was passed during the Weimar period. This *Verordnung gegen Missbrauch wirtschaftlicher Machtstellungen* came into force in 1923 and was directed against abuse of economic power by (groups of) firms.[43] It did not contain a prohibition of anticompetitive combinations such as cartels but allowed collusive agreements to be declared null and void when contractual terms were the consequence of monopolistic conduct by one or more members.[44] The ordinance was enforced by both the Reich minister of economics and a newly established *Kartellgericht*, a cartel court that effectively operated as an administrative agency. This court was not very efficacious, however, and, if anything, enhanced the overall positive image of cartels in the Germany of that time.[45]

As the 1923 cartel ordinance was a control measure and not a prohibition, there was a natural connection with the preceding enforcement system. Since the German unification in 1871, cartel agreements were commonly assessed like any other contract under the German civil code. In this context, the main issue was whether the cartel contract must be considered contrary to good morals and customs (*contra bonos mores et decorum*). In the last few decades of the nineteenth century, the dominant view was that such organizations should be permitted or even encouraged, in particular during economic depressions:[46]

> it was not contra bonos mores for business men belonging to a branch of industry which is suffering from a depression to get together and enter into agreements regulating the ways and means of operating their industry with a view to promoting recovery. On the contrary such course of action would seem to be incumbent upon prudent business men.

In a similar spirit, cartel contracts were widely viewed as an effective means to avoid ruinous competition. This was made explicit in a case concerning wood pulp manufacturers in 1897. A defecting member sued the cartel, the *Sächsischen Holzstoff-Fabrikanten-Verband*, for limiting its freedom of trade (*Gewerbefreiheit*).[47] The German Supreme Court (*Reichsgericht*) took the side of the conspirators, however, by arguing that the cartel did not actually harm the public interest or individual freedom. The *Reichsgericht* thus choose the freedom of contract over freedom of trade. It further reasoned that:[48]

> 'when prices continue to be so low that business men are threatened with ruin, combination is not merely a legitimate means of self-preservation but also serves the public interest.'

This wood pulp decision was taken to mean that cartels should, in principle, be considered legal.

After a brief intermezzo in the years following the 1923 ordinance, the legal acceptance of cartels was further enhanced when the Nazi regime came to power in 1933. A few years prior, an ordinance to meet financial, economic, and social emergencies was already enacted. This ordinance strengthened government involvement by enabling the economics ministry to directly interfere with cartel agreements (see Schwarz 1957). In 1933, the so-called *Zwangkartellgesetz* was passed, a decree that authorized the Reich minister of economics to virtually force firms into cartels in any industry. Not surprisingly, many industries got cartelized in the ensuing years (see McGowan 2010). By the end of the 1930s, cartels were widespread and effective agencies in a centrally controlled German economy.

In the decade following the Second World War, German competition policy came from the Allied Powers. Already at the Potsdam Conference in 1945, there was great consensus that the power of German combinations should be diminished. Specifically, in paragraph 12 of the Report on the Tripartite Conference of Berlin it was stated that:

> the German economy shall be decentralized for the purpose of eliminating the present excessive concentration of economic power as exemplified in particular by cartels, syndicates, trusts and other monopolistic arrangements.

This formed the foundation for the first cartel prohibition in German history. These types of organizations were declared unlawful through the so-called deconcentration laws of 1947, which also allowed for the decomposition of powerful companies into smaller units.[49]

After a series of drafts resulting from the complex political interactions between several parties, the *Gesetz gegen Wettbewerbsbeschränkungen – Kartellgesetz* (GWB) was passed and came into effect on January 1, 1958.[50] Apart from some specific exemptions, the GWB outlawed horizontal anticompetitive conduct as well as abuse of dominance. More generally, this legislation contained many elements that can be found in the German competition policy of today.

Interestingly, it took quite a bit longer before a merger policy was introduced. Several business interest groups repeatedly and, in some sense, successfully put forth the argument that a stringent merger control would harm the competitive position of German firms in international markets. The opportunity for adopting a merger control regime arose after the Social Democrats and the Free Democrats took office in 1969. Together with the first major reform of the GWB that came into force in 1973, a system of merger control was installed.

The evolution of German competition law since 1973 is characterized by a series of reforms of the GWB. The third and fourth revision in 1976 and 1980 shaped the novel merger policy, whereas the fifth in 1989 focused on enhancing the position of modestly sized industries. Moreover, the number of sectors that were exempted from competition law prohibitions was slowly but surely reduced.

Overall, there has been a clear tendency to bring German competition policy more and more in line with its counterpart at the European level. The seventh amendment that was adopted in June 2005 is illustrative in this respect. This amendment centred on the application of European antitrust rules in the German jurisdiction and significantly reduced the scope of national competition law (see Klees 2006). The ninth major reform entered into force on June 9, 2017. This last reform was enacted primarily to better cope with the digitalization trends in many markets and corresponding network effects.

8.2.2.2 German market competition: From hierarchy to coordination?

Together with some small countries like the Netherlands, Germany has had a long reputation for being a cartel's paradise. The brief description of German competition policy history confirms this picture up until the end of the Second World War. During the decade thereafter, however, the legal view on such anticompetitive combinations changed dramatically. In particular, the loose control measures from before the war were replaced by tight prohibitions. Ever since the late 1950s, German and European competition policy are very similar.[51]

This development can be positioned within the hierarchical and coordinated market traditions. Arguably, German competition policy is primarily compatible with the hierarchical market model until the end of the Second World War. Until then the system was supportive of big business, for example, which in turn made it easier for the German state to steer industries in its preferred direction. The *Zwangkartellgesetz* of 1933 is perhaps most illustrative in this regard as it allowed the Nazi regime to effectively use its domestic industries as weapons of war.

The adoption of the first German competition act, the cartel ordinance of 1923, is also consistent with this argument. Not only was the enforcement of this law, for a large part, in the hands of the economics ministry; it was not very effective either. For an important part, this was simply due to the refusal by the Reich minister of economics to apply the abuse provisions:[52]

> Decisions were rare and of little importance, primarily because these provisions could only be used by the economics minister, and he seldom chose to use it. To do so would have been inconsistent with the 'co-operative' arrangements between the ministry and the cartels that constituted the informal system for achieving compliance with the statute.

Finally, it is noteworthy that both banks and families were frequently among the dominant shareholders of large German corporations and consequently held key decision-making positions (see Resch 2005). This too is characteristic of the hierarchical nature of German market competition up until the Second World War.[53]

This radically changed during the decade thereafter, however, primarily under the pressure of the United States and the increasingly popular ordoliberal philosophy (see also Chapter 4). From the late 1950s onwards, Germany has embraced a market competition model that is characterized by a strong competition law framework and an equally strong enforcement policy implemented by an independent competition authority, the *Bundeskartellamt.* Since the start, officials working for this authority have had little discretion in interpreting the new German competition law. Thus, there has been a clear switch in German competition policy history from a hierarchical-based model to a coordinated-based model. Indeed, the current policy framework is arguably quite close to the ordoliberal ideal, particularly regarding the combat of anticompetitive conduct.

When it comes to issues of industry structure, however, the competition statutes still contain some clear hierarchical elements. Specifically, Section 42 of the GWB arranges the so-called Ministerial Authorisation for industry concentrations. Among other things, this provision enables the economics ministry to clear a merger even after it has been blocked by the *Bundeskartellamt.* This may occur when the benefits of the concentration to society are considered to outweigh the costs. Examples of such an overriding public interest include the protection of jobs in economically weak regions and the safeguarding of energy supplies.[54] Although to date this provision has been rarely applied, its presence does imply that in matters of an industry structure the German state is still around the corner.[55]

8.2.3 The French case

8.2.3.1 A brief history of French competition policy

Competition policy in France can be traced back to at least the late 1700s. Not long after the awakening of the French Revolution, the National (Constituent) Assembly adopted the *Loi Le Chapelier.*[56] The name of this law refers to one of its most prominent initiators, Deputy Isaac-René-Guy Le Chapelier, who considered associations and groups in principle incompatible with the spirit of the Revolution. Several organizations, such as the professional guilds and trade unions, were thought to defend their own collective interest rather than that of individuals or society as a whole and were therefore declared illegal. This law also prohibited market participants to make agreements designed to set common prices.

In 1810, under the regime of Napoléon Bonaparte, a new *Code Pénal* saw the light of day. The central part of competition was Article 419, which was primarily directed at pricing practices and, in particular, prices not resulting from *the free and natural competition of trade.*[57] This soon appeared to be a complex criterion to apply in actual cases and by no means ruled out anticompetitive actions per se. Moreover, a body of case law developed throughout the nineteenth century that distinguished between good and bad cartels. Good ones (*bonnes unions*) were defensive coalitions which attempted to stabilize the market, while avoiding ruinous competition resulting from excessive supply. By contrast, bad cartels (*mauvaises unions*) were offensive coalitions, which attempted to limit competition through monopolistic conduct. Since relatively few agreements were considered bad, this law had less and less bite. Article 419 was ultimately amended in 1926, in part, to clarify that price collusion is illegal precisely when it has *the purpose* of creating profits that would not result from the natural play of demand and supply (see Riesenfeld 1962; Pace 2007).

This revision did not lead to a stricter policy towards cartels, however. On the contrary, France increasingly and explicitly recognized this type of anticompetitive agreement as an effective means to control industries and to ensure economic stability. In fact, the French government even required them in some industries during the crisis of the 1930s.[58]

In the Second World War, the Vichy government additionally made extensive use of industry associations, some of which remained active in the immediate post-war period (e.g., in the coal and steel sector). After Germany signed a surrender at the Allied headquarters in the French city of Reims, France convincingly chose to follow such a state-led route to rebuild the country.

This planning-oriented approach manifested itself in at least three ways. First, the *Commissariat Général du Plan* was established, a planning board which was given the task to design plans to support the recovery of the French economy. The first board, led by Jean Monnet, addressed the urgent issue of how to allocate scarce resources right after the end of the Second World War. It further advocated the need for systematic and large-scale investments, particularly in six so-called priority sectors: coal, steel, electricity, cement, agricultural machinery, and transportation (see Djelic 2001). Second, there was a series of nationalization decrees, which effectively restricted competition in key sectors including aviation, insurance, banking, electricity, and gas.[59] Third, the government issued an ordinance in June 1945, which enabled the extensive use of price controls and wage freezes.[60]

The 1945 ordinance additionally prohibited a collection of what was referred to as *illicit pricing practices*, which included refusals to deal and several forms of price discrimination.[61] Combined with a series of amendments enacted in the ensuing years, this culminated in a failed attempt to adopt a general competition law in the early 1950s (see Pace and Seidel 2013). This attempt was unsuccessful not least because of a deeply rooted conviction among French politicians that the planification policy was the best way to allocate resources and to support home industries in emerging global markets.

As a substitute, the French government issued a decree that extended the 1945 price control ordinance.[62] This provision appeared not very effective in practice, however, which was partly due to two clear exemptions. Exempted were agreements (i) which result from the application of a legislative or regulatory measure, or (ii) which are demonstrated by the parties to have the effect of improving production, or assuring the continuance of economic progress by means of rationalization and specialization.[63] Moreover, the enforcement of this decree was primarily reactive and cases were mostly dealt with on an ad hoc basis.[64]

A more convincing move towards contemporary competition law enforcement took place a few decades later. Partly driven by the international oil crises, France faced a severe economic downturn with high inflation and unemployment during the second half of the 1970s. The response by the government was, however, radically different compared to the crisis years of the 1930s. Competition policy was intensified rather than relaxed and more resources were made available to the newly installed *Commission de la Concurrence*.[65] Additionally, France adopted a merger control regime.

This change in direction was reinforced by a reform in 1986, which effectively removed price controls altogether. The 1986 ordinance further transformed the *Commission de la Concurrence* into the *Conseil de la Concurrence*. In addition to its advisory task, this new body was given the right to start proceedings and to impose penalties without the minister of economy being involved. Moreover, it brought the French competition rules in line with the European ones as laid down in the Treaty of Rome.

Some amendments in 1987 allowed for appeals against the authority's decisions at the *Cour d'appel de Paris*, thereby enhancing the separation between the economic ministry and competition law enforcement. The *Conseil de la Concurrence* was allocated even more power in 2001 when French competition laws were restated and codified in the *Nouvelles Regulations Economique* (NRE).[66] Among other things, it provided more scope for proactive competition law enforcement and allowed for more severe fines. In addition, a system of self-reporting was installed that induces those who are acting in breach of competition laws to inform the authority in exchange for a reduction of the antitrust penalty.

The last substantial change took place about a decade ago. In 2009, a new competition authority, the *Authorité de la Concurrence*, was established.[67] This independent administrative authority combines the several enforcement tasks that were still allocated among the *Conseil de la Concurrence* and the economic ministry. Important implications of this reform are that it enables the authority to proactively form opinions on (draft) competition legislation and that it has become responsible for merger control (see Lasserre 2009).

8.2.3.2 French market competition: From hierarchy to coordination?

The short historical overview of French competition policy sketches a picture of a slow but sure move towards the ordoliberal model of coordinated market competition. Most notably, competition policy has become increasingly independent from state politics. Akin to the German case, however, its origins contain important elements that arguably have a better fit with the hierarchical market tradition. In particular, French competition policy has repeatedly favoured big business over labour (see also Chapter 5).

Indeed, one characteristic feature of the hierarchical market model is that organization of labour is weak. This was certainly the case in the early years of French competition policy. For instance, right from the beginning, Le

Chapelier Law banned strikes and ruled out any association of workers. Unions and other types of cooperation were allowed again after 1864 when the coalition offense of Article 419 was abolished (see Souam 1998). In most cases, however, French businesses benefited more from this than did their employees.

In the years directly following the Second World War, labour was again marginalized. Several 'modernization commissions' were installed by the planning board, for example, which brought together representatives of capital and labour as well as planning staff and experts. Yet it quickly became apparent that the influence of the working class would be very limited. In fact, this cooperative set-up enhanced ties between big companies and the French state (see Michalet 1974). And although the first actual French competition law was around the corner, the 1953 decree soon appeared ineffective in protecting market competition and, in particular, in mitigating the power of big businesses (see Jenny 1990: 150). For a significant part, this was due to the widely held belief that French firms were too small to be competitive on a global scale (see Djelic 2001: 137).

This positive perspective on industry concentration manifested itself in several ways. First, the French government largely ignored small and medium-sized companies and primarily focused on the creation of national champions. Second, the number of multinational companies active in France substantially increased during the 1960s (see Michalet 1974). Third, external growth through mergers was actively encouraged by offering tax deductions to the parties involved (see Jenny 1981: 478). Not surprisingly, France witnessed a large number of mergers in the 1960s and 1970s.

The combination of big (diversified, multinational) companies and atomistic, weakly organized labour makes French market competition primarily compatible with the hierarchical capitalist model, at least until the late 1970s. As mentioned above, however, there was an important competition policy reform in 1977 and this reform pushed France in the direction of the European coordinated market model. For a significant part, this switch was due to the impetus of Prime Minister Raymond Barre. Not only was he a trained economist and former chairman of the European Commission; he had also published on, at the time relatively novel, the ordoliberal philosophy in the 1950s.

As mentioned above, the coordinated market model requires a strong and autonomous competition authority. Regarding resources, these were very limited until 1977. Those who were given the task to enforce French competition laws were few in number, only partly specialized and typically had many other tasks to fulfil (see Clement 1974). The establishment of the new *Commission de la Concurrence* implied more resources and a severe enhancement of French competition law enforcement.

Regarding autonomy, this was de facto absent in decades following the Second World War as the economic ministry was the main enforcer and ultimately had the final say in competition cases. However, the French competition authority became more and more independent since the late 1970s. After a hesitant start in which the *Commission de la Concurrence* remained primarily an advisory body, a major step towards independence occurred in 1986 with the establishment of the *Conseil de la Concurrence* (see Gerber 1998, and Lachnit 2016). Yet, it was not until a decade ago that French competition law enforcement was put in the hands of a single competition agency, the *Authorité de la Concurrence*. There is little doubt that this organizational reform has strongly supported the independence of the competition authority and consequently can be considered an important step towards the ordoliberal ideal.

This does not mean that the current system is completely immune to government interference, however. Indeed, similar to the German counterpart, the French minister of economic affairs can still intervene in merger processes or overturn the authority's decision when public interest demands it. Reasons for this include industrial development, employment, and the competitiveness of French companies operating in international markets.[68] Thus, even though the economic ministry undeniably has lost terrain in terms of decision-making power, particularly in cases dealing with anticompetitive conduct, it did not completely vanish from the market competition scene. Specifically, when it comes to competition matters dealing with industry structure, the French state has never been far away.

8.2.4 Concluding remarks

On February 6, 2019, the European Commission communicated that it had blocked the proposed merger by the French *Alstom* and the German *Siemens Mobility*. The main reason for preventing this merger is that it would result in excessive industry concentration in some signalling markets as well as in the very high-speed train market. The European commissioner for competition, Margrethe Vestager, additionally clarified that the companies did not adequately address the Commission's competition concerns. The French economy minister Bruno le Maire was quick to respond that he, together with the German economy minister Peter Altmaier, will soon put forward a proposal to reform the European competition law system. In particular, this new policy should incentivize European companies to grow and be ready to compete on a global scale.

This recent case, on the one hand, illustrates that contemporary European competition policy functions largely like the ordoliberals envisaged. The competition authority independently assessed the proposed merger and concluded that approval would harm the competitive order in the particular markets. On the other hand, the same case also shows that competition policy may be under severe pressure from the state. We have shown that this is anything but new.[69] In both Germany and France, politicians and big business representatives have frequently challenged competition policy. One recurring argument is that industrial giants are required to stand the test of competition in international markets.

There is little doubt that today's competition policy in both countries is mainly compatible with the coordinated market model. Yet, when it comes to industry structure, we have seen there are some elements that fit more naturally within the hierarchical market tradition. Jean Monnet, one of the founding fathers of the European Union, once stated: 'Make men work together. Show them that beyond their differences and geographical boundaries there lies a common interest.'[70] The political response to the European Commission's decision on the Alstom–Siemens merger reveals that France and Germany may indeed have a common interest beyond their differences and geographical boundaries. This common interest, however, need not necessarily be a competitive order safeguarded by a strong competition policy.

Notes

1 I acknowledge the valuable comments of Ivan Boldyrev, Roland Fritz, Johan Graafland, Eelke de Jong, Igor van Loo, and participants at the workshop 'What Good Markets Are Good for: World Views and Practices' in Nijmegen, May 2019.
2 It is generally not easy to define 'competition policy' and one can find a wide variety of descriptions in the literature. Motta (2004: 30) offers the following definition: 'the sets of policies and laws which ensure that competition in the marketplace is not restricted in a way that is detrimental to society.' In this chapter, the (potential) restrictions that we have in mind are horizontal and vertical agreements, abuse of a dominant market position, and mergers.
3 Akin to the varieties in capitalism literature, Poli (2015) provides a detailed discussion on why competition policies may differ across free market-based societies.
4 Appalachian Coals, Inc. v. U.S., 288 U.S. 344 (1933).
5 U.S. v. Topco Assocs., Inc., 405 U.S. 596 (1972).
6 It is noteworthy that some free market scholars have defended competition law enforcement by comparing it to more intrusive forms of government intervention such as regulation and ownership.
7 It should be noted that there was quite some variety in the way in which industries transformed into centres of business power, including monopolization, cartels, pools, and trusts. First introduced in the oil industry, a *trust* was (at the time) a legal form of business organization where participants gave up control over their companies in exchange for a fixed share of profits generated by the trust.
8 The emergence of powerful trusts was widespread. As Heilbroner and Milberg (2002: 86) state: 'It was not just the railroad industry that used economic power to create a monopoly position. In whiskey and sugar, in tobacco and cattle feed, in wire nails, steel hoops, electrical appliances, tinplate, in matches and meat, there was an octopus similar.'
9 George Gunton, a known defender of trusts at the time, stated that the situation was 'surcharged with an indefinite but almost inexpressible fear of trusts.' See Stocking and Watkins (1951).
10 See Thorelli (1955).
11 Quite a few states had already adopted competition laws prior to 1890 as did Canada in 1889. See, for example, Stigler (1985).
12 Hylton (2003) provides an extensive discussion of the relation between the antitrust acts and the common law.
13 Central Ohio Salt Co. v. Guthrie, 35 Ohio St. 666 (1880). For similar examples, see Thorelli (1955) and Kintner (1980).
14 These cases are: Standard Oil Co. of New Jersey v. U.S. 221 U.S. 1 (1911) and U.S. v. American Tobacco Co., 221 U.S. 106 (1911).
15 This happened primarily through two case decisions: U.S. v. Trenton Potteries Company *et al.* 273 U.S. 392 (1927) and U.S. v. Socony-Vacuum Oil Co. *et al.*, 310 U.S. 150 (1940).

16 Kleinwächter (2017) coined the phrase 'Kartelle sind Kinder der Not' ('Cartels Are Children of Distress') as far back as 1883. A general discussion on cutthroat competition can be found in Scherer (1980: 212–216).

17 U.S. v. Socony-Vacuum Oil Co. *et al.*, 310 U.S. 150 (1940).

18 Senate Report 698, 15.657, 63rd Cong., second session, 1914, page 1. A detailed description is provided in Scherer (1980).

19 The Hart-Scott-Rodino Antitrust Improvements Act came into force in 1976 and contains premerger notification provisions. Prior to a merger (or acquisition), parties involved are required to file a notification with the Federal Trade Commission and the U.S. Department of Justice.

20 Ghosal and Sokol (2014) show that US competition law enforcement has become more severe in terms of total corporate fines collected and years of imprisonment. Yet, Philippon (2019) argues that US antitrust enforcement has weakened substantially over the last two decades.

21 It should be noted that this trend was non-monotonic. For example, merger control became temporarily less strict under the presidency of Ronald Reagan in the 1980s as it was viewed an unnecessary form of government intervention. For more details about changes in US competition policy practices in this time period, see Ergen and Kohl (2019). There are also strong signals of a decrease in antitrust enforcement under the Trump administration. See the recent report by the American Antitrust Institute: 'The State of Antitrust Enforcement and Competition Policy in the U.S.', April 14, 2020.

22 As Philippon (2019) argues, this has indeed been the case in the United States during the last decades.

23 This result is, however, commonly referred to as the Bertrand paradox, see Tirole (1988).

24 See *20 Cong. Record 1457* and *21 Cong. Record 137*. Italics emphasis is ours.

25 See United States v. Aluminum Co. of America, 148 F.2d 416 (2d Cir. 1945).

26 In reflecting on the American industry composition in the second half of the nineteenth century, Stigler (1985) remarks: 'The average business is not capable of achieving effective cartelization or monopoly, simply because the small relative size of an efficient enterprise and the absence of entry barriers make such goals unattainable.'

27 As Alexis de Tocqueville stated in his *Democracy in America*:

> I think that democratic communities have a natural taste for freedom; left to themselves, they will seek it, cherish it and view any privation of it with regret. But for equality their passion is ardent, insatiable, incessant, invincible; they call for equality in freedom.

28 As observed by Lande (1982):

> Decisionmaking was transferred from traditional power centers to the great industrialists. Self-reliant farmers, business owners, and local leaders became dependent on the discretionary power of a few very rich men. Local control of society ended as numerous small power centers were swept away by the new class, one perceived as greedy and evil.

29 U.S. vs. Aluminum Co. of America, 148 F.2d 416 (2d Cir. 1945). In the same case, it is stated that:

> Throughout the history of these statutes [the antitrust laws] it has been constantly assumed that one of their purposes was to perpetuate and preserve, for its own sake and in spite of possible cost, an organization in small units which can effectively compete with each other.

30 See, for example, Millon (1988).

31 See Lande (1982). Notice that, even though the *intent* is to ensure a fair playground, this does not yet imply that competition law enforcement is indeed effective. In fact, there is

some evidence that large corporations use the antitrust system to their own advantage. See, for instance, Philippon (2019).

32 Hofstadter (1965: 209).

33 The Small Business Committee of the Senate, cited in Bunzel (1962).

34 For the United States, this is described in detail by de Tocqueville (1998).

35 For a detailed discussion, see Baker and Salop (2015) and the references therein.

36 Mill (2003).

37 May 9, 1950. Full text is available at: https://europa.eu.

38 This organization was the outcome of a treaty signed by Belgium, France, Germany, Italy, Luxembourg, and the Netherlands in Paris on April 18, 1951.

39 The ECSC Treaty contained both a cartel prohibition and merger provisions, see Chapter VI of this Treaty – Agreements and concentrations, Articles 65 and 66.

40 See Article 9 of the ECSC Treaty.

41 This framework is based on the Treaty of Rome that was signed on March 25, 1957, and came into force on January 1, 1958. A few years later, Regulation 17/62 granted substantial power to the European Commission as competition law enforcer.

42 See, for instance, Whitley (1999), Hall and Soskice (2001), Schneider (2009), and Schneider and Soskice (2009).

43 This *Kartellverordnung* was enacted on November 2, 1923, and is, in fact, considered the first actual competition law in Europe.

44 It also contained a provision on (un)reasonable pricing. See Schwarz (1957) for a detailed discussion and English translation of this ordinance.

45 Cartels were viewed effective and ethical organizational forms by many. See Gerber (1998).

46 Quote by Wolff (1935) cited in Martin (2010).

47 The core of the cartel agreement was to sell exclusively through a joint sales agency and non-abiding members were obliged to pay a fine. The defecting cartel participant sold its wood pulp directly to several paper producers.

48 B. v. den Sächsischen Holzstoff-Fabrikanten-Verband, Reichsgericht, February 4, 1897, 38 R.G.Z. 155 cited in Schwarz (1957). This argumentation by the former German Supreme Court confirmed the reasoning by the Bavarian appeal court about a decade earlier. In Oberstes Landesgericht Bavaria, April 7, 1888, Entsch. des Ob. L. G. 12, 67, this court argued: 'when prices are for a long time so low that financial ruin threatens the producers, their combination appears to be not merely a legitimate means of self-preservation, but also a measure serving the interests of society.' Citation taken from Martin (2010).

49 It should be noted that these laws were enacted by the Western allies and consequently only applied to their occupation territories.

50 The GWB was adopted on July 27, 1957.

51 Somewhat symbolically, the first actual German cartel prohibition and EEC competition policy both came into force on the same date: January 1, 1958.

52 See Gerber (1998: 129).

53 On the importance of family ownership and management within the hierarchical market tradition, see Schneider (2009).

54 More examples can be found in Verloop and Landes (2003).

55 About two handfuls of applications have been granted thus far. See, for example, the German Negotiated M&A guide available at: www.ibanet.org.

56 This law was passed on June 14, 1791.

57 The other main competition rule, Article 412, was directed at anti-competitive conduct at auctions. See, for instance, Clement (1974).

58 See OECD (2003) and Riesenfeld (1960), which also provides several concrete examples.

59 See Riesenfeld (1960) and Djelic (2001). This increased state control included well-known companies such as Air France, Renault, and Crédit Lyonnais.

60 Ordinance No. 45-1483.
61 See, for instance, OECD (2003). A detailed discussion can be found in Riesenfeld (1960).
62 This decree, No. 53-704, was passed on August 9, 1953. It was amended to include an abuse of dominance provision ten years later, law No. 63-628.
63 These exemptions were arranged in Article 59 *ter*. See Pace and Seidel (2013) and Riesenfeld (1960).
64 Also, some commentators have argued that the French government agreed only on the condition that 'no one would ever hear about it.' See Dumez and Jeunemaître (1996).
65 This commission effectively replaced the *Commission Technique des Ententes*, an advisory body that was active since 1953.
66 See OECD (2003) and Lachnit (2016).
67 It was installed on March 2, 2009, by reforming the *Conseil de la Concurrence*. See the Law of Modernisation of the Economy, No. 2008-776, and the Ordinance of Modernisation of Competition Regulation, No. 2008-1161.
68 See Article L. 430-7-1 of the French Commercial Code (*Code de Commerce*).
69 In this respect, see also the recent study by Dinc and Erel (2013) who find empirical evidence for economic nationalism in European merger and acquisitions cases.
70 See, e.g., http://www.historiasiglo20.org/europe/monnet.htm.

References

Baker, J. B. and S. C. Salop (2015) Antitrust, competition policy, and inequality, *Georgetown Law Journal* 104(1): 1–28.

Bunzel, J. H. (1962) *The American Small Businessman*, New York: Alfred A. Knopf.

Clement, B. (1974) An appraisal of French antitrust policy, *Antitrust Bulletin* 19(3): 587–603.

De Tocqueville, A. (1998) *Democracy in America*, London: Wordsworth Classics of World Literature.

Dinc, S. and I. Erel (2013) Economic nationalism in mergers and acquisitions, *Journal of Finance* 68(6): 2471–2514.

Djelic, M.-L. (2001) *Exporting the American Model: The Postwar Transformation of European Business*, Oxford: Oxford University Press.

Dumez, H. and A. Jeunemaître (1996) The convergence of competition policies in Europe: Internal dynamics and external imposition. In S. Berger and R. Dore (eds.), *National Diversity and Global Capitalism*, Ithaca, NY: Cornell University Press.

Ergen, T. and S. Kohl (2019) Varieties of economization in competition policy: Institutional change in German and American antitrust, 1960–2000, *Review of International Political Economy* 26(2): 256–286.

Gerber, D. J. (1998) *Law and Competition in Twentieth-Century Europe: Protecting Prometheus*, Oxford: Oxford University Press.

Ghosal, V. and D. D. Sokol (2014) The evolution of U.S. cartel enforcement, *Journal of Law and Economics* 57(3): 51–65.

Hall, P. A. and D. Soskice (eds.) (2001) *Varieties of Capitalism: The Institutional Foundations of Comparative Advantage*, Oxford: Oxford University Press.

Heilbroner, R. L. and W. Milberg (2002) *The Making of Economic Society*, 11th Edition, Upper Saddle River, NJ: Prentice Hall.

Hofstadter, R. (1965) *The Paranoid Style in American Politics and Other Essays*, New York: Random House Publishers.

Hylton, K. N. (2003) *Antitrust Law: Economic Theory & Common Law Evolution*, Cambridge: Cambridge University Press.

Jenny, F. (1981) From price controls to competition policy in France: The uneasy alliance of economical and political considerations, *Annals of Public and Cooperative Economics* 52(4): 477–490.

Jenny, F. (1990) French competition policy in perspective. In W. S. Comanor, K. George, A. Jacquemin, F. Jenny, E. Kantzenbach, J. A. Ordover and L. Waverman (1990) *Competition Policy in Europe and North America*, New York: Harwood Academic Publishers GmbH.

Kintner, E. W. (1980) *Federal Antitrust Law, Volume 1: Economic Theory, Common Law, and the Introduction of the Sherman Act*, Cincinnati, OH: Anderson Publishing Co.

Klees, A. M. (2006) Breaking the habits: The German competition law after the 7th amendment to the act against restraints of competition (GWB), *German Law Journal* 7(4): 399–419.

Kleinwächter, F. (2017) *Die Kartelle. Ein Beitrag zur Frage der Organisation der Volkswirtschaft*, London: Forgotten Books.

Lachnit, E. S. (2016) *Alternative Enforcement of Competition Law*, Ph.D. Dissertation, The Hague: Eleven International Publishing.

Lande, R. H. (1982) Wealth transfers as the original and primary concern of antitrust: The efficiency interpretation challenged, *Hastings Law Journal* 34: 65–151.

Lasserre, B. (2009) The new French competition law enforcement regime, *Competition Law International* 5(3): 15–20.

Martin, S. (2010) *Industrial Organization in Context*, Oxford: Oxford University Press.

McGowan, L. (2010) *The Antitrust Revolution in Europe: Exploring the European Commission's Cartel Policy*, Cheltenham: Edward Elgar Publishing.

Michalet, C.-A. (1974) France. In R. Vernon (ed.), *Big Business and the State*, Cambridge, MA: Harvard University Press.

Mill, J. S. (2003) *On Liberty*, New Haven, CT: Yale University Press.

Millon, D. K. (1988) The Sherman Act and the balance of power, *Southern California Law Review* 61: 1219–1292.

Motta, M. (2004) *Competition Policy: Theory and Practice*, Cambridge: Cambridge University Press.

OECD (2003) *Country Studies: France – The Role of Competition Policy in Regulatory Reform*: 1–54, Paris: OECD.

Pace, L. F. and K. Seidel (2013) The drafting and the role of Regulation 17: A fragile balance. In K. K. Patel and H. Schweitzer (eds.), *The Historical Foundations of EU Competition Law*, Oxford: Oxford University Press.

Pace, L. F. (2007) *European Antitrust Law: Prohibitions, Merger Control and Procedures*, Cheltenham: Edward Elgar.

Philippon, T. (2019) *The Great Reversal: How America gave up on Free Markets*, Cambridge, MA: The Belknap Press of Harvard University Press.

Poli, E. (2015) *Antitrust Institutions and Policies in the Globalising Economy*, London: Palgrave Macmillan.

Resch, A. (2005) *Phases of competition policy in Europe*, Working Paper, AY0504, Berkeley, CA: Institute of European Studies, University of California.

Riesenfeld, S. A. (1962) Antitrust laws in the European economic community, *California Law Review* 50(3): 459–481.

Riesenfeld, S. A. (1960) The legal protection of competition in France, *California Law Review* 48(4): 574–595.

Scherer, F. M. (1980) *Industrial Market Structure and Economic Performance*, 2nd Edition, Boston, MA: Houghton Mifflin Company.

Schneider, B. R. (2009) Hierarchical market economies and varieties of capitalism in Latin America, *Journal of Latin America Studies* 41(3): 553–575.

Schneider, B. R. and D. Soskice (2009) Inequality in developed countries and Latin America: Coordinated, liberal and hierarchical systems, *Economy and Society* 38(1): 17–52.

Schwartz, I. E. (1957) Antitrust legislation and policy in Germany – A comparative study, *University of Pennsylvania Law Review* 105(5): 617–690.

Smith, A. (1977) *An Inquiry into the Nature and Causes of the Wealth of Nations*. E. Cannan (ed.), Chicago, IL: University of Chicago Press.

Souam, S. (1998) French competition policy. In S. Martin (ed.), *Competition Policies in Europe*, North-Holland: Elsevier.

Stigler, G. J. (1985) The origin of the Sherman Act, *Journal of Legal Studies* 14: 1–12.

Stocking, G. W. and M. W. Watkins (1951) *Monopoly and Free Enterprise*, New York: The Twentieth Century Fund.

Thorelli, H. B. (1955) *The Federal Antitrust Policy: Origin of an American Tradition*, Baltimore: Johns Hopkins University Press.

Tirole, J. (1988) *The Theory of Industrial Organization*, Cambridge, MA: MIT Press.

Verloop, P. and V. Landes (eds.) (2003) *Merger Control in Europe: EU, Members States and Accession States*, 4th edition, The Hague: Kluwer Law International.

Withley, R. (1999) *Divergent Capitalisms: The Social Structuring and Change of Business Systems*, Oxford: Oxford University Press.

9 Central bank independence and monetary policy in the United States, Germany, and France

Have they converged?

Eelke de Jong

9.1 Introduction

During the last decades, the appropriate design of a central bank and the preferred way of conducting monetary policy have been discussed intensely. The preferred way of designing a central bank has been the main substance of the discussion about the set-up of the European Central Bank (ECB). Here, the discussion centred on the difference between the French and German tradition of central bank independence. The financial crisis of 2008 has triggered a debate about appropriate monetary policy in extreme situations and has led to non-conventional monetary policy in the sense that central banks have bought different types of financial assets, a policy which was started by the Federal Reserve System (FED) but has been followed by other central banks, among them the ECB. These extraordinary monetary policies illustrate the large impact these institutions' policies can have on economic activities in the countries concerned. Moreover, as a reaction to the financial crisis, the responsibilities of central banks and areas to be overseen by them have been broadened. Consequently, these institutions can encounter conflicting interests and thus have to judge which objective obtains priority.

This chapter describes the history of three national central banks, with a view to discovering the motives for establishing a central bank and the way each central bank has operated. In particular, attention will be paid to the development of the degree of central bank independence, that is, the degree to which a central bank can and is expected to operate without the direct influence of politicians. In all systems, politicians appoint members of the board. The systems can differ, however, with respect to the direct influence of politicians on monetary policy: has the central banker to follow the instructions of politicians (mostly the minister of finance) or are politicians supposed to refrain from making any comment on the central bank's policy? The latter situation reflects a very independent central bank. Countries with a very independent central bank often have procedures for the appointment of the central bank's board members that are aimed at guaranteeing that no single politician can have an undue influence on the appointment procedure, and that board

DOI: 10.4324/9781003208549-9

members cannot be fired because of disagreement between the politician and the central banker about the banker's policy.

The next section describes the history of the Federal Reserve System of the United States. Striking a balance between the federal and state level and between commercial and public interests have been important in the design of the FED's governance structure. Although there is a raft of rules in place to ensure the independence of the FED's monetary policy, at times the actual freedom to manoeuvre appears to depend on the relationship between the FED's chair and the president. Section 9.3 is devoted to the history of the German Bundesbank, which developed into a very independent institution. For the German population, the stable value of the Deutsche mark and the independent Bundesbank were the most important tokens of the country's economic success after the Second World War. Consequently, for them, and thus for German politicians, it was hard to replace the Bundesbank by an institution which had not yet established an anti-inflation reputation. This became even more difficult because the other important partner in this new institution (the European Central Bank) was France. As will be discussed in Section 9.4, the French central bank was one of the most dependent central banks among the industrialized countries: it often acted as a branch of the ministry of finance. Given these large differences between Germany and France with respect to their history and attitude towards central bank independence, one might wonder how they would cooperate within the ECB. Section 9.5 is devoted to this question. Section 9.6 concludes.

9.2 The Federal Reserve System

The Federal Reserve Act of 1913 founded the United States' Federal Reserve System (FED). The need for a federal financial institution was felt in 1907 when once again a financial crisis hit the country and the government was unable to stem the panic. Opinions on the preferred governance of the new institution differed along two dimensions: the degree of centralization, and private versus public governance. The southern Democrats and the Midwestern Populists wanted a decentralized system, which would serve small farmers (rural Populists) and small-city bankers (Democrats). Their ideal was one reserve bank per state and they preferred control by the government. The Republicans representing northeast states preferred a centralized system without influence from Washington (Binder and Spindel 2017: Chapter 3). In 1913, President Woodrow Wilson convinced the parties to agree to a compromise, namely the Wilsonian Compromise. This consisted of a government-controlled supervisory board, the Federal Reserve Board, based in Washington DC, and essentially private, decentralized central banks. The Board would include the secretary of the treasury, the comptroller of the currency, and five presidential appointees, who would serve ten-year terms. The rest of the system would consist of 8 to 12 Reserve Banks headed by a governor and a board of nine persons. The Reserve Banks represented the private features of the system. Decisions on the number of Reserve Banks and the cities in which they were to be located were delegated to an independent committee.[1] The resulting system struck a balance between centralization versus decentralization, and between private and public governance (see Figure 1.1 in Comte Brown 2016).

The history of the foundation of the FED teaches us at least three lessons. Firstly, the American aversion to the concentration of power hampers nationwide solutions. Only after the country was hit by a severe crisis again were politicians willing to consider a central bank-like organization. Secondly, the power of local rural constituencies is important in sketching the manner in which the FED was formed. In the end, the Wilsonian Compromise was closer to the wishes of the Democrats (small cities) and Populists (rural areas) than those of the Republicans representing the financial centres.[2] Thirdly, partly due to the complexity of the solution, the position of the FED was vulnerable for criticisms and thus for attempts to change it.

The FED's governance was a compromise and hence quite complex. From the very beginning, tensions arose between the Board and the Reserve Banks. Due to its complexity, it became almost impossible to place definite responsibility anywhere. The crisis of the 1930s led to criticism of the FED's policy for not preventing the crisis and was even accused of having led to it. As a result, the Glass-Steagall Act of 1933 created the Federal Open Market Committee (FOMC) as the central body for making proactive decisions on the purchase of market securities, among them government bonds. President Roosevelt invited Marriner S. Eccles as governor of the Federal Reserve Board. Eccles was a successful banker who was of the view that a lack of demand had caused the Great Depression. Eccles refused the offer and made clear to the president that, in his view, the Federal Reserve System needed fundamental changes. Roosevelt invited Eccles to propose the changes he deemed necessary. An important element of Eccles' opinion was that in the past the Federal Reserve Banks had acted too much in the interest of the bankers and at the expense of public interest. These ideas were implemented in the Banking Act of 1935. This act abolished the Federal Reserve Board created in 1913 and replaced it with the Board of Governors of the Federal Reserve System. The position of the heads of the Federal Reserve Banks was demoted, and the secretary of the treasury was no longer member of the Board. As a consequence, the Banking Act of 1935 moved the FED towards more centralization and governance in the public interest (Comte Brown 2016: Figure 1.2). This resulted in a more independent central bank, in particular more independent from private bankers.

After the Second World War, the relationship between the FED and the government (president) came under pressure. When Eccles was appointed in 1935, he followed a monetary policy that stimulated growth during the Depression and supported the war efforts. In order to finance the government's expenses during the war, the FED introduced the 'peg', which fixed the interest rate on government debt at a low level. Monetary policy was thus in unison with the US president's policy. This mutual support ended after the Second World War. At that time, Eccles had changed his mind and thought that growing inflation was becoming a problem. He therefore wanted to remove the peg and let the markets decide on an appropriate level for the interest rate. President Truman wanted support to fight communism in Asia, and in 1948 refused to reappoint Eccles. A war of public speeches took place as the administration wanted to keep the peg and the FED was in favour of increasing the influence of markets in determining the interest rate in order to fight inflation. Over time, the position of President Truman became weaker. In 1951, a compromise was reached, namely the Treasury–Federal Reserve Accord, which honoured the FED's desire to fight inflation and the administration's fear that uncertainty about interest rates would hamper the fight of communism in Asia.[3] It made the FED independent from the government in that it could set interest rates independent from the wishes of the fiscal authority. The Accord reaffirmed the FED's dependence on Congress (Binder and Spindel 2017: Chapter 5).

Some developments during the post-war years appeared to sow the seeds of a change in the FED's goal in the 1970s. In 1913, the FED's mandate was 'to furnish an elastic currency, to afford means of rediscounting commercial paper, to establish a more effective supervision of banking in the United States, and for other purposes.' In the 1930s, Eccles summarized it as to 'supply the credit needs of commerce, agriculture and industry' (Binder and Spindel 2017: 172). This reflects the concerns of that time that not enough liquidity would be available. During the Second World War, employment increased. After this war, politicians wanted to maintain a high level of employment. This resulted in the Employment Act of 1946. The bill emphasized production and unemployment and required a countercyclical policy. In essence, this meant that the FED should help the government to manage the economy, although the bill, as such, did not change the position or goals of the FED. This came in the 1970s when the economy was in stagflation: high inflation and high unemployment. The FED was blamed for this bad economic situation. Congress reacted by explicitly including maximum employment in the FED's mandate. The new mandate requested the FED 'to promote effectively the goals of maximum employment, stable prices, and moderate long-term interest rates.'[4] This amendment explicitly required the FED to follow a policy in accordance with that of the administration and Congress (Binder and Spindel, 2017: 176).

In order to obtain these final goals, a central bank can use different instruments such as reserve requirements, the interest rate, and open market operations. The announcements of targets for interest rates, money growth, or inflation can inform private actors about the central bank's priorities. The FED has used all these instruments (see, e.g., Bernanke and Mishkin 1992). At the end of the 1970s, FED's president Paul Volcker implemented a major change in policy. In order to fight inflation, he decided to focus on the growth of money and let the interest fluctuate (see also later). At times, other central banks also took movements in the exchange rate into account. Except for rare occasions, such as the second half of the 1980s, the FED disregarded the consequences of its policy for the US dollar's exchange rate; an attitude known as benign neglect.

The Federal Reserve Act of 1913, the Banking Act of 1935, and the Treasury–Federal Reserve Accord of 1951 have set the governance structure of the Federal Reserve System. Over the years, the structure has become more centralized and more focused on public aims. Here, we briefly confront the actual practice with Congress's aims in setting the rules for the appointment of the chair and members of the Board. The rules set in 1935 aimed at preventing dominance by the president. Governors therefore have a term of 14 years so that the president can appoint one member every two years. The chairperson of the Board is appointed for a four-year term. The idea is that the FED is independent but in the end accountable to the government. Practice differs, however. Members often do not serve their full term, so that a president can appoint on average more than one member every year, so more than twice the number the legislator had in mind (Conti-Brown 2016: Table 8.1). The chair on the other hand often serves more than four years. A chair has a four-year renewable term and another 14-year non-renewable term as a governor. Moreover, each governor can serve the unexpired term of his predecessor. These combinations can imply that a FED chair could serve for almost 28 years (Conti-Brown 2016: 187, 188). Consequently, the US president can have more influence on appointing members of the Board than foreseen by law, whereas the chair can act more independently than expected. The terms of Martin, Volcker, and Greenspan illustrate the great influence of the FED's chair.

William M. Martin Jr. is the longest-serving chairperson of the FED. He served as chair from April 2, 1951 until February 1, 1970 and acted more independently than President Truman had expected. Conti-Brown (2016) distinguishes three major changes during Martin's reign of which two are important for the present story. First, Martin restricted the type of financial assets used for open market intervention to short-term public debt. Previously, assets with different terms to maturity were used. Second, he succeeded in convincing others that monetary policy should be conducted independently from fiscal policy (see the Treasury–Federal Reserve Accord).

President Carter appointed Paul Volcker, who served as chair from August 6, 1979, to August 1987. When Volcker became chair, the industrialized countries had already experienced a relatively long period of stagflation. It seemed as if monetary authorities could not get inflation under control. Until then these authorities had used the interest rate and restrictions on bank credit to fight inflation. Volcker changed course and focused on money supply. He restricted the supply of money without directly taking the consequences for the interest rate into account. Interest rates increased a lot, the exchange rate of the US dollar appreciated, growth declined, and unemployment increased. More important, inflation also decreased. Although the recession was deep, many understood that it was necessary for killing inflation.

In August 1987, Greenspan, who served as chair until January 31, 2006, succeeded Volcker. President Ronald Reagan appointed Greenspan. The Greenspan era is seen as a period characterized by liberalization of financial markets and without any serious recession. The latter is ascribed to Greenspan's accommodating monetary policy. Moreover, he hinted that in case of serious financial crises the Federal Reserve would help financial markets, also known as the so-called 'Greenspan put.' During his reign, Greenspan was praised for his achievements and any criticism (e.g., Rajan 2005) was overlooked. Immediately, after his resignation, the financial crisis of 2007–2008 emerged and criticism was levied over lax monetary policy, weak supervision, and neglect of signals indicating problems in certain markets, in particular the mortgage market.

These examples show that, indeed, the term of the chair can last almost two decades (Martin and Greenspan). They also show that the chair, and thus the Board of the FED, can have a significant influence on economic events. It is important to note that in all three cases, the policies, at least partly, were in accordance with developments in economic theory and often had the support of the administration. Martin's plea for an independent monetary policy fitted the contemporary discussion about the relative effectiveness of monetary and fiscal policy, according to which monetary policy should focus on inflation and fiscal policy on employment. Volcker's move came after a decade of frustration over the inability to control inflation. Moreover, his anti-inflation policy corresponded with a plea for the appointment of a conservative central banker who would be more anti-inflation than the population (Rogoff 1985). In this way, the central banker could solve the problems associated with time inconsistency (Kydland and Prescott 1977).[5] Finally, Greenspan's policies, to a large extent, were in accordance with the mood in the 1990s that tended towards liberalizing markets and self-supervision of financial institutions. For extensive periods, the administration and Congress applauded these policies as they delivered the results politicians had hoped for. However, when the results were disappointing, Congress blamed the FED and thereby Congress began a process of reform. This was a blame game repeatedly played by Congress (Binder and Spindel 2017).

In conclusion, over the years the FED became more centralized and increasingly represented public interest more than private interest. Moreover, the FED's goals changed over time in accordance with the most urgent needs. Until the 1930s, its goal was financial stability. Starting with the Second World War came a period in which it facilitated fiscal policy with an aim to enhance employment. From the mid-1970s until the Great Crisis of 2008, controlling inflation became the main goal.[6] It is during this latter period that the bank was regarded as independent, although Congress always had the power to change this.[7]

9.3 The Bundesbank

At the time the German empire was established (1871), it had more than 30 banks issuing notes and coins.[8] In order to stem potential chaos, in 1875 the

Reichstag decided to transform the Prussian bank into a Reichsbank. The bank obtained central control but no monopoly of the issue of notes. It remained a privately owned bank with a semi-public character in that its director had to obey the rulings of the chancellor. After Germany's defeat in the First World War, in May 1922, the Allies created a new Reichsbank in order to handle the moratorium on Reparations. This new Reichsbank was formally independent of the government. Despite its independence, the bank continued discounting government and private sector bills, due to which inflation rose to unprecedented levels. After a currency reform, the new Banking Law of 1924 confirmed the Reichsbank's independence from the government, and foreign representatives obtained seats in the governing council. During the Nazi regime, the bank frequently criticized the government's fiscal policy but also played an important role in the rearmament of Germany. In January 1939, the bank informed Hitler that it would no longer provide credit to the government. Hitler dismissed the bank's president, Schacht, appointing in his place the minister of economic affairs who remained head of the bank until the end of the war. Moreover, the new Reichsbank law of June 1939 brought the Deutsche Reichsbank under the full control of Hitler.

After the Second World War, the Allied Forces occupied Germany. The Americans were in favour of a decentralized central bank, similar to the FED, whereas the British wanted a centralized system. At the beginning of 1947, the Americans pushed through their ideas and established *Landeszentralbanken*, central banks for each Land, in their zone. The French followed in February 1947, whereas the British did not do so until March 1948, after they had convinced the Americans to establish the Bank deutscher Länder (BdL), which was founded on March 1, 1948 (Bibow 2009: 157). The *Länder* held all the assets, the majority of the voting rights, and distributed the BdL's profits (Berger and de Haan 1999: 24). The Allied Banking Commission (ABC) supervised the BdL. In particular, in its initial years, this commission adopted a hands-on approach and intervened in personal matters as well as policy determination. The BdL did not like this and at the time sought confrontation with the ABC (Bibow 2009: 159 and 160). The Bundesrepublik was not formed until 1949, so that the central bank (BdL) was founded before a federal government was established, a unique event.

The fact that the central bank, which was largely influenced by the *Länder*, was established before the federal government meant that the latter had to fight the vested interests of the *Länder* in order to obtain a say over the central bank. In 1951, the Allies wanted to stipulate the legal powers of the bank. At that time, 1950–1951, Germany was confronted with a balance of payments crisis and the federal government wanted the BdL to follow a less restrictive policy. The bank refused. The minister of finance, therefore, wanted to bring the central bank under government control, which was legally possible. According to legal experts, a dependent central bank was more in accordance with Germany's *Grundgesetz*, which describes a division of labour between the federal government and the *Länder*. However, the minister of economic affairs and the bank were against the idea of a dependent central bank. In their view, the balance of payments problems were due to a lack of flexibility at the supply side (labour market). Making the central bank dependent would only introduce an inflationary bias. The *Länder* were also opposed to changes that would diminish their role. In the end, a compromise was reached that resulted in two laws, namely the Transformation Act and the Law on Bundesbank Seigniorage. The federal government obtained 20% of the profits over 1951–1952, was allowed to attend the bank's council meetings but had a restricted veto power; it could only suspend (postpone) decisions. The federal structure of the bank remained intact. These laws were regarded as temporary, awaiting a permanent solution.

Public opinion played a decisive role in forming that permanent solution in 1957 (Berger and de Haan 1999: 25–27). In 1955, the German central bank raised the interest rate and criticized the federal government for too loose a fiscal policy. This stimulating fiscal policy was a way for the incumbent government to increase spending and hence chances of re-election in 1957. In March 1956, the central bank announced a further increase in the interest rate. For the first time the government used its veto to postpone the decision by eight days. The federal government was divided, however. Chancellor Adenauer was of the opinion that the bank's policy was too strict, whereas the ministers of economic affairs and of finance agreed with the central bank's view. Soon after the meeting, the latter two and the president of the central bank drafted a stabilization programme and presented that to the cabinet. Adenauer did not know about it. The next day the two ministers joined the central bank's council meeting. During this meeting, the central bank decided to increase the interest rate. Chancellor Adenauer was furious. In a speech to industrial interest groups, he attacked the two ministers and the central bank. This speech became known as the Gürzenich speech, since it was held in the Gürzenich hall in Cologne. At that point, public opinion turned against him. German newspapers and representatives of different interest groups chose to be on the side of the two ministers and the central bank. As a result, the Bank Act of 1957, which replaced the 1951 Transformation Act, did not affect the de facto autonomy of the central bank. The role of the *Landeszentralbanken* was reduced to local departments. The Bundesbank was taken into ownership by the federal government, which also received the seigniorage profits.

Since the Bundesbank had become more legally independent than Audenauer had in mind, he used his right to appoint a new president, Karl Blessing. This new president was supposed to stand closer to the industrial interest groups and thus to follow Adenauer's line more than the previous one had done. In his inaugural speech, Blessing made clear to the public that he would follow the policies of the previous president. This is an illustration of the attitude of later presidents. The president of the Bundesbank has often been someone who previously had a career outside the bank. Nonetheless, the strong organizational culture of the Bundesbank ensures that politically motivated appointees quickly become independent-minded presidents (Sturm, 1995: 35).

According to the law, the Bundesbank's main goal is 'safeguarding the currency' (Amtenbrink 1998: 196). Although this is a vague term, for many it means price stability in the sense of a low inflation rate (e.g., Sturm 1995: 30). When executing its policy, the bank should also take into account the effects on other policy areas: 'Without prejudice to the performance of its functions, the Deutsche Bundesbank is required to support the general economic policy of the government' (Bundesbank Gesetz, §12, cited in Amtenbrink 1998: 198). In 1967, these macroeconomic goals were defined in the Stability Act (Stabilitätsgesetz) as price stability, high rate of employment, foreign trade equilibrium, and steady and adequate economic growth. Hence, the Bundesbank can support government policy if this support does not jeopardize its main goal, that is, maintaining price stability. This order of priorities laid down in law, however, did not prevent conflicts arising between the Bundesbank and the government at times, in particular when it came to the question whether to change the parity of the Deutsche mark's exchange rate (see de Haan 2018: Section 5). Another conflict arose at the time of Germany's reunification. The Bundesbank regarded the one-to-one conversion rate between the Ost mark and the Deutsche mark unrealistic and too much in favour of the Ost mark. This conversion rate would undermine the competitiveness of the *Länder* in the former Deutsche Demokratische Republik (DDR). Over the years, the Bundesbank has gained respect among the German population. Before 1999, its independence was associated with the high value of the Deutsche mark and low inflation. For many these were symbols of Germany's economic success after the Second World War (*Wirtschaftswunder*).

During the Bretton Woods period that lasted until March 1973, the exchange rate of the Deutsche mark was pegged to the US dollar. At times, the Bundesbank had to impose monetary targets. It started with a point target in order to limit any perception that output could also be a final goal. After these point targets had been breached, the Bundesbank switched to publishing ranges (Houben 1999: 147). The method the Bundesbank used was very interesting: 'The calculation of the targets is public and explicitly takes into account the Bundesbank's long-term inflation goal, estimated potential output growth, and expected velocity trends, which are combined using the quantity-theory equation to determine the desired money growth' (Bernanke and Mishkin 1992: 200). Short-term considerations such as the unemployment rate were not formally included. Nevertheless, the implementation was flexible enough to take changes in these variables into account. The Bundesbank accepted deviations outside the target range of money growth. As a result, during some periods actual money growth was higher than its target (Houben 1999: Appendix VI). Exchange rate movements were often the reason for short-term deviations from the monetary target. A reason for this is the importance of the Deutsche mark's exchange rate for the German exporting sector (see Bernanke and Mishkin 1992: 202).

This brief description of the Bundesbank's history reveals that its authority is rooted in the population's preference for a stable currency, and this can most likely be explained by the period of hyperinflation of the 1920s (Issing 2005). In the 1950s, the authorities did not want an independent central bank as its policy might come into conflict with the government's policy. Moreover, no economic theory gave support to an independent central bank. The ordo-liberals, for example, found it important that the different policy areas supported each other, not that monetary policy should be independent from political influences (Bibow 2009). The population's reaction to Ardenauer's Gürzenich speech moved the balance towards an independent central bank. The 1967 Stabilitätsgesetz illustrates the German wish to balance the responsibilities between the different layers of the federal system, which can be characterized as 'co-operative federalism: separation of power and institutionalisation of joint responsibilities between different levels' (Quaglia 2008: 57).

9.4 Banque de France

The Banque de France was founded in 1800.[9] Its original charter gave it the status of a private bank and restricted its operation to Paris. Napoleon Bonaparte supported its foundation in order to seek a contribution to economic recovery and a source of lending to the treasury. In 1803, the Banque obtained the exclusive right to issue notes in Paris for the next 15 years. In 1806, the Banque's directors were unable to prevent a credit crisis and had to suspend the convertibility of its notes. For Napoleon, this opened an opportunity to put the Banque under the control of a governor and two deputy governors appointed by the head of state. During the nineteenth century, the note-issuing powers were increased. The bank's own rights were extended, and during the 1848 crisis it absorbed the remaining regional banks of issue so that it covered the whole of France.

In 1938, the Banque's judicial status was changed so that the government's influence was expanded at the expense of that of private interests. The representatives of the latter at times had had great influence on the policies of the Banque and even on the government. The new status removed the tie between the shareholders and the governor and deputy governor of the Banque. The government gained considerable influence over the bank, although the legal status remained that of a corporation under private law. On January 1, 1946, the bank was nationalized and the shares were transferred to the government. In large part, it continued to operate under the old statute until the implementation of the Bank Act 1973. From 1946 to 1973, the government had considerable influence over the bank's operations. This did not change under the Bank Act of 1973: the Banque de France executed the monetary policy of the French government (Amtenbrink 1998: 72).

The Bank Act was a compromise. The government personified by the minister of finance, Valéry Giscard d' Estaing, wanted to have full control of monetary policy, whereas the central bank was striving for its own independence. The bank remained very much dependent on the government, though the composition of the General Council changed. From this point, members were selected because of their competence, whereas previously they had been representing interest groups and in many cases did not have any financial expertise. On various occasions, the president of the central bank voiced his concern about price stability and the value of the currency to the government. However, he rarely made his opinion public and was replaced when he did, as in 1974 (Howarth 2009). As a result, the French share with the Americans a Keynesian view on monetary policy, which means a more expansionary monetary policy than that of Germany, where the Bundesbank had price stability as its singular objective (Brunnermeier *et al.* 2016: 250). The German position reflects its relatively high score on Long-Term Orientation (see Chapter 2: Table 2.1).

The French aversion to an independent central bank is in accordance with the dominant role that elected politicians play in the French system. The importance of this political elite corresponds with France's high score on Power Distance (see Chapter 2). According to Howarth (2009), at least four additional factors are important in explaining the French aversion to an independent central bank. First, the negative experience of an independent central bank just before the Second World War. As mentioned above, during that period the interests of the private sector dominated the central bank's policy and even, on occasion, that of the government. Secondly, the belief that monetary and fiscal policy should not be separated but should work in unison and thus be in the hands of one entity – the government. As the discussion of the other two central banks reveals, many share the opinion that monetary and fiscal policy should be coordinated. The third French objection against an independent central bank is that, in the French view, it is democratically elected politicians, guided by bureaucrats, who can obtain stability (see also Chapter 5). Finally, Howarth refers to the significant effect of opposition from the treasury, and in particular the network of graduates of the specialization *Inspecteurs des Finances* of the École National d'Administration.[10] They typically start their career at the ministry of finance and then move to top management roles in banking, among them the central bank, and later to top positions with industrial groups. In all likelihood, political motives also played a role in the decision to appoint Jean-Claude Trichet as governor in 1993 and Christian Noyer in 2003 (Howarth 2009). Both had served in ministerial cabinets in centre-right French governments and been educated at the École National d'Administration. This French hostility to an independent central bank made it difficult for them to accept the independence of the European Central Bank: '[f]or France, accepting the Bundesbank model was a major concession' (Szász 1999: 147).

The French central bank directly controlled the supply of funds to the banks via its refinancing facilities in the 1960s, and by credit restrictions from 1973 to the mid-1980s. Until 1990, France frequently used capital control in order to shield the economy from foreign influences (see Chapter 7). After the U-turn in the policy of March 1983, French monetary policy changed towards maintaining a fixed exchange rate with the Deutsche mark. As did the other central banks, from the mid-1970s France targeted monetary aggregates. From 1977, it publicly announced these targets (Houben 1999: 142). Different monetary aggregates have been used. The central bank started by using M2, but during a few years in the 1980s and from 1991 onwards it used M3 (idem, Appendix V). This change from M2 to M3 was motivated by the instability of M2. It was financial innovations resulting from the removal of quantitative credit controls and the abolishment of capital controls that caused this instability (see also Chapter 7). After a pronounced velocity shock in 1996, the definitions of the monetary aggregates were vague.

9.5 The European Central Bank

A few months after the fall of the Berlin Wall, during a meeting of heads of states and ministers of foreign affairs, the German Chancellor Helmut Kohl expressed his desire for a united Germany.[11] Many of the other heads of states did not appreciate a large Germany in the centre of Europe, as they feared that it would become too dominant. Kohl, however, was very persistent and emotional about his request; a united Germany had always been the ultimate goal of his political career, he claimed. Mitterrand felt that the discussion could go nowhere and suggested a break during which he talked with Helmuth Kohl. After the break, Mitterrand announced that Kohl and he had reached a Historical Compromise. France would accept a united Germany and in exchange Germany would stop its opposition to a common currency. This move by Kohl to accept a common currency surprised many, including his own advisers. For the German population giving up the Deutsch mark for a common currency felt like a sacrifice. The Deutsch mark and the independent Bundesbank were the symbols of Germany's post-war success. Consequently, Kohl could accept a common currency if its central bank were as independent as the Bundesbank. Moreover, at that time, the 1990s, many regarded an independent central bank as a guarantee of low inflation. Since the Bundesbank was already very independent, only a few and minor changes in the law had to be implemented.

For France an independent central bank was much more difficult to swallow. This started to become evident during the law-making process. The French Constitutional Council blocked the proposal in 1993 on the basis that the Constitution did not allow the delegation of policymaking power to an independent institution. The support of three-fifths of the members of both chambers was needed to amend the Constitution. In addition, French law did not contain the core elements of an independent central bank, namely that the government is not allowed to give instructions on monetary policy and that the bank should strive for price stability. In the end the fact that these provisions were not included did not have any effect, as they were part of the Maastricht Treaty, which had already been signed by the French government (Howarth 2009).

In the years after the formal independence of the Banque de France, that is, since about 1993, leading politicians repeatedly criticized and 'scapegoated' the Banque de France and the ECB for French economic difficulties (Howarth

2009; van Esch and de Jong 2013), or argued for more *room de manoeuver* for national governments (Howarth 2007). The French resistance to an independent central bank is nicely illustrated by a quote from President Chirac of May 1998. Chirac wanted Duisenberg, who had been selected as the first president of the ECB, to sign saying that he would step down after four years. That would introduce the possibility of the French candidate Trichet succeeding Duisenberg in January 2002. As such, this request went against the idea of an independent central banker who serves a long term in order to prevent political influence. Duisenberg agreed to sign to the effect that he would not serve the entire term of eight years, but he refused to announce a date on which he would step down. This upset Chirac who declared '*Je ne me laisse pas faire chanter par un petit fonctionnaire*' (I don't let myself be blackmailed by a little civil servant) (de Haas and van Lotringen 2003: 25). This '*un petit fonctionnaire*' illustrates the French idea that, ultimately, decisions had to be taken by elected politicians. Hence, decisions by non-elected officials, or those taken automatically according to preset rules, are unthinkable for the French.

The opposition to automatic rules without political interference came to the fore in October 2010. At that time, the Euro-member states were negotiating more strict conditions within the Stability and Growth Pact (SGP) in order to prevent government debt from once again increasing to unacceptable levels. Germany had already enacted its own rule on debt brake *Schuldenbremse* in 2009. The proposal was to establish a similar procedure in Europe. This would entail the European Commission automatically imposing fines of up to 0.2% of GDP on countries breaching the SGP's debt and deficit rules. Only a qualified majority of the EU governments could reverse the Commission's decision. This rule-based mechanism was suggested in order to stop the political barter that had previously characterized European decision-making and thus undermined its credibility. Germany was among the most fervent defenders of this automatic mechanism, whereas the French supported it only half-heartedly. The then French minister of finance, Christine Lagarde, accurately summarized the French position during a meeting of the taskforce chaired by van Rompuy on October 18, 2010. In her view, the rules to be agreed upon referred to economic governance, and the word 'governance' originates from the Latin word 'governare' which means to rule. Ruling belongs to politics. Hence, the beginning and the end of economic governance has to be political and thus automatic sanctions cannot be implemented since, according to her, they disregard the essential role to be played by politicians (Bohn and de Jong 2011: 13).[12]

Whereas French politicians, sometimes joined by Italy's prime minister, Berlusconi, had problems with the independence of the ECB, its automatic sanctions, and its anti-inflationary policy, the Germans (and Dutch) had problems when these – for them – crucial characteristics of the ECB came under fire. This was the case in 2010. On this occasion, Sarkozy urged the ECB to follow the example of the US Federal Reserve System and buy government bonds. In the case of the ECB, this would mean Greek bonds. The German chancellor

Merkel and the Dutch government joined ECB President Trichet in denouncing the French calls as a direct violation of the ECB's independence. Shortly afterwards, the ECB's Governing Council introduced the Securities Market Programme (SMP) that was intended to ensure depth and liquidity in malfunctioning segments of the debt and securities markets. In practice, it implied that the ECB would buy Greek government bonds. This decision, which according to Trichet was made entirely autonomously from French pressures, elicited fierce criticism from the president of the Bundesbank, Axel Weber. In his eyes, the ECB interventions constituted a form of quantitative easing which, in his view, is a direct violation of the Maastricht Treaty. Moreover, he argued: 'But the SMP risks blurring the different responsibilities between fiscal and monetary policy. As the risks associated with the SMP outweigh its benefits, these securities purchases should now be phased out permanently as part of our non-standard policy measures' (Weber 2010: 2). It was widely speculated that it was these interventions that led to the resignation of Weber. In August 2011, the ECB went even further and bought up Italian and Spanish bonds pre-emptively in an attempt to prevent their borrowing costs from spiralling out of control. Again this led to a wave of criticism from the German political and financial elite, and the resignation of the German member of the ECB Executive Board, Jürgen Stark (Young and Semmler 2011). Weidmann, the successor of Weber, raised similar concerns when in March 2016 he said: 'this [government bond purchases] will lead to a dangerous commingling of monetary and fiscal policy' (Weidmann 2016). The quotes from speeches by Weber and Weidmann illustrate that in the German worldview, each institution has its own responsibilities and one should not mix these responsibilities.

This division of responsibilities also holds internationally. Each government is responsible for its own behaviour and thus also for its own finances. The no-bail-out clause in the Maastricht Treaty reflects this view. In addition, private actors are responsible for their behaviour and therefore should not be bailed out. These principles explain why in 2010 Merkel was against a European solution for the Greek crisis and in favour of private sector involvement.[13] A European solution would have meant the other members of the euro-area sharing part of Greece's debt. Moreover, in the German view, taking over the responsibilities (in this case, debt) of one country might create expectations that in the future these governments would again be willing to step in. In their view, the resulting moral hazard would increase the chance of a new crisis in the future. Once again, this German focus on the long-term consequences of policy reflects its high score on Long-Term Orientation (Table 2.1).

The French hold the opposite view. It was their opinion that the members of the euro-area had to solve the Greek problem themselves. The European elite should solve European problems just as the French elite solves French problems (see France's high score on Power Distance in Table 2.10). The French solution would imply a way of sharing Greece's debt among the member states and not require the involvement of the International Monetary Fund (IMF). Moreover, they were concerned that matters could become worse if the crisis were not solved swiftly. They did not share German worries about moral hazards.

The typical German approach came to the fore in July 2015. The Greek government had organized a referendum with respect to the requests of the troika.[14] By far the majority of the voters had rejected the troika's proposals, so the Greek government came up with alternative proposals. The then German finance minister Wolfgang Schäuble presented a non-paper in which he suggested that in the event that Greece could not guarantee debt sustainability and credible implementation of the troika's proposal upfront, then it should be offered a timeout from the eurozone. During this period of at least five years, it should obtain debt restructuring. This timeout solution should be accompanied by growth-enhancing, humanitarian and technical assistance provided by the EU over the following years. In Schäuble's view, 'only this way forward could allow for sufficient debt restructuring, which would not be in line with the membership in a monetary union'.[15] His position clearly illustrates the German attitude that a member of a club has to adhere to the rules of the club. A nice example in everyday life is the distinction between the people who are allowed to say 'du' to someone and those who are not. Of course within the members of the eurozone, these differences are too subtle, so Schäuble's proposal did not obtain any support.

This brief description of some events during the first two decades of the ECB illustrates that deeply embedded national culture and economic ideas about the role of monetary authorities still play an important role. An important difference between the two main players, Germany and France, is the extent to which the public at large accepts differences in political power and wealth. Hofstede's Power Distance represents this characteristic (see Table 2.1). De Jong (2002a) found that within a group of OECD countries, Germany and France were at the two extremes of this dimension. In de Jong (2002b), he already warned that these differences could lead to a clash of cultures within the ECB and thus to difficulties at the time crises would emerge. Persistence of these differences is found in a study of the European national central banker's opinions on central bank independence (van Esch and de Jong 2019). Another relevant aspect is the relative importance German players attach to future consequences (the issue of moral hazard). This is reflected in their relatively high score on Long-Term Orientation (see Table 2.1). This focus on the long-term consequences is also in accordance with the fact that the ordoliberals are the only academic school that explicitly pays attention to the long-term consequences of markets (see Chapter 4).

9.6 Conclusions

This chapter describes the history of central bank independence and monetary policy in the United States, Germany, and France. It appeared that until the 1970s–1980s no theory pleaded in favour of a central bank that could act independently and, under certain circumstances, against fiscal policy. It seems that the common view of academics was that the two fields of economic policy should operate in unison and hence that government should also be involved in monetary policy. An important insight of the 1960s was that fiscal policy was effective in reducing unemployment and monetary policy in controlling inflation. This did not mean that they should operate independently. The position of economists with respect to independent central banks changed simultaneously, or after Volcker's successful anti-inflation policy. In 1985, Rogoff published a well-known paper in which he pleaded for a conservative central banker who had a higher preference for fighting inflation than the population at large. In this paper, Rogoff applied the concept of time inconsistency, developed in the 1970s, to monetary policy. The argument became that rational agents would foresee that politicians would not adhere to their promise of a low inflation and hence these agents would expect a high rate of inflation and act upon that expectation. In order to break this vicious circle, one needed an outsider: the independent central banker. These theoretical developments were inspired by the inability of the authorities to reduce inflation and unemployment in the 1970s, the period of stagflation.

Despite this lack of a theoretical foundation for an independent central bank, in the 1950s the FED and the Bundesbank acquired a high degree of independence. In the United States, the independence was a result of an agreement between the treasury and the FED and it meant independence from the president. The FED does not operate independently from Congress. 'Congress is our boss', according to former chair Bernanke.[16] In Germany, support at all levels of the population backed the move to independence. This support was associated with a wish for price stability. An independent central bank could prevent a government from spending its way out of political problems. Many regard this widely held preference for price stability to be rooted in the devastating experience of the period of hyperinflation of the 1920s.[17]

The aims of the central banks differ. Among these three central banks, the Bundesbank's stands out as the only one that has price stability as its single goal. The other two central banks focus more on the short term. The FED has a broad mandate and thus has to make a choice between economic growth and price stability. In the French case, the Banque de France was highly dependent on the minister of finance and thus had to implement the monetary policy preferred by the politicians, who mostly have a short-term time horizon. The German focus on the long term is in accordance with Germany's score on Long-Term Orientation and the ordoliberals' focus on long-term consequences of economic policy. Its pragmatic implementation of monetary policy resonates with the ordoliberals' 'open-minded, non-dogmatic form of liberalism' (Chapter 4). The fact that American monetary policy is often focused on the short term is not directly in conflict with the free market theory as described in Chapter 3. It corresponds with the short-term orientation of the American culture (see Table 2.1). One can also argue that it compensates for the weak social security system. In times of economic downturn, monetary and fiscal policy have to provide a shield for the weak.

Since the inception of the Economic and Monetary Union (EMU), the French and Germans have had to cooperate in a common institute, the ECB. We have argued that the national differences in attitude towards independent non-elected officials and in their views on the preferred monetary policy still exist. There are also no signs that the differences are reducing any. Embeddedness cannot easily be swept away. The best solution, then, is to be prepared and where possible to take action before a crisis erupts.

Notes

1 See Binder and Spindel (2017: 62–79) for more details.
2 Binder and Spindel (2017) argue in various places that the fact that many parts of the country were represented by means of the District Reserve banks has helped the Fed to protect its position.
3 The Treasury - Federal Reserve Accord consists of the following statement:

> The Treasury and the Federal Reserve System have reached full accord with respect to debt management and monetary policies to be pursued in furthering their common purpose to assure the successful financing of the Government's requirements and, at the same time, to minimize monetization of the public debt.
>
> (Conti-Brown, 2016: 35)

4 https://www.federalreserve.gov/aboutthefed/section2a.htm, consulted at January 14, 2020.
5 Time inconsistency arises when agents know at forehand that a decision-maker, especially a policymaker, prefers one policy in advance but later has incentives to enact a different one. Note that Volcker's policy preceded Rogoff's paper on the conservative central banker. Theory seems to have followed practice in this regard.
6 This division into three periods can be found in Reinhart and Rogoff (2013).
7 'Congress is our boss', according to Ben Bernanke (Binder and Spindel, 2017: 26).
8 The history before the Second World War is based on De Haan (2018).
9 The description of the Banque de France's history is based on Serre and Cobham (1992) and Amtenbrink (1998: 69–78).
10 See Chapter 5 for the role of the *Grandes écoles* and the economic engineers.
11 A brief description of this meeting is on the website of the then Belgian minister of foreign affairs, Mark Eyskens; www.eyskens.com – Een historisch compromise (A Historical Compromise).
12 This French position is also nicely illustrated by the next quote from the French economist Thomas Piketty: 'The idea that it might be preferable to replace democratic decision making with rigid and automatic rules expresses a nihilist disillusionment with democracy (which no historical experience justifies)' (Piketty 2020: 912).
13 See Brunnermeier *et al.* (2016: 29–33) for a description of the Deauville agreement in which Merkel and Sarkozy agreed upon private sector involvement.
14 The troika consisted of representatives of the IMF, the ECB, and the European Commission. It regularly investigated whether the Greek government implemented policies as agreed upon in the different programmes.
15 The full text of this part of the German comments on the Greek proposal is:

> In case, debt sustainability and a credible implementation perspective cannot be ensured upfront, Greece should be offered swift negotiations on a time-out from the Eurozone, with possible debt restructuring. If necessary, in a Paris Club-like format over at least the next 5 years. Only this way forward could allow for suf-

ficient debt restructuring, which would not be in line with the membership in a monetary union (Art. 125 TFEU). The time-out solution should be accompanied by supporting Greece as an EU-member and the Greek people with growth enhancing, humanitarian and technical assistance over the next years. The time-out solution should also be accompanied by streamlining all pillars of the Economic and Monetary Union and concrete measures to strengthen the governance of the Eurozone.

(Grexit, Bundesregierung non-paper, July 10, 2015; https://www.auditamosgrecia.org/wp-content/uploads/2015/07/grexit_bundesregierung_non_paper_10_juli_2015.pdf.

16 The quote is from Bernanke's Press Conference at December 18, 2013, and can be found on page 29 of the corresponding transcript. file://cnas.ru.nl/U402107/Documents/My%20Documents/Templeton/monetary%20policy%20and%20Fin%20systems/FOMCpresconf20131218.pdf

17 See Taylor (2013) for an extensive description of this period and the consequences of hyperinflation for the German middle class.

References

Amtenbrink, F. (1998) *The Democratic Accountability of Central Banks: The European Central Bank in the Light of Its Peers*, Ph.D. thesis, Groningen: University of Groningen.

Berger, H. and J. de Haan (1999) A state within a state?: An event study of the Bundesbank, 1948–1973, *Scottish Journal of Political Economy* 46(1): 17–39.

Bernanke, B. and F. Mishkin (1992) Central bank behavior and the strategy of monetary policy: Observations from six industrial countries. In O. J. Blanchard and S. Fischer (eds.), *NBER Macroeconomics Annual* 1992, 7: 183–238.

Bibow, J. (2009) On the origin and rise of central bank independence in Germany, *The European Journal of the History of Economic Thought* 16(1): 155–190.

Binder, S. and M. Spindel (2017) *The Myth of Independence: How Congress Governs the Federal Reserve*, Princeton, NJ and Oxford: Princeton University Press.

Bohn, F. and E. de Jong (2011) The 2010 euro crisis stand-off between France and Germany: Leadership styles and political culture, *International Economics and Economic Policy* 8(1): 7–14.

Brunnermeier, M. K., H. James and J.-P. Landau (2016) *The Euro and the Battle of Ideas*, Princeton, NJ: Princeton University Press.

Conti-Brown, P. (2016) *The Power and Independence of the Federal Reserve*, Princeton, NJ: Princeton University Press.

De Haan, J. (2018) The struggle of German central banks to maintain price stability. In R. Edvinsson, T. Jacobsen and D. Waldenström (eds.), *Sveriges Riksbank and the History of Central Banking*, Cambridge: Cambridge University Press: 388–417.

De Haas, B. and C. van Lotringen (2003) *Wim Duisenberg: Van Friese volksjongen tot Mr. Euro (Wim Duisenberg: From Frisian Folk Boy to Mr. Euro)*, Amsterdam: Uitgeverij Business Contact.

De Jong, E. (2002a) Why are price stability and statutory independence of central banks negatively correlated?: The role of culture, *European Journal of Political Economy* 18(4): 675–694.

De Jong, E. (2002b) De ECB onder vuur: een botsing van culturen? (The ECB under attack: A clash of cultures?), *Tijdschrift voor Politieke Economie* 23(4): 20–40.

Houben, A. C. F. J. (1999) *The Evolution of Monetary Policy Strategies in Europe*, PhD thesis, Groningen: University of Groningen.

Howarth, D. J. (2007) Making and breaking the rules: French policy on EU 'gouvernement économique', *Journal of European Public Policy* 14(7): 1061 –1078.

Howarth, D. J. (2009) Bank of France: The challenge of escaping politicization. In K. Dyson and M. Marcussen (eds.), *Central Banks in the Age of the Euro: Europeanization, Convergence, and Power*, Oxford: Oxford University Press: 111–129.

Issing, O. (2005) Why did the great inflation not happen in Germany? *Federal Reserve Bank of St. Louis Review* 87(2): 329–336.

Kydland, F. E. and E. C. Prescott (1977) Rules rather than discretion: The inconsistency of optimal plans, *Journal of Political Economy* 85(3): 473–491.

Quaglia, L. (2008) *Central Banking Governance in the European Union: A Comparative Analysis*, London: Routledge.

Piketty, T. (2020) *Capital and Ideology*, Cambridge, MA: The Belknap Press of Harvard University Press.

Rajan, R. J. (2005) *Has financial development made the world riskier?*, NBER Working Paper Series no. 11728, Cambridge, MA: National Bureau of Economic Research.

Reinhart, C. M. and K. Rogoff (2013) Shifting mandates: The Federal Reserve's first centennial, *The American Economic Review Papers and Proceeding* 103(3): 48–54.

Rogoff, K. (1985) The optimal degree of commitment to an intermediate monetary target, *Quarterly Journal of Economics* 100(4): 1169–1189.

Serre, J.-M. and D. Cobham (1992) Banque de France. In J. Eatwell, M. Milgate and P. Newman (eds.), *The New Palgrave Dictionary on Money and Finance, Part 3*, London: Macmillan: 177–180.

Sturm, R. (1995) How independent is the Bundesbank? *German Politics* 4(1): 27–41.

Szász, A. (1999) *The Road to European Monetary Union*, London: Macmillan.

Taylor, F. (2013) *The Downfall of Money: Germany's Hyperinflation and the Destruction of the Middle Class*, New York: Bloomsbury Press.

Van Esch, F. A. W. J. and E. de Jong (2013) Institutionalisation without internalisation. The cultural dimension of French-German conflicts on European Central Bank independence, *International Economics and Economic Policy* 10(4): 631–648.

Van Esch, F. A. W. J. and E. de Jong (2019) National culture trumps EU socialization: The European central bankers' views of the Euro crisis, *Journal of European Public Policy* 26(2): 169–187.

Weber, A. (2010) *Monetary Policy After the Crisis – A European Perspective*, keynote speech at the Shadow Open Market Committee Symposium, New York City, October 12.

Weidman, J. (2016) *A Look at the Euro Area from a Central Bank Perspective*, keynote at the Second Finance Forum, Vaduz, Liechtenstein, March 23.

Young, B. and W. Semmler (2011) The European sovereign debt crisis. Is Germany to blame? *German Politics and Society* 29(1): 1–24.

Part IV

Concluding remarks

10 Conclusions and discussion

Eelke de Jong

10.1 Introduction

In this volume, we have discussed economic ideas on markets and competition, and related these to national cultures and policies in three countries: the United States of America, Germany, and France. Although we are aware that one cannot relate every single policy measure to an underlying value or economic theory, our starting point has been that the economic theories, national culture, and policy measures are related. In general, policy is embedded in values held by the majority of the population. Since economists are human beings and are influenced by the same value system as their fellow citizens, economic theory is also expected to reflect the same set of values. The three views on the market are that of the free market, the coordinated market (ordoliberal), and the hierarchical market. The population of the United States and its policies are assumed to reflect the preferences and practices of a free market economy. Germany represents a coordinated market economy, and France a hierarchical market economy.

We link the three parts of the book in this concluding chapter. The next section summarizes the main elements of the three theories. Section 10.3 briefly describes the context within which each of these theories has been developed. The subsequent sections summarize the findings as follows: with respect to the individual and the market (Section 10.4); hierarchy (Section 10.5); time preference (Section 10.6); and uncertainty (Section 10.7). Section 10.8 discusses the performance of the United States, Germany, and France on income and wealth, education, and health. Section 10.9 concludes with a general discussion.

10.2 The three economic ideas

The free market view sees competition as good in itself. In Chapter 3, Candela contrasts catallactic competition with non-catallactic competition. Catallactic is derived from the Greek verb *katallattein*, which means 'to exchange', 'to admit into the community', and 'to change from enemy into friend.' These meanings nicely express the idea that the adherents of free markets see markets as places of voluntary exchange that benefit both parties and thus can generate

DOI: 10.4324/9781003208549-10

friendship. Non-catallactic competition is based upon legal status and privilege. Catallactic competition, which corresponds with the free market view, liberates the individual from arbitrary assignments of resources and income based on gender, race, or legal status. Non-catallactic competition restricts the individual from self-actualization by means of arbitrary assignments. The government must guarantee a legal system with well-defined and well-enforced exchangeable private property rights.

The ordoliberal view provides the theoretical foundation of the coordinated market economy. Ordoliberals do not emphasize free exchange as the free market theorists do, but the peaceful coexistence of free individuals within a functional legal order (Fritz and Goldschmidt in Chapter 4). They see the disadvantages of concentration of power, with respect to both private agents and government. One must find the right balance between the concentrations of power with each of these agents. This explicit consideration of the distribution of power and a concern about the effects of the economic process are the most important distinctions between the ordoliberal and the free market school.

For the French economists of the economic engineering tradition, competition is favoured because, in theory, it can deliver optimal results. The theoretical insights derived from mathematical models of market competition can be used for policy advice to governments and regulators. In this way, economists can calculate the prices to be set by providers of public goods such as water and electricity. The contracts should reflect the conditions that would be optimal under free competition. This does not imply that the actual economy must be organized as a free market, but only that those who are in power must set prices that would also have been arrived at under market competition.

10.3 The context

The ideas of economists on markets and competition presented in the previous section are quite diverse, and differences in historical circumstances offer an important explanation for each of these views. In particular, the Second World War is a key factor in explaining the three different views on the market economy that are considered in this volume. This war was fought, among others, on French and German soil. The United States was an important partner of the Allies, but the North American continent was only marginally part of the battlefield. The war also did not originate in the United States. Japan bombed the United States into the war, one could say. Moreover, there was no change of political regime and the incumbent was not replaced because of its role during the war. These facts might explain why no pressure for a fundamental change in the economic order was felt in the United States. Consequently, there was no need to find another theoretical concept. The discussion on market economies continued. This discussion had started already in 1776 when the *Wealth of Nations*, written by Adam Smith, was published. As the quotes in Chapter 3 illustrate, the authors of the free market tradition are mainly concerned with unjust privileges and restrictions that are harmful to the poor and non-white ethnic groups. Government intervention always favours one group so that it becomes a source of inequality. The free market economists therefore plead for an institutional set-up in which the government 'enforces *exchangeable private property rights*' (Candela: Chapter 3).

Matters were quite different for Germany, the originator of the Second World War. From the moment that Hitler acquired power in 1933, the Nazi regime started centralizing the economy. The state obtained a central role in directing the economy, which at the end of the war was a command economy. For some German economists, the Nazis' rise to power was the impetus to redirect their work and focus on the link between freedom and the economy. The *Freiburg Schule* and Walter Eucken were prominent in this process. After the war, these economists helped in organizing the German economy and proclaimed the social market economy. According to Ludwig Erhard, the economy must be liberated from governmental orders and the red tape of the ever-swelling bureaucracy.[1] The market is the structure that can limit the powers of both a powerful and large government and that of large companies. Many ordoliberals favoured small companies. Moreover, for ordoliberals some form of material equality is seen as necessary for the beneficial functioning of a market.

> All in all, they thought that a society producing extremely non-egalitarian outcomes, and even more so starting positions, will, apart from being less desirable from a normative viewpoint, also create problems for the long-term viability of a market order and a free society.
>
> (Fritz and Goldschmidt: Chapter 4)

The French experience is a continuation of a trend towards greater centralization of power. Before the Second World War, the French economy was freer and more like a market economy than the German economy. In some areas even more market oriented than the US economy. For example, in 1913, the French stock market capitalization to GDP ratio was twice that of the United States (Rajan and Zingales 2003: Table 3). This illustrates that at that time, financial markets were more important in France than in the United States. During the 1930s, criticism arose about the behaviour of the private sector. Many felt, for instance, that the private banks had too much influence on the French central bank's monetary policy. After the war, the French moved towards a highly regulated economic system. Economists became instrumental in implementing the government's policy. The theories described in Chapter 5 helped the state in finding an efficient solution in cases where no actual market was operating.

10.4 The view on the individual and the market

Although on a worldwide scale these three countries are quite individualistic, the three traditions take different views on the individual. The individual's freedom to act is held in high regard in the free market tradition. The exchange of goods and services is between independent persons, who voluntarily participate in the transaction. Each individual enters a transaction in order to realize a certain goal (preference). The counterpart judges the offer being made based on the characteristics relevant to him or her. Since the exchange is voluntary, each partner can decide whether to participate or not. In this way, individuals can realize their potential, if the government protects property rights. The concentration of power on the demand or supply side will hamper a fair process and a fair deal. This explains a preference for markets consisting of a large number of relatively small agents. In the United States, this meant a preference for unit banking. Every bank has only one branch in one city. It also explains why the United States was among the first countries to introduce competition law enforcement, the Sherman Act, to reduce the power of large firms.[2] Competition is essential for a fair exchange and hence should be preserved at all costs. In the 1930s, competition was thought to have become 'ruinous' in the United States. Regulation was implemented to restrict free competition in order to save competition. In sum, in the free market tradition the individual can realize his or her potential if the government protects property rights and prohibits concentration. The latter two, protection of property rights and lack of concentration, are prerequisites for the well-functioning of markets and the self-realization of individuals. Market institutions will teach the participants to behave properly: the *doux commerce* hypothesis.

The ordoliberal view extends these economic prerequisites with cultural or moral norms. One of these preconditions is that the population has a basic knowledge of economic processes so that they know what they do when entering transactions. The government must stimulate economic education. Moreover, whereas free market economists concentrate on equality in opportunities for individuals, the ordoliberals add equality in outcomes. They are in favour of a redistribution of income and wealth and some of them suggest a prohibitively high inheritance tax to fight the concentration of wealth. In their view, an extremely non-egalitarian society is undesirable because, in the long term, it will undermine the market order and a free society. Therefore, the ordoliberals share the idea with the adherents of the free market ideology that the best economic order is one in which individuals are free to act. However, they differ in that these individuals must possess economic knowledge and that the government must intervene to redistribute income and wealth.

The hierarchical view differs from the previous two in that the market is not necessarily real. Theories about the functioning of markets are instruments for economic planning. Market principles determine the prices set by the authorities. The market itself is not a coordination mechanism constituted of a set of small independent entities as in the other two streams. Coordination is more a social contract according to which the elite provides the necessary goods and services. In this view, the elite must take care of the population at large. Of course, the best the elite can do is to implement policies that use scarce resources in an efficient way. Economic theory about markets can help in this respect. The preference of the individual and his or her freedom is implicit. It is assumed that the consumers appreciate an efficient allocation by the state and prefer a Keynesian type of demand policy.[3]

Various studies on cross-country differences in values find that the relative importance of the individual versus the group is the first and most important value that differentiates societies. On the one side are societies in which the individual is less important than the group. The latter can be large or be restricted to an extended family. Many countries in Asia and Latin America belong to this collectivistic group. All Western societies score high on the Individualism scale, which means that the interest of the individual prevails over that of the group. The United States has the highest score, whereas France and Germany are number 15 and 20 out of 91 countries. America's high score on Individualism corresponds with the important role individual agents play in the free market view. Both the free market economists and the ordoliberals see the individual as the core agent in the economy.

10.5 Hierarchy

The attitude towards concentration of power is another value often found in cross-country studies. With it goes a willingness to delegate power and to cooperate. Cooperation and willingness to delegate are high in countries where people consider a concentration of power as bad. The various indicators consistently show that the French population sees a concentration of power and wealth as a more natural state than the inhabitants of the other two countries do. This attitude is accompanied by a large difference between social classes, in particular between the elite and large parts of the population. The elite is expected to take care of the others and be generous to them. In a survey about virtues organized in eight industrial countries, the French respondents were the only ones who mentioned 'generosity' as an important virtue (van Oudenhoven *et al.* 2014 and Chapter 2). They even regarded it as the most important one. In France, the elite consists of political leaders. Elected politicians are in charge and non-elected specialists or civil servants are unimportant as decision-makers.

Several places in this volume bring forward the idea that in France a concentration of power in the hands of a few is acceptable. After the Second World War, the state became the principal agent in the economy, both as the regulator and often also as the owner of firms. The French economic engineers use the idea of a market equilibrium in order to facilitate the state in its task of setting prices. French politics prefers national champions: large companies that are partly owned by the government. Moreover, the alumni of the *Grandes écoles* easily exchange membership of the board of these (private) companies with leading positions in the administration or politics. At the beginning of the 1980s, the financial sector was so tightly regulated that the sector no longer functioned and a restructuring was needed. The French president at that time, Mitterrand, had no intention of privatizing the financial sector nor leaving reform to private forces. Instead, his government nationalized all the banks and implemented a restructuring of the banking sector under the guidance of the ministry of finance. Some years later, this ministry also took the lead in organizing an exchange for derivative products. During the European sovereign debt crisis, the French government wanted to implement a European solution, without IMF involvement. As well as revealing an Anglo-Saxon antipathy, this preference also reflects the French attitude that a problem must be solved by the government (elite).

Of course, tensions arise if problems are not solved, or if the majority of the population does not agree with the solution suggested. The distance between the different classes makes finding a solution cooperatively rather difficult. The hostile attitude of trade unions and employers' associations towards each other is an example of this lack of cooperation. The Yellow Vests movement that started in 2018 is also an expression of the French social cleavage. Although similar movements exist in other European countries, the French Yellow Vests movement is much more violent and persistent.

The other two traditions have a much more egalitarian view on society. As described in Section 10.2, these traditions have the individual in high regard. The United States is extreme in both its high appreciation of the individual and its aversion to a concentration of power. The latter is nicely illustrated by a quote from the United States' former president, John Quincy Adams: 'Power for good, is power for evil even in the hands of Omnipotence' (cited in Timberlake 1993: 39). The aversion to a concentration of power is reflected in the policy of keeping banks small; ideally a bank only has a branch in one city (unit banking). The American competition policy is also directed at reducing the might of large companies. In principle, the state (neither federal nor individual state) does not own companies. An exception to this are Fanny Mae and Freddy Mac, two government-sponsored private enterprises that operate on the secondary market for mortgages. Since the credit crisis, these companies have been fully owned by the federal government. Although in principle the United States is characterized by an aversion to concentration of power, in practice, companies can be very large. This reflects an emphasis on equality of opportunity and a neglect of equality of outcomes. Moreover, large companies finance lobby activities and political parties so that they can unduly influence policy, including competition policy (Philippon 2019).

Germany takes the middle position when it comes to the concentration of power and hierarchy. It shares with the United States a focus on the individual. Like the United States, it is a federal state with a delicate balance of power between the *Länder* and the federal state (*Bund*). Although companies are private, the government can have a stake in firms (Volkswagen, for example). The *Sparkassen* are owned by the local government and operate in predesigned regions. Local politicians often play an important role in these banks' supervisory boards. Moreover, the government plays an active role in negotiations between trade unions and representatives of the employers.

10.6 Time preference

Differences in time preference are another important distinction in values between people of various countries. It refers to the wish to consume now (low score on Hofstede's Long-Term Orientation) and a willingness to postpone consumption (high score on this cultural dimension). Inhabitants of countries that score high on Long-Term Orientation save more and care more about the consequences of present action in the long term. Of the countries considered, Germany has the highest score on Long-Term Orientation whereas the United States has the lowest. This orientation in the long term is also found in the ordoliberals' argument that extremely non-egalitarian outcomes will create problems for the long-term viability of a market order and a free society. The German attempt at fostering a stability culture also reflects the concern for consequences in the long run. Long-term relationships between different agents are appreciated. A relatively large proportion of the workers will be employed with the same firm for a long time. This trend is reinforced by the German educational systems, which, via vocational training, focus on specific skills. The resulting high level of specialization hampers workers when they want to change jobs. The opposite holds for the United States. The American educational system emphasizes acquiring general skills, and employees easily switch jobs and even switch between different types of industry.

The difference between the German and American financial system also illustrates the differences in time orientation. The important role given to financial markets in the United States results in an at-arm's-length relationship. Consequently, partners can choose to engage in such relationships only for a short period. Since the mid-1990s, Germany has moved towards a more market-based financial system. However, it still has many characteristics that are typical of a bank-based system, such as long-standing relationships between local banks and their customers. Local firms finance their activities by means of bank loans. When their owners become rich, they remain with this local bank for the management of their assets. As mentioned in Chapter 7, it is difficult for outsiders to acquire a share of this private asset management.

The difference in time orientation between Germany and France came to the fore during the European sovereign debt crisis. In the discussions around finding a solution to this crisis, Germany always stressed the consequences of a solution for moral hazard; a possible effect that could occur in the long term. France, on the other hand, emphasized the importance of solving the present crisis in order to prevent the next one from happening.

10.7 Uncertainty

The attitude towards uncertainty is an important factor in explaining differences between industrialized countries (de Jong 2009: Chapter 5). Uncertainty, here, is Knightian uncertainty; that is, an event's outcome, as well as its distribution, is unknown. Psychologists use the term 'ambiguity' for this phenomenon. Hofstede's Uncertainty Avoidance measures the degree to which a country's population accepts ambiguity. In Chapter 2, we argued that uncertainty can be approached in three ways: acceptance, reducing it by means of rules, or reducing uncertainty by means of delegating authority to another who will reduce it for us. Uncertainty is high in a full-fledged free market economy. The argument is that uncertainty is accepted in the free market economy (the United States), reduced by means of rules in a coordinated market economy (Germany), and reduced by means of delegation of power to an elite in a hierarchical market economy (France).

Indeed, the theory of free markets stresses the possibility for individuals to realize themselves and does not pay much attention to the consequences of the market process. The focus is on the voluntary exchange between equivalent partners. No partner has a larger say than the others and no government rules should be implemented that change the natural position of individuals. So, implicitly, the two ways of reducing uncertainty are rejected. Consequently, the free market theorists accept uncertainty. In practice, it means that in the United States many sectors are organized as markets. Investors invest a relatively large share of their portfolio in equity or start-ups (venture capital). Employees can easily be fired. The exception to the aversion to government intervention is in the field of competition law, which originates in the desire to reduce the power of dominant firms.

The ordoliberals emphasize 'the necessity of basic principles for the establishment of an economic order which must be created and maintained by the state as a *legal framework* in order to guarantee a free, prosperous and humane society' (Fritz and Goldschmidt in Chapter 4, italics added). The phrase 'legal framework' illustrates the importance Germans pay to the law and adhering to rules. Note that the difference with the other two countries does not refer to the fact that Germany has more or better regulation. No, the difference concerns attitude towards these rules, the importance they have when decisions are being made. The German preference for adhering to rules and their prominence in the German mindset is very evident when it comes to European cooperation. When problems within the framework of European monetary coordination occur, Germans tend to propose new rules. In some cases, they even argued for amendments to the European Constitution. During the European sovereign debt crisis, they pleaded for automatic sanctions, sanctions that would automatically be imposed on the governments (sovereigns) of member states.

The French take the opposite position. For them, might trumps right. The elite decides. This attitude reflects the high score of France on Power Distance, but as we have argued in Chapter 2, can also be regarded as a way of coping with uncertainty. The idea is that leaders are responsible for dealing with uncertainty. Consequently, these leaders cannot be restricted by means of rules. Hence, the proposal for automatic sanctions to be imposed on leaders was unacceptable to the French.

10.8 How do they perform?

In the end, the important question is whether one system performs better than the others do. We therefore evaluate the performance of the three economies on some indicators of human flourishing in this section. In Chapter 6, Delsen has already described each country's performance when it comes to wages, unemployment, and the quality of jobs. In this section, we use the components of the Human Development Index (HDI) as a yardstick: income per capita, education, and life expectancy. The two liberal views (the free market view and ordoliberals) explicitly state that their aim is to reduce inequality. A society characterized by large inequalities is unjust and, in the end, will not function properly (according to ordoliberals). We therefore provide indicators for both the level and the distribution of material possession (income and wealth), education, life expectancy, and the healthcare sector in general.

The scores of the three countries on the Human Development Index (HDI) are in the same range (see Table 10.1). Over the period 1990–2017, the United States has had the highest score on the general index and on the sub-indices of income per capita and education (Table 10.1). Life expectancy is the highest in France. The German scores are always between those of France and the United States. The development over time reveals that France's score on the HDI has always been the lowest and that from 2004 onwards, Germany has scored higher than the United States (Figure 10.1a and 10.1b).

The change in the German position is due, in particular, to the improved score of Germany on education (Figure 10.1c). Of the three countries,

Table 10.1 Characteristics of the three countries

Characteristic	*USA*	*Germany*	*France*
Human Development Index	0.89	0.88	0.86
HDI-income	0.93	0.90	0.89
GDP per household	40.126	26.569	25.649
HDI life expectancy	0.88	0.90	0.92
Life expectancy in years	74.36	74.60	75.79
HDI education	0.87	0.85	0.75
Education: years in education	17.13	18.08	16.43
Indicators of inequality			
Gini coefficient	0.37	0.28	0.29

Sources and periods

The HDI figures are from United Nations Development Program for the period 1990–2017. GDP per head is for 1990–2017 from the AMECO database:

https://ec.europa.eu/economy_finance/ameco/user/serie/SelectSerie.cfm.

Life expectancy is the average from 1950 to 2017; years in education cover the years 2014–2017.

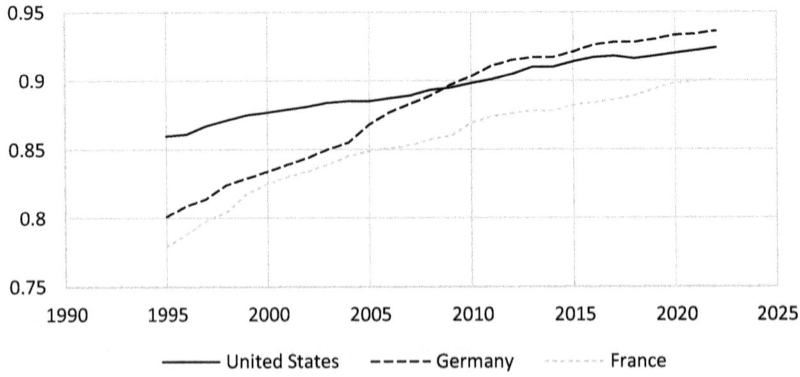

Figure 10.1a The Human Development Index in the three countries

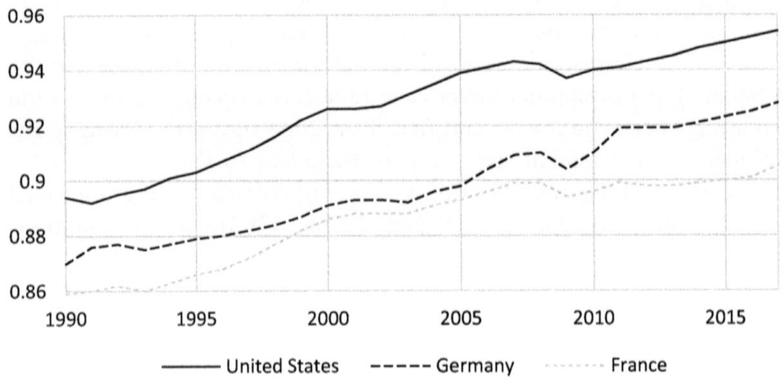

Figure 10.1b Evolution of income per capita as part of the Human Development Index.

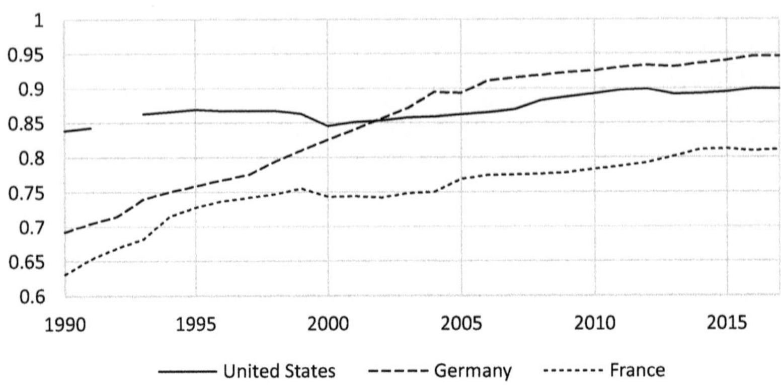

Figure 10.1c Education as part of the Human Development Index.

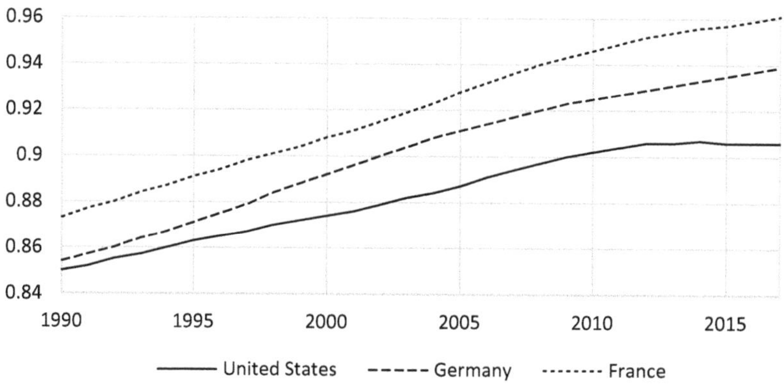

Figure 10.1d Life expectancy as part of the Human Development Index. Source: United Nations Development Programme; http://hdr.undp.org/en/content/human-development-index-hdi.

Germany is the only one that belongs to the high-performing countries, those that had an above-average share of students performing at the highest levels (Level 5 and above) in science, reading, or mathematics (OECD 2018: 43).

It is furthermore remarkable that, from 2010 onwards, life expectancy in the United States flattens, whereas it still increases in the two other countries (Figure 10.1d). In 2017, life expectancy at birth (total for men and women) was 82.6 years in France, 81.1 in Germany, and 68.6 years in the United States (OECD 2019). This finding is in accordance with the results of studies on the quality of healthcare systems. The Global Burden of Disease Study 2016 has developed an index for healthcare access and quality. This index ranges from 97 for Iceland to 23 for Guinea-Bissau. France and Germany score 92, which corresponds with positions 16–20, and the United States scores 89, which corresponds with positions 28 and 29 (GBD 2016 Healthcare Access and Quality Collaborators 2018: 2243). The 2015 edition of the Global Burden of Disease Study reports a similar ranking. Once again, France (score 88) and Germany (score 86) have a higher score than the United States (score 81) (GBD 2015 Healthcare Access and Quality Collaborators 2017: 238). The score of the United States is worse than that of many European countries including formerly centrally planned economies such as Slovenia, the Czech Republic, Croatia, and Estonia. According to Philippon (2019: Chapter 12), the United States' relatively poor performance is a consequence of America's competition policy. This policy has led to a concentration of hospitals, which generated monopoly power. As a result, American healthcare is very expensive and is thus not affordable for the lower income levels. The costs are also high due to the high salaries medical doctors receive. The high costs of a medical education fuel the high salaries of doctors.

The Gini coefficient is a frequently used measure of inequality. The average of the Gini coefficient for income per capita over the period 1980–2017 is the highest in the United States (Table 10.1). The difference between France and Germany is relatively small. In the United States, income inequality increased particularly in the 1980s and at the beginning of the 1990s (Figure 10.2a). In Germany, it increased from the mid-1990s to 2010. The Gini coefficient has some limitations in that it is a very general measure and does not clearly indicate the distribution over the different deciles. Thomas Piketty and his team have therefore collected data on income for different groups. The share of the top 10% income earners increased from 1980 onwards in the United States and from 2005 onwards in Germany (Figure 10.2b). In 2014, the share of national income of the top 10% earners was 42% in the United States, 35% in Germany, and 32% in France. In 2014, the top 1% of income earners had 20% of national

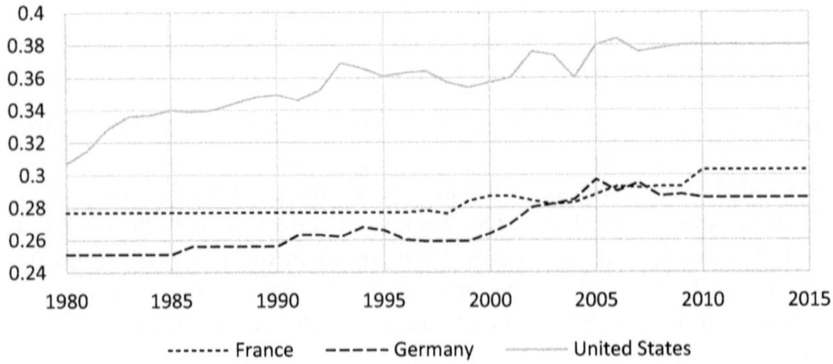

Figure 10.2a Inequality of income: Gini coefficient. Source: OECD, Gini at disposable income, post taxes and transfers, from the total population.

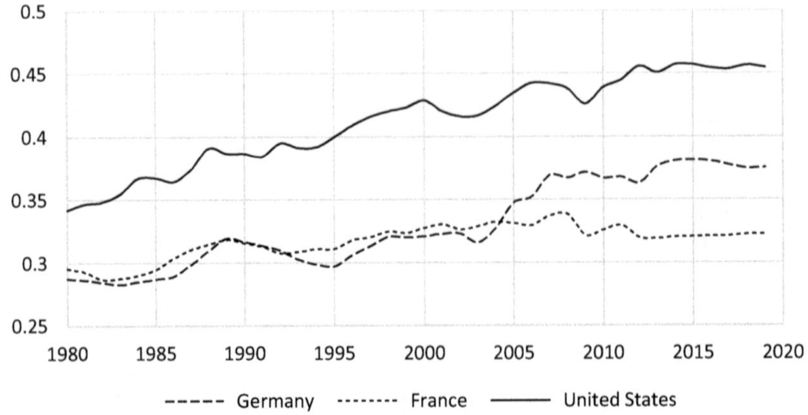

Figure 10.2b Share of top 10% in income. Note: The 'equal-split adults' series distribute income to all adult individuals, while splitting income equally within a couple or a household.

income in the United States, whereas the equivalent figure for Germany and France was about 11%.

Data about the size and distribution of wealth are less precise than those on income because the latter are more systematically collected for tax purposes. Vermeulen (2014) uses the US Survey of Consumers Finances (SCF), Europe's Household Finance and Consumption Survey (HFCS), and Forbes 400 list of wealthy people to calculate the share of the top 1% of households in total wealth. If he uses all three sources, then the estimates range from 35% to 37% for the USA, 32% to 33% for Germany, and 19% to 20% for France (Vermeulen 2014: Table 9). These estimates are based on data for the years around 2010. Piketty and co-authors collected times series of the share of the wealthiest persons of the total stock of wealth. Unfortunately, these data are available for the United States and France only. In the 1950s and 1960s, the top 10% held about 70% of all assets. Starting from the mid-1960s, France saw a steep decline of this share after which it stabilized at about 50% (Figure 10.3a). Since about 1995, it has been increasing again but remains at a level slightly above 50%. The United States saw a decline in this regard during the same period but the size of the decline was less. Moreover, from the mid-1980s onwards this share increases again and at the end of the period is even higher than in the 1950s. When zooming in at the very top (the top 1%), we see that in the United States in the 2010s about 40% of all wealth is held by the top 1% (Figure 10.3b). This corresponds with about 50% of the total wealth of the top 10%. These figures clearly illustrate the American tendency to concentrate wealth at the very top. In France, this pattern is much less marked. The top 1% of households owned slightly more than 20% of all assets. Both estimates are in line with those by Vermeulen.

In general, access to education is less for disadvantaged groups in almost all societies. A study among 15-year-olds reveals that Germany performs better than the average of all OECD countries (OECD 2016: Figure 1.6.2). The participation rate among 15-year-olds is high and the number of students

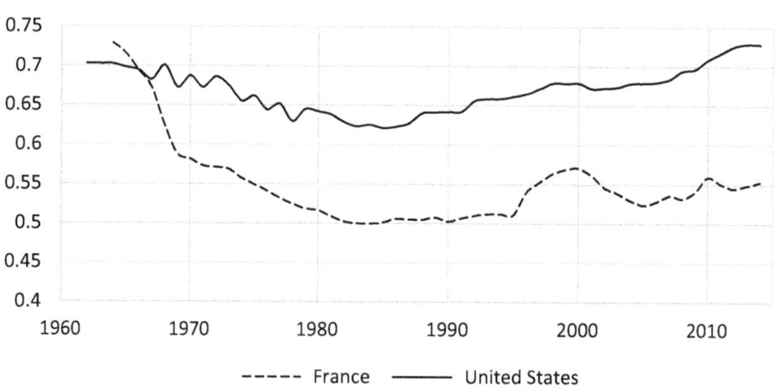

Figure 10.3a Wealth inequality (share of top 10%). Source: WID.world.

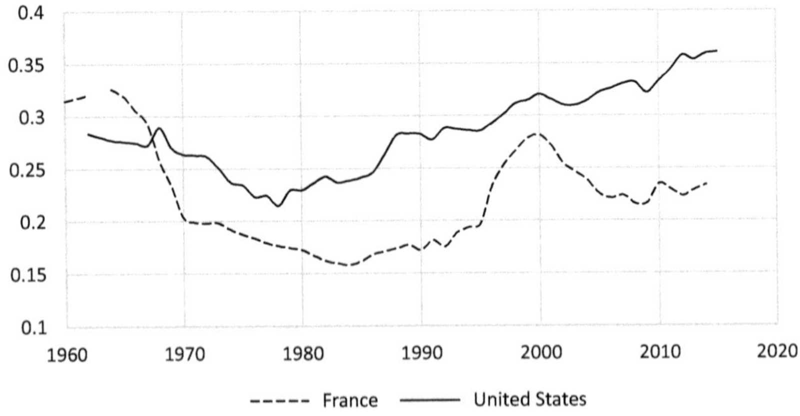

Figure 10.3b Wealth inequality (share of top 1%). Source: WID.world.

performing poorly is low. France and the United States score slightly worse in that they belong to the group of countries that do not differ significantly from the OECD average. For those scoring low on economic, social, and cultural status, access to tertiary education, university, and colleges is also better in Germany than in the other two countries. In the United States, the high tuition fees of prestigious private universities and the opaque admission procedures work against outsiders, such as students of poor parents or parents without an academic degree. In France, the educational system is very hierarchical, with *Grandes écoles* at the top. These institutes are very selective, and students often must attend special preparatory classes in order to be admitted. The *Grandes écoles* prepare students for careers in business and public administration. Lower in the hierarchy are universities, which are not allowed to select students. Finally, technical universities offer shorter curricula of two or three years (Piketty 2020: 752).

The United States also performs poorly when it comes to access to healthcare for the disadvantaged groups. Much of healthcare is privately funded and costs are high. A relatively large number of people cannot afford health insurance and thus have no easy access to health facilities. The differences between France and Germany are small. In both countries, a high share of health expenditure is publicly funded. In Germany about 10% of the healthcare is privately insured (Baeten *et al.* 2018: 17). These private schemes can be targeted to the individual's wishes. Often, privately insured patients get priority access and are treated by the *Chef Artz*, which, by the way, is not necessarily an improvement on what lower-ranked but more experienced staff can provide. Surveys about unmet needs in healthcare show a slightly better score for Germany than for France (Figures 6 to 12 in Baeten *et al.* 2018). A noteworthy

5% of the French population do not have complementary coverage. This is mainly the case for the unemployed and retired people with low pensions.

In sum, the United States outperforms the other two countries when it comes to income per capita and education (until 2000). France always scores best on life expectancy and from 2000 onwards, Germany outperforms the others on education. Inequality is higher in the United States than in Germany and France. The top income households earn a much larger share of national income and possess a greater part of national wealth than in the other two countries. Accesses to education and healthcare are also more unequal in the United States than in France and Germany.

10.9 Concluding remarks

The aim of this volume is to illustrate that a particular worldview dominates each nation's economic theories, its population's preferences (national culture), the design of the economy, and the policy measures taken. This book has focused on views on the role and functioning of markets. It distinguishes three types of market economies: the free market, the coordinated market, and the hierarchical market. We have illustrated that these worldviews on markets differ with respect to the degree to which one accepts uncertainty, the role and importance of the individual, hierarchy, and time preference. Although all the theories and societies are market economies, they differ in at least these aspects.

Although we emphasize a consistency between the dominant values and economic theories and practices, the reality might be different, certainly from an outsider's point of view. The measures taken in the 1930s in the United States serve as a good example. At that time, it was felt that competition had become ruinous. In order to save competition, measures were taken which restricted competition. As argued in Chapter 7, these measures may have caused problems in the 1960s and 1970s. In accordance with the plea for free competition, the American government does not have a stake in companies, as is common policy in other countries. Nevertheless, the US government's involvement in the secondary market for mortgages, via Fanny Mae and Freddy Mac, companies that have been government owned since 2008, suggests that this market is dominated by government involvement. Much more so than many European mortgage markets. Note that until the credit crisis of 2008, these institutions were called government-sponsored private enterprises, a term containing many contradictory messages.

The main message of this volume is that in many fields – academia, politics, and practice – one dominant view prevails so that one can speak of a country's culture. This does not imply that this culture is set in stone. This volume illustrates that dramatic events can change people's attitude and hence the dominant view in a country (or group in general). For France and Germany, the Second World War acted as such a trigger event. Whereas before the Second World War, the market in France was freer than that in Germany, the countries switched positions after this war. In both cases, discontent with developments in the 1930s and 1940s fuelled the demand for change. That said, this volume's main message is that during any period, the way that economic developments are interpreted and the measures that are taken are dependent on that individual country's dominant worldview. No universal optimal solution prevails, although, of course, bad examples always exist.

Notes

1 In German 'die Befreiung von der staatlichen Befehlswirtshaft' and 'einer alles Leben überwucherenden Burokratie' (Vogel 2015: 168).
2 The Sherman Act dates from 1890, whereas Canada had its first competition law in 1889.
3 Note that in the 1960s, Keynesian types of policies were popular around the entire industrialized world. An element of this is the aim for full employment. This policy goal has been enacted in many countries among which the United States and Germany.

References

Baeten, R., S. Spasova, B. Vanhercke and S. Coster (2018) *Inequalities in Access to Healthcare: A Study of National Policies*, Brussels: European Commission.
De Jong, E. (2009) *Culture and Economics: On Values, Economics and International Business*, London: Routledge.
GBD 2015 Healthcare Access and Quality Collaborators (2017) Healthcare Access and Quality Index based on mortality from causes amenable to personal health care in 195 countries and territories, 1990–2015: A novel analysis from the Global Burden of Disease Study 2015, *The Lancet* 390: 231–266.
GBD 2016 Healthcare Access and Quality Collaborators (2018) Measuring performance on the Healthcare Access and Quality Index for 195 countries and territories and selected subnational locations: A systematic analysis from the Global Burden of Disease Study, *The Lancet* 391: 2236–2271.
OECD (2016) *PISA 2015 Results: Excellence and Equity in Education, Volume I*, Paris: OECD.
OECD (2018) *Effective Teacher Policies: Insights from PISA*, Paris: OECD.
OECD (2019) *Health at a Glance*, https://data.oecd.org/healthstat/life-expectancy-at-birth.htm, downloaded at March 18, 2020.
Philippon, T. (2019) *The Great Reversal: How America Gave Up on Free Markets*, Cambridge, MA: The Belknap Press of Harvard University Press.
Piketty, T. (2020) *Capital and Ideology*, Cambridge, MA: The Belknap Press of Harvard University Press.
Rajan, R. G. and L. Zingales (2003) The great reversals: The politics of financial development in the twentieth century, *Journal of Financial Economics* 69: 5–50.
Timberlake, R. H. (1993) *Monetary Policy in the United States: An Intellectual and Institutional History*, Chicago, IL: The University of Chicago Press.
Van Oudenhoven, J. P., B. de Raad, M. E. Timmerman, F. Askevis-Leherpeux, P. Boski, C. Carmona, [….] , M. Yik (2014) Are virtues national, supranational, or universal? *SpringerPlus*, 3(1): 223. doi:10.1186/2193-1801-3-223.
Vermeulen, P. (2014) *How fat is the top tail of the wealth distribution?*, ECB Working Paper Series No 1692, Frankfurt am Main: European Central Bank.
Vogel, J. (2015) *Der Souveränitätseffekt*, Berlin-Zürich: Diaphanes.

Index

Note: Page numbers in *italics* indicate figures, **bold** indicate tables and page numbers with "n" indicates the end notes in the text.

For Product Safety Concerns and Information please contact our EU
representative GPSR@taylorandfrancis.com
Taylor & Francis Verlag GmbH, Kaufingerstraße 24, 80331 München, Germany

www.ingramcontent.com/pod-product-compliance
Ingram Content Group UK Ltd.
Pitfield, Milton Keynes, MK11 3LW, UK
UKHW020008200926
475702UK00015B/2547
* 9 7 8 1 0 3 2 0 7 7 3 0 7 *